A HISTORY
OF THE
S.A.S. REGIMENT

A HISTORY
OF THE
S.A.S. REGIMENT

By

JOHN STRAWSON

SECKER & WARBURG
LONDON

First published in England 1984 by
Martin Secker & Warburg Limited
54 Poland Street, London W 1 V 3 D F

Reprinted 1984

Copyright © John Strawson 1984

British Library Cataloguing in Publication Data
Strawson, John
A History of the S.A.S. Regiment
  1. Great Britain. *Army. Special Air Service Regiment*—
  History
  I. Title
  356'.167'0941   UA659.S67

ISBN 0-436-49992-4

Printed in Great Britain by
Butler & Tanner Ltd, Frome and London

By different methods different men excel;
But where is he who can do all things well?
Charles Churchill

CONTENTS

LIST OF ILLUSTRATIONS

Between pages 176 and 177.

Between pages 240 and 241.

Maps

AUTHOR'S NOTE

This is not the official history of the Special Air Service Regiment. Indeed there can be no such thing for too many of the S.A.S.'s activities are *un*official. This is a book about the S.A.S. and it is important for the reader to understand why it has been written. Shortly before Tony Geraghty's admirable volume, *Who Dares Wins*, appeared, a senior officer of the S.A.S., who had some close contacts with the publishing world, happened to be dining with me at a friend's house in Herefordshire. Knowing something of my former connections with the S.A.S. and of my former writings, he asked me whether I would consider doing a book about the Regiment. This led to further discussions, after the appearance and success of *Who Dares Wins*, between Headquarters S.A.S., the publishers and myself, when it was agreed that despite this latest book and all the others that had been written, there might be room for another one. It was further agreed that the S.A.S. would themselves lend their support in two ways. They would make available certain material to help me and they would acknowledge their association with the book. Although clearly not an official history, therefore, this book may be called an authorized history, although it was made clear at the outset that there were certain S.A.S. activities about which I was *not* authorized to write.

It is also deliberately quite short. To present an account of every action in which the S.A.S. had been engaged in their forty-odd years would be to weary even the most indulgent, let alone the general, reader. What I have therefore tried to do is to recount the S.A.S.'s broad contribution to campaigns in which they have taken part and about which it is permissible to write. But rather than tell the same sort of tale - however full of sound and fury each one might be - a dozen times, I have selected tales which will, it is to be hoped, signify

something. There are also appendices with facts and figures designed
to fill gaps in the narrative. Such an account of the S.A.S.'s history
cannot be comprehensive. But it can perhaps be representative. It has
not been possible to mention all those who so distinguished themselves
in peace and war. But the story is about the Regiment and, as every
man of the S.A.S. knows, the two are identical. Thus every time one
man's story is told, the Regiment is depicted, and every time the
Regiment is portrayed, it personifies *all* those who served with it.
These stories are essentially those of the S.A.S. in action, and therefore
no attempt is made to give a detailed account of what the two Territorial Regiments, 21 and 23, have done. Yet if the book is sufficiently
representative to have presented a Regiment unique in its men, its
daring and its victories, then the purpose of writing it will have been
realized.

But it could not have been even attempted, still less realized, without
the help given to me by a number of people. First and foremost I wish
to thank Colonel John Waddy, former Commander of the S.A.S., who
has assisted me with all the research. Without his knowledge, his
judgment, his S.A.S. entrée and his perseverance, it would have been
impossible for me to assemble the raw material from which the narrative springs. Moreover, he compiled the appendices, drew the maps
and selected the illustrations. I am wholly in his debt. There now
follows a list of those, all of whom have some direct connection with
the S.A.S., who have assisted me with and supported the production
of this book. The particular form of their assistance and support is
designedly omitted. But there was no winter in their bounty; it grew
the more by reaping. My appreciation of being permitted to be asso-
ciated with them all in this endeavour is infinite. My deep gratitude is
therefore offered to: Brigadier Peter de la Billière, CBE, DSO, MC,
Brigadier John Foley, MC, General Sir Robert Ford, GCB, CBE,
General Sir John Hackett, GCB, CBE, DSO, MC, Jeffrey Holland,
Colonel I.G. Jack, General Sir Frank Kitson, GCB, CBE, MC,
Lieutenant-General Sir George Lea, KCB, DSO, MBE, Major-
General David Lloyd Owen, CB, DSO, OBE, MC, Major Dare
Newell, OBE, Lieutenant-Colonel Michael Rose, The Viscount Slim,
Colonel David Stirling, DSO, CBE, Colonel Mike Wingate-Gray,
OBE, MC, Lieutenant-Colonel John Woodhouse, MBE, MC.

My thanks are due to the following for permission to quote from
the books mentioned: Virginia Cowles, *The Phantom Major*, Harper
& Row; Winston S. Churchill, *The Second World War*, Cassell;
Roy Farran, *Winged Dagger*, Collins; Tony Geraghty, *Who Dares Wins*,
Arms & Armour Press, and *Ten Years of Terrorism*, RUSI; General

Sir John Hackett, Foreword to *Providence Their Guide*, Harrap; D.I. Harrison, *These Men Are Dangerous*, Cassell; Tony Jeapes, *SAS Operation Oman*, W. Kimber; Frank Kitson, *Bunch of Five*, Faber & Faber; John Lodwick, *The Filibusters*, Methuen; David Lloyd Owen, *Providence Their Guide*, Harrap and *The Desert My Dwelling Place*, Cassell; Sir Fitzroy Maclean, *Eastern Approaches*, Cape; Jan Morris, *Heaven's Command*, Faber & Faber; Malcolm James, *Born of the Desert*, Collins; Claire Sterling, *The Secret War of International Terrorism*, Weidenfeld & Nicolson; John Verney, *Going to the Wars*, Collins; Philip Warner, *The Special Air Service*, W. Kimber.

I am most grateful to Headquarters Special Air Service and their staff for permission to use and quote from certain documents which they made available to me, including their Regimental Journal, *Mars and Minerva*, and to reproduce as illustrations the photographs which appear in this book together with copies of some original S.A.S. orders and citations. I am grateful to Mr James Lucas and his colleagues at the Imperial War Museum for all their help in selecting photographs.

I would like to add a very special word of thanks to Major Dare Newell. Just as David Stirling can properly be called the father of the Regiment, so Dare Newell, as John Waddy has put it, may be thought of as the Regiment's godfather, for he saw to it that their education and upbringing were carefully watched. From his position at S.A.S. Headquarters, his help and encouragement have been continuous and unstinting. In a similar way I am particularly grateful to Peter de la Billière, who, as the Commander S.A.S. at the outset of this project and for most of its execution, gave his enthusiastic and indispensable support. Michael Rose has also been especially helpful.

The responsibility for any errors of fact, serious omissions of event or expressions of opinion - unless specifically attributed elsewhere - is mine. The author and publishers wish it to be known that a percentage of the royalties of this book go to the S.A.S. Regimental Association Fund.

1

IN DEFEAT: DEFIANCE

A time when it was equally good to live or die.

Churchill

If there is one sphere of military enterprise in which the British have excelled again and again, it is that of avoiding defeat. They have, of course, had much practice. Scarcely a single major European or indeed colonial conflict into which they have entered with such careless confidence has been one where the British were not unready, unequipped, unrepentant or unaware of what the consequences would be. And on each occasion the European or non-European power with whom Britain was arguing the toss - no matter how striking or swift their initial successes might have been - was in the end worsted by the presence and activity of the Royal Navy, which enabled the gentlemen in khaki (or in former days more colourful and less practical accoutrements) to do their stuff. So it was with Spain, with France, with the Boers, with India, with Germany. Only in North America did the formula fail, and this was because of an eventual realization that America could not be defeated rather than a refusal to modify the familiar pattern of initial military incompetence.

At no time was the danger of defeat, nor the almost sublime indifference to its likelihood, greater than it was in 1940. There were then, to our extreme good fortune, a number of powerful cards in an otherwise wholly inadequate British hand. First and foremost was the chance that these cards were held by 'a man larger than life ... a man superhumanly bold, strong and imaginative ... an orator of prodigious powers ... a mythical hero who belongs to legend as much as to reality'* - in short by Mr Winston Churchill. Second was his ability,

* *Mr. Churchill in 1940*, Sir Isaiah Berlin, John Murray.

and it is not too extravagant a word, to inspire the nation. Third was the integrity of the Royal Navy and our merchant fleet; fourth the gallantry, skill and sufficiency, albeit by a hair's breadth, of the Royal Air Force, fifth the resolution of the Dominions and Colonies, sixth the partiality of the United States. These were all positive features of a story which is still a source of pride and honour. Of equal, perhaps of even greater, significance was the nature of the danger itself as represented by the person and purposes of Adolf Hitler.

When in *Mein Kampf* Hitler called for one last decisive battle with France, he was speaking as an adventurer. When much later on, after the war had started, and he was trying to urge the General Staff to steel themselves actually to assault the Western Allies, he was nearer the mark when he declared, in November, 1939: 'I place a low value on the French Army. Every army is a mirror of its people ... After the first setbacks it will swiftly crack up'. Yet even Hitler was surprised by the rapidity and totality of his success. Fortunately for the British it left him strategically off balance. The French defeat, of course, was total. As Vercors* put it:

> The wholesale retreat towards Dunkirk turned into an epic, but it was a sombre epic. The disaster was immeasurable. The French army was smashed to pieces, cut to shreds by the tanks, nailed to the ground by the enemy's Stukas. A hundred miles from the front dazed soldiers were still streaming back. There was no more mention in the press of Corap or even of Gamelin, the defeated C.-in-C. I was convinced that, disgraced by their own incompetence and responsible for their country's collapse, they had committed suicide. Today I can only wonder at my naivety. Gamelin was very much alive and quite self-satisfied: he put the entire blame on his subordinates.

When Hitler realized how absolute his victory was to be, he praised emotionally the army and its leaders. He predicted the peace arrangements which he would conclude with France and so make up for all the injustices inflicted on the German people since the Thirty Years War. He would return ignominy for ignominy, and humiliate the French nation by conducting peace negotiations in the same railway carriage at the same place in the forest of Compiègne as the French had done twenty-two years before. As for the British – they could have peace as soon as Germany's colonies were returned.

But the British were not interested in peace. On 10 May, on the very same day that von Rundstedt's sickle began to cut down the

* *A Bataille du Silence* by Jean Bruller, pseudonym Vercors.

Allied armies, Churchill became Prime Minister and three days later made a memorable declaration in the House of Commons:

> I have nothing to offer but blood, toil, tears and sweat. You ask, What is our policy? I will say: It is to wage war, by sea, land and air, with all our might and with all the strength that God can give us: to wage war against a monstrous tyranny, never surpassed in the dark, lamentable catalogue of human crime. That is our policy. You ask, What is our aim? I can answer in one word: Victory - victory at all costs, victory in spite of all terror; victory, however long and hard the road may be.

At all costs! The cost was indeed to be all-embracing - the decline of the British Empire, the hegemony of the United States, the huge expansion of the Soviet Union, the bankruptcy of Britain. Yet there was no doubt about the aim - victory, and it was at length achieved. But what of the policy? How was war to be waged? It could no doubt be done at sea and in the air in a desultory and half-hearted fashion. But how was it to be done on land? The miracle of Dunkirk might have saved the British Army. But where and with what was it to fight? This dilemma of what to do next was not Churchill's alone. It was Hitler's too. Perhaps Hitler would solve the problem by coming to England and finishing the thing off there. But if not to England, where was the *Wehrmacht* to go? So great was this dilemma for Hitler that in the end the *Wehrmacht* was to go to the one place which guaranteed its defeat and withdrawal, and which thereby ensured also that the British Army would never be required to take on the real power of its principal adversary. But much was to happen before that.

There are two great rules of war, and throughout its history each has been more honoured in the breach than the observance. The first rule is correctly to select your main objective. The second is so to concentrate your forces that you achieve this objective. Neither one will do by itself. It is indispensable to do both and do them together. In 1940, no matter how difficult or hazardous the undertaking might have been, Hitler's main objective was clear - the elimination of England. There was, after all, no other enemy until Hitler set about finding some. Churchill might have spoken of carrying on the struggle from elsewhere - should the British Isles be overcome - but the truth was, as General Fuller has pointed out, that the war's centre of gravity, in other words the true line of operations to strategic objectives whose possession would yield decisive prizes, lay through London. Yet Hitler would not or could not see it. Churchill himself was in no doubt. 'Hitler knows,' he declared, 'that he will have to break us in this island

or lose the war.' Once the Battle of Britain was over however, and
Hitler had decided that, however desirable might be the overthrow of
Britain by direct assault, it could not be done without air supremacy,
even the Führer hesitated. It might be too hazardous an operation even
for the *Wehrmacht*, and so he turned aside and sought, as Bonaparte
had done, to facilitate the eventual downfall of the British by removing
from the scene one of her potential allies, Russia. At the same time,
one of Germany's actual allies was conveniently placed in both geo-
graphical and military circumstances for Churchill to begin his policy
of waging war.

It was not until Italy's position in North Africa became precarious
that Hitler really turned his attention to it, but as early as November,
1940, his War Directive No. 18 showed the way his mind was moving
and how many alternatives to Operation *Sea-Lion*, the invasion of
England, were being considered. There were few parts of Europe
which did not figure in his broad strategic survey. France was to be
persuaded to secure her African possessions against the British and de
Gaulle, and so begin to participate in the war on Germany's side.
Spain, too, was to be brought into the war in order to help drive the
British from the western Mediterranean. Gibraltar was to be captured
and the Straits closed. In order to assist the Italians in their offensive
against Egypt, the *Wehrmacht* would make certain preparations – a
panzer division would stand by for service in North Africa, certain
German shipping would be made ready to transport troops and equipment, the *Luftwaffe* would plan for attacks on Alexandria and the Suez
Canal. But German forces would not be employed until the Italians
had reached Mersa Matruh. Meanwhile the occupation of the Greek
mainland north of the Aegean Sea would be the subject of planning
for the Commander-in-Chief Army.

Perhaps the most significant paragraph in the whole of this Directive, however, was the one dealing with Russia. Paragraph 5 indicated
that 'political discussions for the purpose of clarifying Russia's attitude
in the immediate future have already begun' and went on to direct
that all preparations for the East would be continued. Reluctant ever
to abandon any idea, Hitler also included a reference to *Sea-Lion*,
which might still be possible if there were 'changes in the general
situation'. As usual in such directives, Hitler showed how tight and
complete would be his grip on the reins and finished with these words:

> I await reports from the Commanders-in-Chief on the operations laid down
> in this directive. I will then issue orders on the manner of execution and
> the timing of individual operations.

In this way Hitler demonstrated his rejection of the two master rules of war. He neither chose the single proper objective, nor concentrated his forces. Indeed the very comprehensiveness of this strategic survey presaged the dissipation of the *Wehrmacht*. Paragraph 5, for all its circumlocution, is ominous and simply reinforces what had long been in Hitler's mind – the destruction of the Soviet Union. After all, as long before as July, 1940, Jodl, Chief of Operations at Hitler's head-quarters, had confided to some senior staff officers that an attack on Russia in the coming spring was contemplated. In that same month Hitler had told his Commanders-in-Chief that Russia's elimination would have to be made part of the struggle, for, as he argued, if Russia dropped out of the picture, so would America, since Japan's greatly increased power would then obsess the United States. So, the Führer argued, – and we must be grateful that he did – the strategic line to London lay through Moscow.

Directive No. 18 seemed to keep the options open. Which was it to be – French North Africa, Gibraltar, Libya, Greece, England or Russia? In the event it was to be several of them, but Directive No. 21, which followed hard upon No. 18, made it clear that even before the conclusion of the war against England, the *Wehrmacht* was to be pre-pared to crush Soviet Russia in a rapid campaign. What is more, the Mediterranean question was to be liquidated during the winter of 1940–41 because, as Hitler put it: 'I must have my German troops back in the spring, not later than May 1st'. The Mediterranean question was to persist until May, 1945, and from the British point of view was to provide the very distraction to the main power of the *Wehrmacht*, the very cause of its dispersion in non-decisive areas, so that the British Army, while unable to deliver hammer blows likely to achieve a knock-out, was encouraged to mount a series of small, yet damaging, pin-pricks.

For the British at this time the Middle East was all-important. 'If there was no prospect of a successful decision against Germany her-self,' wrote Professor Michael Howard, 'there was a subsidiary theatre where British forces could be employed to harass the enemy and perhaps inflict serious damage. Italy's entry into the war had turned the Middle East into an active area of operations. As a centre of gravity of British forces it was second only to the United Kingdom.' This turn of events suited Churchill who, fully aware of the strategic weight of the Middle East and prepared to back it with great daring and foresight in the distribution of his limited military resources, was still puzzling as to how he should 'wage war'. His yearning for initiative was shared by another man, who was in no doubt as to his crucial role in forwarding Britain's objectives - General Wavell, Commander-in-Chief, Middle East.

Convinced that the eastern Mediterranean would be a decisive area of operations and accepting that, to start with anyway, the tune would be called by the Axis powers, Wavell judged that, whereas Germany would seek to dominate eastern and south-eastern Europe, Italy would try to do the same in North Africa and the Mediterranean. His task therefore became clear. It was not merely to guarantee the integrity of Egypt, together with other Middle Eastern countries and resources, but to take the offensive as soon as he could in order to gain control of the Mediterranean and mount operations against German forces in eastern and south-eastern Europe. We shall shortly see how Wavell was able to turn the tables on the Italians and bring them so near to total defeat in North Africa that only the emergence of Rommel's Afrika Korps and the distraction of Greece robbed the British of complete possession of the North African coast two years before its actual realization. Shortage of resources was a permanent feature of Wavell's numerous campaigns, yet they were sufficient for him to wage war on land in the desert, in East Africa, Syria, Iraq, Greece and Crete - campaigns not all of which yielded great glory for the gentlemen in khaki. But at least Wavell was able to harass and eliminate enemy soldiers. For soldiers in the United Kingdom, it was a different story. How and where were they to engage the enemy?

Churchill's method of running the war was unique. It was done, as Professor A.J.P. Taylor reminded us, with a flow of chits, 'provoking memoranda, to which he made further written replies. At meetings he did not discuss. He harangued, and others contributed by listening, patiently or not, to his monologues'. As the Prime Minister himself put it, he wanted only compliance with his wishes after reasonable discussion. But the papers for discussion had always been prepared beforehand. It was in this respect that Churchill's paper war - a procedure so often ridiculed and despised by men of action - was both indispensable and supreme. For Churchill was not 'one of the two greatest men of action his nation has produced'* for nothing.

Mountbatten observed once that Churchill had told him to turn the south coast of England from a bastion of defence into a springboard of attack. Some of his famous minutes, many of which called for 'Action This Day', showed how this was to be done; not that defence was altogether forgotten, as was evident from Churchill's early refer-

* Isaiah Berlin, *Mr. Churchill in 1940*. I have always wanted to ask Sir Isaiah who the other one was, but have not yet dared to do so. Would it be Pitt or Marlborough or Wellington?

ence to Commandos, which in their Boer origins were essentially defensive in purpose, but aggressive in nature. What, he demanded of General Ismay, were the ideas of Commander-in-Chief, Home Forces, about Storm Troops? And this in a minute dated 18 June, 1940:

> We have always set our faces against this idea, but the Germans certainly gained in the last war by adopting it, and this time it has been a leading cause of their victory. There ought to be at least twenty thousand Storm Troops or 'Leopards' [later called Commandos] drawn from existing units, ready to spring at the throat of any small landings or descents. These officers and men should be armed with the latest equipment, tommy guns, grenades, etc., and should be given great facilities in motor-cycles and armoured cars.

But even though Churchill was concerned with the dangers of a German landing in England, he had already turned his and others' attention to the desirability, even at a time when many were more conscious of a sense of deliverance from attack and the miracle of Dunkirk than anything else, of mounting 'a vigorous, enterprising and ceaseless offensive against the whole German-occupied coastline'. Deep raids inland, cutting vital communications and 'leaving a trail of German corpses behind them' – these were his lines of thought and these were the measures he required the Joint Chiefs of Staff to take:

1. Proposals for organizing the Striking Companies [ten were initially raised from the Regular Army and Royal Marines and given the name Commandos].
2. Proposals for transporting and landing tanks on the beaches.
3. A proper system of espionage and intelligence along the whole coasts.
4. Deployment of parachute troops on a scale equal to five thousand.

All these ideas about hitting back at the Germans – Commandos, landing craft, coastal intelligence, parachute troops – had at their root the eventual intention of a British return to the continent of Europe.* Indeed the very first return was on 23 June, 1940, when a small reconnaissance raid was mounted by British Commandos on the French coast near Boulogne. Hitler, who had just signed the armistice with France, had elected to declare at the same time, 22 June, that the British had been driven from the Continent for ever. The very next day the British demonstrated that this was not so. It was a small beginning, a raid by a mere 120 men [for suitable craft were hard to

---

* For further details of the origin of Special Forces, see Appendix 1.

come by] who either landed where there were no enemy to be seen or indulged in minor and ineffectual exchanges of fire, with no prisoners taken and little information yielded. Yet the thing could be done. That was the point. So confident was Churchill about the future – or so he gave others to understand – that his establishment of a Combined Operations Command in July, 1940, was followed a few months later by his instructions to the Joint Planning Staff to study the feasibility of offensive operations in Europe, including one which involved seizing a bridgehead in the Cherbourg Peninsula – shades of things to come.

When the time did come, Commandos, parachute brigades, the Special Air Service, all would have their part to play. But there was a lot of waiting, preparation and experiment first. And all these ideas and intentions inevitably contributed to David Stirling's own special adaptation of them. There were more Commando raids. Two small ones in Norway in late 1941 even prompted Hitler to reinforce his naval forces there with the battleships *Scharnhorst* and *Gneisenau* and the cruiser *Prinz Eugen* which were despatched there with a typical display of speed and daring. Norway continued to figure large in Hitler's calculations for the rest of the war. The British had other fish to fry. Churchill continued his search for ways to harass and dismay the enemy, even creating the Special Operations Executive with the idea of setting Europe ablaze by supporting and supplying Resistance movements. Until 1944 there was in fact only one man capable of setting Europe ablaze and he had already done it with a series of *Blitzkrieg* campaigns. Exaction of the price for all the Führer's ruthless violence was a long time in coming. But, in terms of keeping hope alive among those whom Hitler had conquered and oppressed, Churchill's ideas for hitting back at the enemy were of supreme importance.

Yet, for all Churchill's impatience for offensive action, there was still but one area where it was possible on land. Even then it was in the nature of a riposte to enemy initiatives rather than a campaign devised in the agreeable conditions of strategic freedom of choice. In September, 1940, the Italian 10th Army began its ponderous and reluctant advance into Egypt. However much Mussolini might be in pursuit of military success and glory, these aspirations were not shared by the bulk of those required to win them for him, and Ciano noted that no military operation had ever been undertaken so much against the will of the commanders in charge. Nothing could have better suited an irregular British force which Wavell had established a few months before and which became, like the Special Air Service itself, to which, indeed, it contributed so much, one of the most celebrated of all the private armies created during the war, the Long Range Desert Group.

The opportunities for bold enterprise in a desert, which was something to be used, not feared, were infinite, although for the time being
this bold enterprise was confined to gathering intelligence and harassing the enemy. When, therefore, Egypt was invaded, Wavell was able
to despatch patrols hundreds of miles to the west to investigate, report
and interfere with the movement of enemy aeroplanes and transport
columns. It was a process which went on until the whole of North
Africa was in Allied hands. If ever there were an example of looking
for an open flank and making use of it, here it was. It may have been
insignificant compared with what was to happen in the great land
battles between the Red Army and the *Wehrmacht* on the plains of
Russia, the cities of Stalingrad and Leningrad or the approaches to the
Caucasus, but it was at least doing something, when there was little
else that could be done. Wavell was shortly to indulge in some more
spectacular enterprises of his own, which so shocked the Italian Army
that Hitler was obliged to take a hand in the affair and so create the
circumstances leading to a kind of desert seesaw game which endured
for years. It was not for the British Army to take on the power of the
Wehrmacht, and no doubt it was because of this, a strategically fortunate but tactically baffling condition, that the burning enthusiasm for
excitement and action on the part of handfuls of intrepid, imaginative
amateurs found expression in irregular operations. As there was no
choice but the oblique approach, the British made the best of it.

It was not an oblique approach of which the Commander-in-Chief
of the *Wehrmacht* was thinking. In an article remarkable for its prescience and written at the beginning of June, 1941, Sir Arthur Bryant
depicted the strategic dilemma confronting Hitler. 'For all her glittering victories,' he wrote, 'the Third Reich is encircled by steel. And
the instrument of that encirclement is the sea-power of the British
Empire and its still passive but very real and potent supporter, the
United States of America. Germany must break that ring or go down
as surely in the end as she did in 1918.' This great historian went on
to ask himself whether it could be broken, and if so, how and when.
Direct invasion of our own country could hardly be undertaken without command of both the sea and air, neither of which was ever within
the grasp of Hitler's albeit very powerful forces. Breaking the ring by
blocking our supply routes was an alternative, and indeed the greatest
threat to this country in both world wars was in fact posed and pro-
secuted by the U-Boat. But even Hitler, although he fully grasped its
strategic importance, never concentrated sufficiently on it to realize its
ultimate benefit. There had, therefore, to be other ways of breaking
the British ring. If it were not to be by striking west to Britain or the

Atlantic – and there was little to be gained in the north – it had to be either east or south. In the event, it was both – Russia and the Mediterranean. 'Everything points,' Arthur Bryant concluded, 'to an early blow against our encircling lines across and beyond the Mediterranean ... his road to untrammelled power lies across the historic fighting-grounds of Englishmen: sea and desert. Can he cross them?' There probably was a time when he could have done so. Had Hitler listened to the arguments of Admiral Raeder, well before the attack on Russia, that with Malta in Axis hands a successful advance into Egypt, Palestine, Syria and Turkey would make the Russian problem appear in a very different light, to say nothing of all the Middle Eastern oil and the consequent inability of the British to take on the Axis powers anywhere on land – had Hitler done this, it is hard to see how Churchill's policy of waging war could have been executed. We must be thankful that Raeder's arguments did not prevail. Nonetheless, as Arthur Bryant pointed out: 'It is Hitler's fate to strike, and ours to resist and strike back.' But the fact remained that, even after the German assault on the Soviet Union, the only active theatre of operations for the British Army remained the Middle East.

It was here that Fitzroy Maclean took himself and it was here that he first came across David Stirling's ideas for a Special Air Service. There is perhaps no better introduction to these ideas than that given to us in *Eastern Approaches*:

> David was a tall, dark, strongly built young man with a manner that was usually vague, but sometimes extremely alert. He asked me what my plans were. I told him. 'Why not join the Special Air Service Brigade?' he said. I asked what it was. He explained that it was not really a Brigade; it was more like a Platoon. It was only called a Brigade to confuse the enemy. But it was a good thing to be in. He had raised it himself a month or two before with some friends of his after the Commando with which they had come out to the Middle East had been disbanded. Now there were about half a dozen officers and twenty or thirty other ranks.

Stirling went on to tell Maclean that he himself commanded the S.A.S. and was directly responsible to the Commander-in-Chief, at that time General Auchinleck. Everyone in it had to be trained in parachuting, something he personally found disagreeable, but whose advantages in getting you behind enemy lines easily and clandestinely were very great. When there, you would blow up things and then get back to your own lines by other means. Up to this time they had had one disastrous operation, the first one, and since then a number of successes. All of them had been in the desert. They had achieved surprise and done the enemy much harm. There were further possibilities in this area of small-scale raiding. The desert was not the only place. There would be southern and eastern Europe, where small parties could land by parachute, do their stuff and then be removed again by submarine. The possibilities were endless. All this sounded promising to Maclean and he said he would be delighted to join. Such was the impact on one man of David Stirling's idea.

2

THE IDEA

'Anyone might have thought of it ... Instead of sending more strength to the maelstrom where it is expected and where it will meet strength, a thrust is launched at a tender point where it is not expected. The enemy must hastily withdraw strength from the maelstrom to counter the thrust; now it is he who anxiously wonders where the next blow will fall and you who grimly plan it'.

Philip Woodruff

Anyone *might* have thought of it. But it was David Stirling who did. He has himself told us how it came about. He had gone to the Middle East in the first months of 1941 with the Guards Commando. This unit was part of Layforce, a group formed under the direction of Robert Laycock, whose mission in the Middle East was to exploit the success of O'Connor's offensive against the Italians by mounting an operation to seize the island of Rhodes. The plan was very much in keeping with both Churchill's and Wavell's intentions to take the war into south-east Europe. But as was to happen time and time again, the British underestimated and misunderstood both Hitler's loyalty to his Axis ally, Mussolini, and his ability to act with the astonishing speed and ruthlessness which had characterized so much of his relentless pursuit and manipulation of power.

On 7 February, 1941, O'Connor had sent his celebrated signal to Wavell: *Fox killed in the open*, signifying that, in the course of two months, he had achieved what few generals have ever achieved – the conduct of a campaign which concluded in the total annihilation of the enemy set before him. The Italian 10th Army had ceased to exist. O'Connor had reached El Agheila and it seemed to him that the road to Tripoli and the entire conquest of Italian North Africa was open. He therefore proposed to Wavell that he be allowed to execute the plan he had already made for an advance to Sirte and Tripoli. Wavell as usual backed him, although he did so with reservations. In his message to London he indicated that the measure of the Italian defeat at Benghazi made it possible for Tripoli to be taken even by a small force, provided it were despatched without delay. Indeed he was working out what such an operation would involve. Nonetheless, he added, the Balkan situation was bound to give him pause before embarking on it. What did Wavell mean by the 'Balkan situation' and what intelligence did he have to bring about this hesitation?

As early as 21 January, when O'Connor was on the point of taking Tobruk, Wavell had been instructed by His Majesty's Government that he must be ready to capture islands in the eastern Mediterranean, particularly Rhodes, 'that will-o'-the-wisp,' as Ronald Lewin puts it, 'which throughout the Mediterranean war danced before the strategists' eyes, inviting and unattainable'. Churchill, of course, had long been attracted by the idea of a Balkan front. He wanted to form an alliance with Greece, Yugoslavia and even Turkey to take on the Axis powers with an Allied force totalling fifty divisions – 'a nut for the Germans to crack' – and so begin the process which Churchill so ardently desired of inflicting defeat rather than merely avoiding it. Unfortunately, instead of one large and hard nut, there turned out to be a number of small and soft ones, all of which the Germans cracked with consummate ease. The fact was that, even at this time and in spite of the various demonstrations of it, the British had still not grasped what *Blitzkrieg* was all about. They were about to receive some further demonstrations of it, both from Field-Marshal List in the Balkans and from Lieutenant-General Rommel in the Western Desert.

The notion, therefore, of taking Rhodes as part of a generally successful British and Allied effort in the Mediterranean in order to exploit the imminent collapse of Italy was quickly overtaken by the less palatable recipe of propping up a series of operations all of which were going wrong. Sending strength to the maelstrom was to prove unprofitable, although this did not stop the British from doing it. At the same time the minds of those responsible for finding some formula to hit back at the seemingly invincible *Wehrmacht* were more than ever receptive to an idea, any idea, which might lend even the tiniest prospect of inflicting, instead of continuing to avoid, defeat.

It was not intelligence that the British lacked. It was military competence. In his acclaimed book about Ultra, Ronald Lewin points out that, however abundant the flow of accurate and comprehensive intelligence might be, it would not compensate for poor generalship, amateurish training, inferior equipment and less than adequate performance by the soldiers. 'Ultra alone was impotent, if the generals lacked the military strength or the mental ability to apply it in action.' So Greece was lost, and Crete, and despite further reliable intelligence about Rommel and his likely manner of operating – 'aggressive, ruthless, thrusting, daring' – things went badly in the desert too. In two weeks Rommel reconquered Cyrenaica, tried to bounce Tobruk and got to the Egyptian frontier. No wonder the idea of using the Commandos of Layforce to take Rhodes was given up. Indeed before long, after some minor operations which included raids on the Cyrenaican coastline, helping to hold Tobruk and landings in Syria, Layforce was itself disbanded.

It was during the period just before this that David Stirling found himself with time on his hands to develop and then peddle his great idea. The particular Commando of which David Stirling was a part, No. 8, was stationed at Mersa Matruh and had taken part in three operations directed at targets on the Cyrenaican coast. All these were raids, two against communication centres, one on an airfield. Each employed some two hundred soldiers, to be delivered by gunboat or destroyer in the early part of a night giving maximum darkness for the military business. Not one of the raids was successful, either because of bad seas or being seen by enemy reconnoitring aircraft. There was thus in these latter cases no surprise, and for operations of such a nature, surprise was all important. Instead there was intense enemy bombing. These failures made David Stirling contemplate other ways and means of mounting raids. He was provided with an enforced period of contemplation which, as he subsequently recorded, came about like this:

> During the last weeks before the disbandment of Layforce, Brigadier Laycock had authorised Jock Lewis (of the Welsh Guards), myself and six other ranks to experiment with some parachutes we heard had arrived in the Middle East (by error – they had been intended for India). This was on Lewis's initiative. We succeeded in borrowing an old Valencia aircraft for an afternoon and each of us did a jump. The static lines were secured to the aircraft seat legs. I was unlucky and landed on rocky ground and severely injured my back. This resulted in two months in hospital which gave an ideal opportunity to evaluate the factors which would justify the creating of a special service unit to carry on the Commando role, and amass a case to present to the C.-in-C. in favour of such a unit.

The former Commander-in-Chief would have applauded and supported Stirling's initiative, for long before the war started Wavell had observed that you should never allow yourself to be trammelled by the bonds of orthodoxy, that you should always think for yourself, getting as much experience as possible outside the ordinary run of military affairs. The herd, he told Bernard Fergusson, was usually wrong. David Stirling was a man after Wavell's heart, but by the time he put forward his idea, Wavell's *Battleaxe* offensive against Rommel had failed, and Auchinleck had become Commander-in-Chief. Fortunately, he too was a man who admired and cultivated imagination and daring. 'You got through,' he had said to the 7th Indian Brigade after their break-out from an Afrika Korps trap near Benghazi, 'because you were bold. Always be bold.' Boldness was at the very kernel of all that David Stirling was thinking about and wanting to do. It began with an appreciation of the situation. Writing appreciations is a common and useful practice in Staff Colleges and Military Academies. It is less often done in earnest. The essential point of David Stirling's proposal was not so much *what* was to be done, but *how* it was to be done and by whom.

There was still no doubt, he argued, about the enemy's vulnerability. His coastal communications and other installations there, airfields, depots of vehicles, fuel and stores – all these invited attack. So that the *role* which No. 8 Commando had had was sound enough, and properly carried out could yield important dividends. It was the *scale* which had been wrong, together with the method of introducing into the enemy area those who were going to interfere with the enemy resources they would find there. In other words the former idea of trying to introduce a large number of raiders was quite at odds with, a complete contradiction of, what they were trying to achieve. Large numbers necessitated a large effort in respect of movement agencies and all the other supporting activities. Not only did this mean that this effort behind it all inevitably prejudiced the clandestine nature of the operation, on which its success depended, but it also tied up military resources – men, ships, aircraft – whose value in their own right was indisputable and whose dissipation for raiding purposes would never offer advantages compatible with this value. But look at the thing from the point of view of maximum surprise and minimum commitment of men and weapons, two conditions which were not merely compatible but mutually sustaining, and you arrived at a very different answer.

Apply this principle in practice, Stirling's argument went on, and you could make do with a tiny unit of five men to deal with targets such as an airfield or a vehicle park, whereas formerly such targets had been thought of as requiring two hundred men. Take the thing a stage further and it became clear that with two hundred men in all, divided up into these little self-contained groups of five,* you could attack

* The S. A. S. module or sub-unit later became four men.

thirty to forty different targets at the same time. Success by only a few of these small parties would result in far greater damage to the enemy than could ever be achieved by preserving the former organization. In this way two enduring principles of war – economy of effort and surprise – would be exploited to the full. It was true that concentration of force would be left aside, but this did not matter, for you were launching your attack 'at a tender point where it was not expected'. Of course, the men of these small groups would need to be of exceptional calibre; their selection, training and equipment would call for a rigorously high standard. What is more their versatility would have to be such that they would be capable of arriving at the scene of action by any means – air, sea or land. In pursuit of economy, these means of delivery must not be of such a nature that denying their use elsewhere in different kinds of tactical operations would be critical. The new force must be able to use any sort of aircraft and drop by parachute without special modifications to it; the men would have to get themselves to their targets with any type of vessel, from submarine to caique; they would be able to infiltrate the enemy's lines on foot or by vehicle; they would need to cooperate with the Long Range Desert Group (L.R.D.G.) to get them near their destination.

One of the principles which David Stirling was anxious to get right from the very beginning was that of command and control. He was determined to avoid the stifling influence of bureaucratic staff branches at HQ Middle East, and so insisted that his unit should be responsible directly to the Commander-in-Chief himself, and also that he himself should be in charge of all training and operational planning. Having seen what sort of mess was being made by the Middle East equivalent of the Special Operations Executive, which Stirling described as a 'monstrous and inefficient octopus', and being equally opposed to the idea of getting mixed up with the Combined Operations Directorate, he was adamant that the very special way in which he and his outfit was going to operate demanded direct access to the top and minimum interference by others. [How right he was to do so is perhaps best illustrated by the fact that this direct access has survived until today: the Commander Special Air Service Group deals direct with Cabinet Ministers and, during the Princes Gate siege, it was the Prime Minister who gave authority for the S.A.S. to get on with its business].

In order to convince those at GHQ Cairo of the soundness and likely benefits of his proposals, Stirling outlined an actual plan for some raids to coincide with Auchinleck's forthcoming offensive against Rommel, Operation *Crusader*, timed for November, 1941, and about which, such was the lax security in Cairo at the time, everyone seemed to know. Before we see what this was, however, we must turn to his highly unconventional way of getting his idea accepted and how he set about raising, training and equipping his force. It is not given to many subaltern officers to persuade generals as to how war should be conducted. Yet this is exactly what David Stirling did. Virginia Cowles has given us her entertaining account of how Stirling, still wielding, and then jettisoning, the crutches which were the legacy of his back injury, virtually broke into GHQ Cairo, confronted, but managed to outflank a silly, inconsequential staff officer, and found himself at length sitting opposite the Deputy Chief of Staff, Middle East Forces, Major-General Neil Ritchie. Ritchie was a man who was prepared, like the exiled Duke in the Forest of Arden, to judge the uses of adversity sweet and to find good in everything. He had, moreover, that admirable quality, so renowned in Nelson, of being able to find telling employment for his subordinates' ideas, while still acknowledging them to be his subordinates' ideas. When, therefore, David Stirling burst into Ritchie's office in July, 1941, insisting that he had 'vital business' for him and thrusting his ill- and pencil-written memorandum into the general's hand, Ritchie read it. One reading was enough to convince him that the idea contained the seeds of a plan they badly wanted. After all, it had that supreme virtue of offering much and demanding little. What is more, it had the irresistible appeal of being at once original and daring. Ritchie told Stirling that he would discuss it with the Commander-in-Chief, Auchinleck, and let him know their decision in a few days' time.

Sure enough, three days later Stirling was summoned to GHQ and this time he saw not only Ritchie but Auchinleck too. Both his general idea and its particular application to the operation he had proposed (which was for an attack on airfields at Tmimi and Gazala) were discussed. The outcome was that Stirling was instructed to raise his unit, train it and continue to plan the operation. He was made a Captain and authorized to recruit his officers and men from Layforce and, if necessary, from regiments in the desert. Thus at the end of July, 1941, the Special Air Service was born. Its christening by that name was chance, rather than Stirling's design. Brigadier Dudley Clarke headed a staff section at Middle East Headquarters, whose responsibilities included that of trying to deceive the enemy as to the British order of battle, its capabilities and deployment. Clarke was attempting amongst other things to persuade the enemy that there was in the Middle East a complete parachute and glider brigade. He arranged for dummy parachutists to be dropped as if on training exercises for real operations, and did it in such a way that enough was seen by those who would report it back for them to be under the impression that it *was* real. He also had mock-up gliders distributed about the desert for enemy air reconnaissance to take note of. He called this bogus formation the 1st Special Air Service Brigade. When, therefore, he heard of an actual parachute unit being formed, no matter how small, he jumped at the chance of reinforcing his deceptive measures.

'To humour him,' as David Stirling put it, 'we agreed to call our new unit L Detachment, Special Air Service Brigade.' It could hardly have had a more fitting name. So, in a remarkably short time since his proposal, Stirling's idea had been given a 'local habitation and a name'. Nor was it to be so very small. The establishment to which recruitment could get under way was seven officers and sixty men, many of whom would be NCOs. Most of them came from Layforce and included Jock Lewis and Paddy Mayne, [who was later to command the S.A.S. and became Colonel of the Regiment]. As Stirling later recorded, the officers and men he got from Layforce were first class and had already done a lot of night work and other training in skills necessary for what was to come. He also found some men from the Scots Guards, who had a battalion in the desert and which was his own original regiment. By August he had established L Detachment at Kabrit, a village in the Canal Zone about a hundred miles from Cairo. There were three months to go before Auchinleck's November offensive and their own first operation.

One of the most important and urgent aspects of their training was, of course, parachuting. Stirling had repeatedly tried to get help and advice from the British Parachute School at Ringway, but not until two of his men had been killed in what later turned out to be an avoidable accident did Ringway send him notes on training and other information. They also sent a Captain Peter Warr, who greatly helped with the forthcoming operation and subsequently joined the S.A.S. As training proceeded Stirling insisted on two things: first, if the men they recruited did not come up to the required standard, they were sent back to the units they had come from [this is still a frequent occurrence in the S.A.S. because of the exceptional demands on mental and physical toughness which their selection course makes]; secondly, the discipline, cleanliness, turnout and behaviour of L Detachment was to be as high as in the Brigade of Guards. There was to be no acting tough or noisy ill-discipline when on leave or in Cairo. 'Toughness,' David Stirling made plain, 'was to be reserved entirely for the enemy.'

How were these ideals to be achieved? At this point it is necessary to understand a little more of the philosophy on which the Special Air

Service was founded. David Stirling has explained it many times, both in talking and writing, and what he said in essence is this. You had to be clear first of all that the S.A.S. role was quite different from Airborne or Commando forces whose task was to assist in the tactical battle. It was quite different too from the Special Operations Executive, which operated largely out of uniform with local forces. The S.A.S. was designed to carry out strategic tasks, operating almost exclusively in uniform, and its operations can be summarized in Stirling's own words as:

> firstly, raids in depth behind the enemy lines, attacking HQ nerve centres, landing grounds, supply lines and so on; and, secondly, the mounting of sustained strategic offensive activity from secret bases within hostile territory and, if the opportunity existed, recruiting, training, arming and co-ordinating local guerrilla elements.

It followed that the methods of introducing S.A.S. parties into their target areas had to give a very high assurance of surprise, minimize danger to whoever was getting them there and be extremely versatile. Arriving by air meant by parachute; by sea, either submarine or some very small boat; by land, penetrating through or round enemy lines using jeeps or simply walking. It also followed that the time of arrival was nearly always at night, which in turn demanded the highest standards of proficiency in whichever method of entry was to be employed.

One way to make entry easier and so exploit to the full both surprise and ingenuity was to stick to very small groups of men. So it was that a cardinal principle of the whole S.A.S. operational idea was its organization into sub-units of four men. Up to this time the smallest grouping in the British Army had been that of the infantry section, which according to the fashion of the time or numbers available might be anything between eight or ten men, led usually by a corporal, who within the dictates of his platoon, company and battalion, did indeed 'lead' in that he did both the thinking for and the direction of his men, whom David Stirling described as 'the thundering herd behind him'. The S.A.S. group of four men was quite a different thing. There was to be no nominated leader of it in the traditional sense. Each man in it was expertly trained to have, apart from many general skills, a particular proficiency, whether in explosives or radio or weapons or navigation, according to his own fitness and inclination. In an operation, therefore, it would be necessary for each man in the group to make full use of his own special sensitivities, skills and sense. Indeed the success of the operation would depend on his doing so under conditions designed to make the maximum demand on all his faculties.

It was not the intention that a single module of four men would always go into action by itself. Each was ready not only to do this, but also to combine with other modules as the needs of any operation dictated.

Because of the special nature of the tasks, essentially strategic ones, which the S.A.S. set itself and of the special groups chosen to execute these tasks, it was hardly to be expected that other features of the whole range of activities involved would be commonplace. Planning procedures had to be exclusive. L Detachment dealt directly with only the highest level of Middle East headquarters. This was done to ensure that the tasks really were strategic, and not allowed to decline into tactical ones in support of some engagement at the maelstrom, for there were plenty of staff officers at the headquarters whose imagination was limited both in terms of time and space and who saw the S.A.S. as a useful pinprick in tactically quiet periods, but could not grasp its long-term strategic potential. And there were other organizations like S.O.E. which tried to gather the S.A.S. into their own aegis on the grounds that they dealt with strategic operations behind enemy lines. But David Stirling and his team insisted properly on their right to remain untrammelled.

Nor was planning the S.A.S.'s only peculiarity. There was the matter of security. Absolute security was not merely necessary in order not to compromise the success of operations. It was a kind of obligation to those organizations, such as Ultra and other secret sources, which supplied the highly sensitive and closely guarded intelligence sometimes required for an operation by the S.A.S. to be mounted at all. A natural partner for special planning and special security was, of course, special communications. The S.A.S. groups might be operating at a distance of a thousand miles from the headquarters to whom they were reporting. Exceptionally reliable and efficient wireless was therefore needed, and initially this was provided by the L.R.D.G.

Most important of all was the quality of the men themselves, and here a problem of recruitment, which has lasted until today, emerged. Those who were likely to do well as members of the S.A.S. [the witches' recommendation to Macbeth to be 'bloody, bold, and resolute' was as good a formula as any] were likely also to be among the best men of the regiment they already belonged to. Those regiments' unwillingness to part with them is readily understood. But then, as now, S.A.S. recruitment depended on volunteers, and David Stirling was able to obtain general backing from Middle East Headquarters that a few volunteers from each of the experienced regiments in the desert should be allowed to try their hand. Not that volunteering for the S.A.S. meant acceptance into it. First the man concerned underwent a most rigorous and demanding course. Even if he came through this, it was not the end of the story. Once accepted, his training began in earnest. One of the main purposes of this training was to give each man complete confidence in himself and his fellow soldiers – confidence in their fitness, their skills and their determination to win, to outthink, outclass and outfight the enemy. Obviously each man's special aptitude for sabotage, machinery, medicine, enemy weapons, navigation at night, wireless and so on would emerge, so that in the end each group of four men could be balanced to produce a uniquely effective sum of skill and capability.

Unrelenting pursuit of excellence, self-discipline of the highest order – these were, and are, the watchwords of the Special Air Service. This, therefore, was what their training strove for. Apart from compatibility of character, a great deal depended on sheer bodily fitness. 'For days and nights on end,' Fitzroy Maclean subsequently recorded, 'we trudged interminably over the alternating soft sand and jagged rocks of the desert, weighed down by heavy loads of explosive, eating and drinking only what we could carry with us. In the intervals we did weapon training, physical training and training in demolitions and navigation.' There was one other very important aspect of all this preparation. David Stirling had from the start insisted that everyone joining the S.A.S. should be trained in parachuting. This was where Peter Warr, whom we met earlier in this chapter, was of enormous help. Fitzroy Maclean has described some of his activities in his customarily lively manner:

> In common with every other parachute instructor Peter had a considerable natural gift for dramatization. Somehow he contrived to make the unpleasant but relatively simple act of stepping out of an aeroplane appear as the climax of a great drama. While we were still on the ground he would dash round yelling instructions on a noisy and entirely unnecessary motor bicycle, followed by an equally noisy and even more unnecessary Alsatian dog. We fitted our parachutes and climbed into the aircraft amid pandemonium. Once we had taken off he would continue to shout above the noise of the engines, occasionally breaking off to whisper vaguely disturbing and only half-comprehensible technicalities into one's ear. As the moment to jump approached, he would work himself up into such a frenzy of excitement that he almost fell out of the plane, jumping up and down, waving his arms and screaming the order in which we were to jump at the top of his voice.*

* Although this passage is entertaining enough to warrant inclusion, in fact the best parachute instructors were quiet, assured and extremely competent.

All that was to come much later. Indeed, as we have seen, Fitzroy Maclean did not even join the S.A.S. until after some of its early operations had taken place. The first of them was inauspicious. Nonetheless it was the first time that L Detachment, Special Air Service Brigade, went into action.

3

FIRST BLOOD

The regiment is the Man and the man is the Regiment.
David Stirling

As was fitting for the month of November, hunting the Desert Fox began. The purpose of hunting is, of course, first to find your fox, then make him go away*, then pursue, harry, exhaust and finally kill him. Hunting the Desert Fox rarely followed this pattern. Indeed, all too often it was he who made you go away and then subjected you to the harassment, bewilderment and headlong retreat which properly had been intended for him. In the case of the *Crusader* battles, the outcome was something of a draw. During David Stirling's own contribution, first blood was drawn all right, but initially it was the hounds, not the fox, who lost blood.

Conduct of the *Crusader* offensive and what followed it was not enhanced by those circumstances which led Auchinleck to sack his first choice as 8th Army commander, Cunningham, then his second choice, Ritchie. Perhaps his wisest command decision was the one which led to his taking over 8th Army himself. All this chopping and changing, however, did not make for continuity of intention, clarity of direction or coherence of execution. Moreover, the idea of *Crusader*, although not unsound, was, like many British ideas about waging war, deliberate, unimaginative and a long time in germinating. In the very month when David Stirling was putting together his own notions and trying to persuade those steeped in traditional methods to accept something new and singular, the seeds of *Crusader* were being sown. As was customary for Commanders-in-Chief, Middle East, the man who was chucking the seeds about in July, 1941, as on many other occasions, was the Prime Minister. He could hardly be blamed for doing so in this par-

* Except, of course, for cubbing when you dispose of him there and then.

ticular month for the fate of the world was in the balance, not so much in Africa as in Russia.

While Hitler's panzer division raced about, advancing deep into Soviet territory and capturing hundreds of thousands of prisoners, Churchill was passionately concerned that British arms should not stand idle. After all the Soviet Union was at this time Britain's only ally which possessed military power, and this ally was in distress. Something had to be done. Churchill would have been even more urgent in his desire to take action if he could have read Hitler's war directive No. 32, issued eleven days *before Barbarossa* [codename of the German assault on the Soviet Union] began, which laid down how the war was to be conducted after Russia was conquered, that is exactly how the British position in the Middle East would finally be destroyed by converging attacks through Egypt, Turkey and Transcaucasia. But even without this knowledge and this spur, Churchill was longing to encompass and eliminate Rommel's 'small audacious army'. Then what might not follow? With Tripoli in our hands and the German air force busy in Russia, why should not eighty thousand British soldiers descend on Sicily and take it? Where else but in the Mediterranean could the British Empire trouble the Germans? It would be just what was needed to take some pressure off the Red Army and the very thing which Stalin was to demand time and again – a second front! But first Auchinleck would have to defeat Rommel and *he* was thinking far more modestly. He was also making demands on Churchill and asking for such substantial reinforcements that the Prime Minister could scarcely contain his exasperation, reflecting later that generals could only expect to enjoy such comfortable conditions in Heaven – 'and those who demand them do not always get there'.

On 23 July Auchinleck had signalled Churchill saying that if he had 150 cruiser tanks by mid-September, if he still had air superiority and there had been no major enemy reinforcements nor attacks on Syria, he could in November undertake a limited offensive to relieve Tobruk. If, on the other hand, he could have 150 extra American tanks together with trained crews, plus both lorried and air transport, a decisive operation to retake Cyrenaica could be mounted by 15 November. Although Churchill did not like this waiting, he eventually agreed to it. There was, in fact, much to be said for waiting. Whereas Auchinleck's position greatly improved in the months from August to November by virtue of reinforcement and preparation – and we should not forget that the newly appointed 8th Army commander, Cunningham, did not establish his headquarters in the desert until September – Rommel's position worsened. The deterioration in his operational

capacity was brought about largely by conditions created by two fortresses, one on land, one in the sea. Tobruk tied down Axis troops to
the tune of more than four divisions and Malta continued to play its
indispensable part in savaging Axis lines of communication. The key
to the battle of North Africa had always been that of supplies. In
August, 1941, Rommel lost 35 per cent of the supplies and reinforcements despatched to him, in October *63* per cent.

The influence of Malta on the *Crusader* battles gives us an example
of a strategic circle of events which were constantly repeated until the
whole of North Africa was finally captured by the Allies. It was the
sea and air attacks from Malta which had such a drastic effect on
Rommel's supplies, and this weakening of his defensive capability
made it possible for 8th Army to advance. The further the British
advanced, the more they were able to make use of airfields closer to
Malta, bringing it the very protection and sustenance necessary to
make the island's offensive operations against Axis convoys still more
telling. It was therefore of great importance to Rommel to try and
reverse this sequence, to hold the British away from forward airfields,
to sharpen the Axis sting against Malta so that by suppressing it his
convoys *would* get through, his own strength would grow and his own
ability to turn the British out of Cyrenaica and Egypt once and for all
would in turn enable the grand strategic plan of the Führer finally to
be fulfilled. Thus for Rommel it was essential to keep Malta quiet if
he was to advance and it was essential for him to advance if he was
to keep Malta quiet. In all this David Stirling's plans to curtail the
air power available to Rommel's *Panzerarmee* was an important
element.

Unfortunately for the British, the material advantages enjoyed by
Auchinleck and Cunningham were largely neutralized by Cunningham's own concept of conducting the battle. He had been a highly
successful commander in his East African campaign against the Italians, but he had never been in the desert before and had failed to grasp
the point, so fundamental to the Afrika Korps' way of thinking, that
infantry and armoured formations should complement each other to
form a single whole. His plan, therefore, was to have two battles: first,
a decisive tank engagement by 30 Corps, which would outflank Rommel's defences, occupy the Sidi Rezegh escarpment and so draw the
panzer divisions to their destruction; second, an infantry operation
against the enemy's defences to relieve Tobruk. This idea might have
been all right if those two prime battle-winning recipes – singleness of
purpose, concentration of force – had been properly observed. As it
was, attempts to guard against too many possible countermoves by the

enemy so modified plans that both concentration and singleness of aim were fatally compromised. Moreover, the whole concept lacked daring.

David Stirling's proposed contribution to the battle did not. If anything it suffered from being too daring in the face of unpromising circumstances. The task he set himself had not changed from his original suggestion – to attack and destroy enemy aircraft on the five airfields near Tmimi and Gazala just before Cunningham's main offensive, timed for 18 November, started. Since the formation of L Detachment at Kabrit, preparation had gone forward, though not without its setbacks; for during parachute training two men had been killed because of a faulty type of clip which attached the static line to the rail. It was corrected, and Stirling was the first to try out the new clip, a gesture typical of his leadership and his confidence. Meanwhile Jock Lewis, after a good deal of experiment, had invented the bomb which bore his name – small, light, explosive, incendiary and simply made of oil, plastic and thermite, ideal for its purpose. By virtue of the scepticism of an R.A.F. officer, Stirling's men were even enabled to have a dummy run at the Heliopolis airfield, using labels instead of bombs. It was a complete success, the men having taken three days to march ninety miles across the desert by night, rest concealed by day and plaster the R.A.F. aeroplanes with labels quite undetected, to the surprise and dismay of the sceptics. The point was that David Stirling had shown it could be done.

On the night, however, it was not all right. David Stirling's own brief account of what happened just before Auchinleck's offensive began shows that things went very wrong:

> Unfortunately the night on which it took place was almost unbelievably unsuitable for a parachute operation. There was no moon and the wind was so strong that on arriving in our Bombay aircraft over the Gazala coastline, the flares dropped by the Wellington bombers were quite insufficient for our navigators to pick up any fixed point on the coast because the desert sand and dust was obscuring the whole coastline. Therefore, in effect, the navigators had to take pot luck in their dead reckoning and, as far as I know, no party was dropped within 10 miles of the selected DZs. One of the five Bombays never dropped its stick of parachutists at all but landed the next morning on the Gazala landing ground with the whole unit still on board. This fantastic affair was brought about by a chain of mischance. The Captain of the aircraft had decided that conditions were too bad to drop his party and was, therefore, returning to his base when engine trouble occurred. He had to make a forced landing in the desert. After the engine was repaired he radioed a request for a direction beam,

which was promptly provided by the German staff on one of the Gazala landing grounds. Unsuspecting the Captain accepted the course and a little later discovered that his Bombay was being escorted by German fighters, which forced him to put down on the main fighter landing ground at Gazala. The fate of the four other parties was a mixed one. Two men were killed on landing, owing to the severity of conditions, and of the rest only eighteen men and four officers (Paddy Mayne, Bill Fraser, Jock Lewis and myself) got to the L.R.D.G. rendezvous. Thus the operation was a complete failure.

Another account of the affair comes from Warrant Officer Charles West, one of the Bombay pilots. Coming as it does from the Royal Air Force it makes the particular point that David Stirling's plans to destroy the Luftwaffe's latest Messerschmitt 109s on the ground could hardly have been more welcome to the Desert Air Force, who were still struggling to argue the toss with an inadequate number of Hurricanes and even some 'ancient outclassed Gloster Gauntlet biplanes'. He explains that the sixty-four S.A.S. men were to parachute in two groups ten miles inland from the two enemy landing grounds at Gazala and Tmimi. That same night, 16 November, they would move on foot to hiding places near the airfields, from which they could observe all that went on during the next day. Then on that night they would plant the bombs and make their way back inland to their rendezvous with the L.R.D.G. It is easy to blame the weather when things go wrong. David Stirling knew on the morning of 16 November that he might be faced with a gale, but had decided to carry on despite this warning. But as West recorded:

As the aircraft droned on, so the wisps of cloud drifting lazily across the sky thickened and deepened. Soon nothing existed in the world but cloud, rain and flashes of lightning. The smooth passage of the aircraft became a mad, bucketing switchback through the sky, and the pilots needed all their strength and skill to hold the course and airspeed. All the carefully checked navigational calculations were useless. It was impossible even to guess the force and direction of the wind which was driving the aircraft off course, and even less possible to sight the sea over which they were flying.

Small wonder that the five groups were either dropped miles from their selected zones or that one of the aircraft was hit and forced to land. It was all very disappointing but David Stirling was not the man to be put off by difficulties or disappointments. On the contrary, he was a man born to gain reinforcement from hope and draw resolution from despair. His own experiences during this first disastrous raid merely doubled his conviction that he was right and led him to modify his methods so that he and his men could enjoy success next time. The account which David Stirling gave to Virginia Cowles for her exciting book, *The Phantom Major*, would be impossible to better. He had been the first of his own group to jump and after the jerk of his parachute as it opened, he was astonished at how smooth his descent seemed to be:

> He could feel no pressure against his body and he wondered if there really was a high wind blowing or whether by some miracle it had stopped. After a minute he began to prepare for the landing. It was so black there was no prospect of seeing the ground. He braced his body expectantly, but continued to drift through space. Now his whole being was keyed up. Each second he expected to feel the impact of the ground, but it never came. It was almost as though the laws of gravity had stopped working and he was floating away from the earth through infinity.
>
> Then a smashing blow obliterated his senses. He must have been unconscious for two or three minutes. He awoke to find himself being dragged very fast over rough stony ground. He knocked the release harness and rolled over on his back, free. For a moment he lay in a daze. He felt blood trickling down his face but he moved his arms and legs and was relieved to find that no bones were broken. When he stood up he had to brace himself against a raging wind. The air was thick with dust and sand which almost choked him. He could see nothing through the black, noisy night. He shouted but the gale carried his voice away. He flashed his torch. Still he saw nothing. He began to walk waving the torch. After a few minutes a light blinked in the distance; then off to the right was another and yet another. The group was starting to converge.

They did not find much to comfort them. It took an hour to assemble. They were short of one man and most of those there were damaged – sprained ankles and wrists, a broken arm, gashes and cuts; only two of the ten supply parachutes were found, with some food and water, blankets and a few Lewis bombs *without* fuses. Another lesson for learning. They could find neither the missing man nor the other supplies. They were therefore impotent to do any harm to the enemy, but they could at least reconnoitre. The first thing was to find out where they were and to do so meant heading for the coast, but only Stirling and Sergeant Tait did this. The others, despite injuries and uncertainty of whereabouts, were to make for their rendezvous. After walking until dawn, there was no sign of the escarpment which flanks the coast. They pushed on, stopped for some food and rest and went on again. On reaching the escarpment, there was little to tell Stirling where they were, although he judged their position to be east of Gazala and not far from Tobruk. As night approached on 17 November, with 8th Army's offensive to begin shortly, the rain poured down in the cold and dark, conditions hardly propitious for reconnaissance, yet just right for clandestine movement. Stirling decided to make his way to the rendezvous, which was on the Trigh el Abd, an old track in the desert, some forty miles inland and running parallel to the coast road. Stirling's principal anxiety now was not so much that the raid had failed totally in its purpose of destroying enemy aircraft, but rather how many of his specially chosen and trained band of comrades he would find when the rendezvous was reached.

It was not until the following night that they did reach it. A warm welcome from the Long Range patrol commander awaited them, as did also both Fraser and Lewis, who after comparable experiences of realizing they could take no offensive action, finding their bearings and deciding there was nothing more to be done, had made their way to the agreed meeting point with their men. It was at this time that an historic meeting took place, between David Stirling and David Lloyd Owen, who recalls:

The moment I met David in the early light of dawn on 20 November 1941, I was captivated by his charm and self-assurance. Even then he had been through quite a lot. He had suffered the torture of failure, failure of an idea which had cost him much to promote, he had walked a long way in foul conditions of wind and weather, and it was at the hour when the morale of ordinary mortals is seldom high. From our hide-out we saw two figures walking across the desert. I was expecting some of David's party to come in, so walked across with Titch Cave to meet them.

'My name's Stirling,' he said, almost as though we were meeting for the first time outside his Club in London. 'Have you seen any of my chaps?'

'Yes, Paddy Mayne came in with nine men some time ago and they're with Jake Easonsmith. My name's David Lloyd Owen. We haven't met before.'

'I think I will wait here for a bit and see who else comes in. So let's talk if you've nothing else to do.'

'Yes, I'd love to. Are you cold? I expect you'd like some tea. Let's go and get some.'

We drank a mug of tea together and it was laced heavily with whisky. David told me the story of his drop and of all that had gone wrong. He had rotten luck and any lesser man would have had his ardour completely damped. Not so David. He was already trying to analyse what had gone wrong and deciding how it would go right next time. I sensed throughout everything David said that he was not really certain that parachuting was the best way to reach his target. He obviously realized the hazards and that the technique of accurate dropping was not very well developed at that stage of the war. Suddenly an idea came to me. Why should not we in the L.R.D.G. take David's men to their targets, let them do their dirty work and then transport them home again:

'I don't see why you don't let us take you there,' I said to David, 'we can get you with accuracy as near the target as you want to go and will then lie up before coming to pick you up again.'

'Yes, perhaps. But it's a bit slow,' he replied.

'Surely it's better to be certain of getting there rather than risk the whole thing going off half cock like this last show of yours?'

'Can you guarantee to get us anywhere without being seen on the way?'

'Yes. Very nearly. There's always a risk that we may run into trouble but the chances are that we'll get away with it.'

'What about the extra load of men and explosives which we'll want to carry? Will your vehicles take it?'

'I don't see why they shouldn't. After all you can't have all that amount extra as otherwise you would never be able to carry it with you. No, I'm sure there wouldn't be much of a problem over that. I reckon we can get you to within five miles of almost anywhere you want to go, and that's far better than being dropped twenty miles away from where you hope to land'.

David was still a bit sceptical. Perhaps he did not want to abandon his idea of parachuting for he had trained his men to jump under the most difficult circumstances and at a stage in the war when very few people knew much about it. Perhaps also he was not convinced that we could do all that I said we could, for he had not yet travelled with one of our patrols. Anyway this conversation was the birth of an idea which grew to fruition in David Stirling's mind and he never again attempted to reach his objective by parachute.

It should be noted here that parachuting of course continued to feature as an S.A.S. capability for operations elsewhere, but it certainly became clear to David Stirling that there was little need to parachute into desert areas on the enemy's southern flank, when access to this flank was easier and more sure by land. Thus began an association between the S.A.S. and the L.R.D.G. which achieved much. Before we see what it was that they dared and did together, we might note the revealing comments made by David Lloyd Owen about David Stirling and one of his most extraordinary comrades, Paddy Mayne:

Paddy was an enormous man with tremendous physical strength and an attractive Irish brogue. He was a most gentle and kind person who possessed all the qualities of leadership, which made him so successful. He had an aggressive and ingenious brain, which was always seeking new ways to harry the enemy and he was the type of man who would never ask anyone to do anything that he had not done himself. He was a born leader and he flourished under the powers that he could exercise.

Yet his gentle appearance and nature were sometimes deceptive and I would have hated to have found myself on the wrong side of Paddy Mayne. It took little to upset him and then it was very difficult to control him. As a fighter he was unsurpassed for his very presence in the full flood of his wrath was enough to unnerve the strongest of human beings. I'm sure he would have forgiven my saying that many a Provost Marshal has had good cause to remember that it was hardly wise to upset Paddy. I need say no more of his courage other than that he had won four DSOs by the end of the war and I have no doubt that he would have won more if he had not been so modest and if some of his more remarkable feats had not been in single combat. His was a truly lovable personality. ... He had all the colour, dash and attraction of a great buccaneer.

Paddy Mayne was the perfect instrument in the hands of David Stirling's genius. David had many of Paddy's characteristics – his aggressive outlook, his courage, his quite remarkable powers of leadership. I would say that he was probably more balanced, but they both possessed the same disregard and contempt for authority, unless it was the kind of authority that was likely to help them further their aims. David Stirling must have dreamed of ways in which to confuse and embarrass the enemy, for he produced more ideas in a week than would be expected of fifteen normal men in a campaign. Some were undoubtedly quite unsound for they took little heed of the administrative problems connected with them. But others were the ideas of a genius and I have no doubt that David Stirling was a genius in the field of guerrilla warfare.

But not only did David produce these ideas, but he had a burning faith in his ability to carry them out and a quite tireless energy in seeing that they were. Of course, he also picked splendid subordinates to assist him but that, in itself, is only further evidence of his greatness. He also had a power over men which I had never seen before. I believe that if David had asked men to jump into the midst of an enemy Armoured Division in broad daylight, they would have gone with him without question and in the knowledge that David would find a way to subdue the tanks and bring his men out unscathed and the overwhelming victors. Where that power of his lay is hard to define. I came under its spell because I was carried away by his enthusiasm, by his energy, by his oratory – for he could convince any man that black was white! – by his sheer determination,

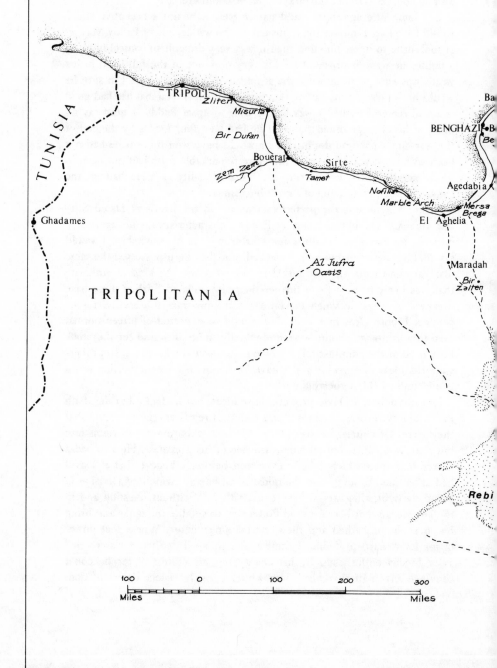

WESTERN DESERT

1941 - 1943

TUNISIA

TRIPOLI
Zliten
Misurta
Bir Dufan
Bouerat
Zem Zem
Sirte
Tamet
Nofilia
Marble Arch
El Aghelia

Ba
BENGHAZI B
Be
Agedabia
Mersa Brega

Ghadames

TRIPOLITANIA

Al Jufra Oasis

Maradah

Bir Zalten

Rebi

100   0   100   200   300
Miles   Miles

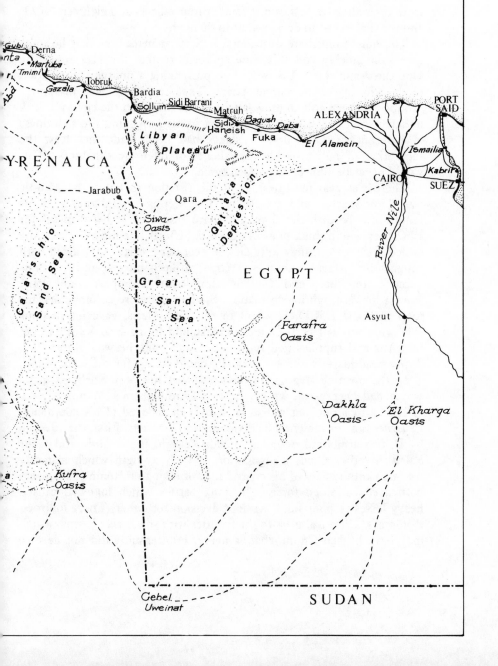

CRETE

Kastelli Heraklion
Maleme Timbaki

Gubi
nta Derna
Martuba
Tmimi
Abd
Gazala Tobruk
Bardia
Sollum Sidi Barrani
Matruh
Sidi Bagush Daba
Haneish
Fuka El Alamein

ALEXANDRIA

PORT
SAID

Ismailia
Kabrit
CAIRO
SUEZ

Libyan
Plateau

Y R E N A I C A

Jarabub Qara
Siwa
Oasis

Qattara
Depression

Calanschio
Sand Sea

Great
Sand
Sea

E G Y P T

River Nile

Farafra
Oasis

Asyut

Dakhla
Oasis

El Kharga
Oasis

Kufra
Oasis

a

Gebel
Uweinat

S U D A N

courage and endurance. I know full well that David knew what fear was. He could recognize the symptoms and he did not like them. But he could control that fear, which was very real to him, and that is the measure of true courage and supreme self-confidence. David had both. I know of no other man who did more to deserve the Victoria Cross and who was so inadequately decorated for his exploits.

Such then were the two men who, together with the other survivors from their abortive first raid, a total of four officers and eighteen NCOs and men, now had to decide what to do next.

The most immediate decision that Stirling made was that he must try again quickly and this time succeed, so that the idea would be vindicated and the S.A.S. would go on making a unique contribution to the winning of the war in Africa. That he and his men in various groups had been able to move about in the desert on the enemy's flank undetected and unharassed reinforced in his own mind the soundness of his concept. Of course, mistakes had been made, not least the separation of indispensable ingredients of offensive capability. This would never be allowed to happen again.

There was also the question of the reaction to failure by Middle East Headquarters and 8th Army. The sceptics would rejoice at his failure and be disinclined to put more resources at his disposal for what they would think of as more wasted efforts. He must outflank the gilded staff. Two things were clearly necessary: first, to try again with roughly his present resources; second, to keep himself and his command at the sharp end, so that administrative support could come from a forward fighting formation. Stirling therefore accompanied his men with the L.R.D.G. patrol to the Siwa Oasis, gave instructions that what was left of L Detachment should fly back to Kabrit to get weapons and supplies and return to Siwa, while he would go to 8th Army headquarters and see what he could fix up for the next round.

In the opening stages of *Crusader* it was not only Stirling's game which had been going wrong. So had Cunningham's. Within a week of the battle's opening moves he had been relieved of his command. *Crusader* can conveniently be divided into four parts. First, the advance by British armoured brigades to Sidi Rezegh, Bir el Gubi and Gabr Saleh, in other words a dissipation of tank strength which instantly robbed Cunningham of his central idea of taking on Rommel's panzers with a concentrated force. The tank battles which followed caused heavy losses to both sides, without decision for either. There followed Rommel's whimsical dash to the frontier with the Afrika Korps, which may have broken Cunningham's nerve, but certainly did not deceive

Auchinleck. Rommel's return to his supply areas between Tobruk and
Bardia was followed by further Sidi Rezegh battles. Finally Rommel
withdrew to Agheila. The British were left in possession of the field,
had relieved Tobruk, taken back Cyrenaica and won a token victory.
Its Pyrrhic nature was to be demonstrated by Rommel's subsequent
advance, devastating in its speed and boldness, and very nearly decisive
in its results.

Stirling arrived at 8th Army Headquarters at the time when Rommel
was making his dash to the frontier and trying by sheer bluff to panic
the British commanders into fatal moves. So obsessed with these problems were the higher commanders that, during Stirling's two brief
encounters with Cunningham, and then Ritchie, the extent of his own
difficulties was never really understood. What all this amounted to was
that weightier matters than L Detachment's next moves preoccupied
those who were directing 8th Army to such an extent that Stirling was
given carte blanche - with the assistance of Brigadier John Marriott
who commanded 22nd Guards Brigade, a man wholly sympathetic to
Stirling's ideas and both willing and able to give real help just when
it was most needed. Having heard that what Stirling wanted was to be
attached to a fighting unit which would supply L Detachment and
allow his complete freedom of operation, if possible in an area remote
from headquarters, control and red tape, Marriott sent Stirling to the
so-called Saharan oasis of Jalo (or Gialo), which was well away from
the main arena used by 8th Army and Rommel's *Panzerarmee* for
shuffling backwards and forwards in the relatively narrow strip of
desert near the coast. A hundred and fifty miles inland, it only occasionally demanded the attention of one side or the other, and at this
particular moment was in the hands of another imaginative and thrusting soldier, Brigadier Denys Reid, together with a squadron of the
Long Range Desert Group. Thus there grew up between these two
special organizations a relationship which flowered into great military
exploits. They complemented each other exactly, and no one tells us
why more elegantly than Fitzroy Maclean:

> Henceforward the Long Range Desert Group provided expert knowledge
> of the desert, skilled navigation and first-rate administration - vital necess-
> ities where one's life and the success of the operation depended on getting
> to the right place at the right time and on carrying with one a sufficient load
> of food, petrol and water to last the trip. David, for his part, brought to
> these ventures the striking power and, to their planning and execution,
> what Lawrence has called 'the irrational tenth ... like the kingfisher flash-
> ing across the pool': a never-failing audacity, a gift of daring improvisation,

which invariably took the enemy by surprise. The resulting partnership was a most fruitful one.

The best targets were aerodromes. From these the Luftwaffe and their Italian allies regularly attacked our convoys, fighting their way through the Mediterranean to Malta and Eighth Army. ... Situated hundred of miles behind the front, these desert airfields were not heavily defended: some wire, some machine-gun posts and an occasional patrol were considered sufficient protection. After carefully studying the lie of the land, it was possible to slip through the wire under cover of darkness, and surreptitiously deposit charges of high explosive in the aircraft where they stood dotted about the airfield. The high explosive, mixed for better results with an incendiary substance, was made up into handy packages and provided with a device known as a time-pencil which could be set to detonate the charges after an interval of a quarter or half an hour. This gave the attackers time to put a mile or two of desert between themselves and the airfield before their bombs exploded and the alarm was given. After that it only remained for them to make their way back to wherever the L.R.D.G. trucks were waiting to pick them up.

Working on these lines, David achieved, in the months that followed, a series of successes which surpassed the wildest expectations of those who had originally supported his venture. No sooner was one operation completed than he was off on another. No sooner had the enemy become aware of his presence in one part of the desert and set about taking counter-measures than he was attacking them somewhere else, always where they least expected it. Never has the element of surprise, the key to success in all irregular warfare, been more brilliantly exploited. Soon the number of aircraft destroyed on the ground was well into three figures. In order to protect their rear the enemy were obliged to bring back more and more front-line troops. And all this was done with a handful of men, a few pounds of high explosives and a few hundred rounds of ammunition. One thing, perhaps, contributed more than anything else to the success of these operations: that David both planned them and carried them out himself, and that, in the early days at any rate, every man in the unit had been picked by him personally.

It would be impossible to describe more succinctly or more effectively what the early days of the S.A.S. were all about. Now we must turn to the raids themselves and see what was planned, what was done and learn something more of those who planned and did it. In this way we shall be able to understand what David Stirling meant about the synonymity of the Man and the Regiment.

4

VINDICATED

We heard later that Rommel had been in Agedabia that night.
He must have had a bit of a headache.

Brigadier Denys Reid

Jalo was just the place for L Detachment. There Stirling enjoyed
freedom for planning, freedom of manoeuvre and freedom from interference, together with assured supplies, support of the L.R.D.G. and
a number of kindred spirits as enthusiastic as he himself was to act
with imagination and daring and inflict special damage on Rommel's
forces. At about the same time as Stirling was planning his next moves,
there occurred an event which, like the German attack on Russia,
turned the strategic scales upside down and brought new dimensions
both to the war in general and to that particular private battle of wills
being waged in the desert. As the first week of December, 1941, came
to an end, and while the pattern of *Crusader* could best be summed up
in Ronald Lewin's words as one of 'confusion compounded by a leth-
argy or indifference which seems to have prevented either side from
establishing the location or strength of the other', Japan launched its
attack on Pearl Harbor and Malaya. Britain and the United States at
once became allies against Japan and a few days later allies against
Germany and Italy.

To both Hitler and Churchill it seemed like a turning point. Hitler
rejoiced to Walther Hewel that now it was impossible for them to lose
the war, as they now had an ally who had never been conquered in
three thousand years, adding, with the kind of reference to Italy he
could never resist, that their other ally had almost always been conquered, but usually ended up on the right side. With the American
people in the war, Churchill put it more pithily: 'So we had won after

all'. Not that there were many signs of it to start with. It is true that within a month the first joint plans of this new alliance began to be made when Churchill and his advisers went to Washington with the first blueprint for Allied Grand Strategy in their pockets. It is true that in the end the weight of the new world would redress the balance of the old. But it is also true that Japan's entry into the war instantly and precariously stretched Britain's resources to an extent not previously contemplated or experienced. And as far as the desert was concerned, just as the diversion to Greece almost a year before had robbed O'Connor of his opportunity to end the North African campaign once and for all, so the re-direction of military strength from Auchinleck to the Far East did away with any idea that 8th Army would be able to finish off Rommel as *Crusader* ground its way to a close. Rommel, as became a Desert Fox, certainly went away, first to Gazala, then to Al Agheila. When he returned, however, it would be to carry out his most daring and devastating demonstration of *Blitzkrieg* in the desert. Moreover, in reversal of former inhibitions imposed on him by those two fortresses, Tobruk and Malta, he was able to seize one and all but neutralize the other.

At the same time as the Japanese entry into the war Rommel and Marshal Bastico, the Italian commander in North Africa, indulged in one of their not infrequent shouting matches, of which Rommel as usual got the best. According to the Italian Official History Rommel, 'like an overbearing and uncouth boor, yelled that he had struggled for three weeks to win the victory and had now decided to take his divisions to Tripoli and have himself interned in Tunisia.' The real cause of this despondency was once again shortage of supplies. Although before long the Luftwaffe was to restore its superiority in the air, and thus ensure supplies to the *Panzerarmee*, at this point in Rommel's fortunes, when the Italian *Commandosupremo* made it plain that, except for a minimum of essentials, nothing in the way of reinforcements or supplies would cross the Mediterranean before the end of the year, there was no alternative. The *Panzerarmee* had to withdraw.

Under the Desert Fox's direction, however, it was clear that his Army was just as dangerous to the British in withdrawal as it was in advance. As Ronald Lewin put it:

The Afrika Korps was about to demonstrate once again its professional skill and invincible morale, for although it had now lost many of its best officers and men, and a large proportion of its equipment, and though a temporary weariness had affected minds as well as bodies, during the long haul from the environs of Tobruk to the Gulf of Sirte, it retained both cohesion and the will to fight ... and far from racing to the rear it could turn, stand its ground and inflict numbing wounds on the enemy.

Meanwhile David Stirling was about to deliver some numbing wounds of his own. He was lucky in finding at Jalo A Squadron of the L.R.D.G. and its commander, Major Steele, who at once responded to Stirling's ideas. The primary role of the L.R.D.G. was, of course, reconnaissance and getting information, whereas L Detachment S.A.S. was essentially for the destruction of enemy aircraft or other military equipment. It was clear that, although the two could complement each other, the more successful the S.A.S. were, the more difficult would become the information-gathering activity of the L.R.D.G. No one has drawn the distinction between these two better than General Sir John Hackett in his foreword to David Lloyd Owen's book, to which we have already referred:

> These were two very different sets of people. The S.A.S. were raiders. The L.R.D.G. were specialists in deep reconnaissance. The S.A.S. could act as information gatherers too, and the L.R.D.G. ... were the better for an occasional beat-up, but their roles were different and their operations had to be kept apart. The S.A.S. would dash in and destroy enemy aircraft on their landing-grounds, or some other equally tempting target, and wake the whole area up. When they had gone – usually leaving the desert strewn with what they had jettisoned – the enemy's patrols would come out in strength in an energetic search for them, sometimes to find and flush out instead the beautifully sited and carefully concealed observation posts of the L.R.D.G. These two groups had enormous respect for each other, but it was better if they did not operate in close proximity.

In this connection David Lloyd Owen commented:

> There were bound to be some problems in avoiding a clash of aims of the two units. It was never easy to achieve a sensible balance between the requirements of reconnaissance for intelligence purposes and the need to stir up trouble in the rear areas. The enemy's reaction to Stirling's operations was bound to make the work of the L.R.D.G. a little less simple than it might otherwise have been. We were able to reach a reasonable modus vivendi primarily because both parties had considerable respect for the other's achievements and because we grew to understand each other by working so closely together.

In spite of their differences, therefore, these two forces had much in common, above all their ideals of daring and adventure. And as the L.R.D.G. method of operating was to send patrols in trucks hundreds of miles behind enemy lines to lie up in hiding and report enemy road movement, and as their men were experts at travelling and living in the desert for weeks at a time without re-supply, they constituted the perfect guides and means of transport for Stirling's men.

Stirling was also fortunate that Brigadier Denys Reid, whose force had taken Jalo and to whom John Marriott had recommended him, was so enthusiastic to help him. Reid quickly saw that his own mission of supporting 8th Army's left flank when it advanced on Benghazi would be greatly assisted if Stirling could destroy German aircraft at Agedabia and other airfields near Agheila and Sirte. Stirling therefore made his plans assured of full support from Reid and Steele. The idea was that Stirling and Mayne with nine men would raid Sirte [and Tamet] airfields, some 350 miles from Jalo, on the night of 14 December. On the same night Lewis with ten men would attack Agheila airfield, and a week later, on 21 December, Fraser would deal with Agedabia, which would be of particular help to Reid and his force. All these raids were to constitute a first phase. The second phase was designed to mount further attacks on advanced landing grounds between 25 and 28 December. During these two phases all the imagination, training, courage and perseverance of Stirling and his men were to be triumphantly vindicated.

On 8 December Stirling, Mayne and their men set off in seven trucks, fully loaded with explosives, guns and ammunition, petrol, food and water, blankets, tyres, camouflage nets, and all the other military paraphernalia they would need. Captain Holliman, who commanded the L.R.D.G. Rhodesian patrol [he was in fact an Englishman], had been instructed to take Stirling's group to their target, and he and his navigator, Sadler, led the way. The trucks were painted a curious blend of pink and green for camouflage. For some 300 miles nothing untoward occurred, just the normal halts for checking position, eating, mending tyres, and, at night, cleaning weapons and maintaining the trucks:

> In the daytime David was surprised at how little came across their line of vision. The brooding solitude was like being on the high seas. It seemed strange to think that a life and death struggle was going on along the coast while here in the great desert waste was an atmosphere of infinite peace. For the first three days there was not a sign of life, not even a faraway caravan, only an endless vista of sand and rock and gully, with an occasional escarpment streaking across the horizon ... the patrol had maintained such a good average that, when it halted that night, Sadler told the men that they were seventy miles south of Sirte. The next day their luck changed.*

* As told to Virginia Cowles.

Luck went against them in two ways: first, the roughness and rockiness
of the ground slowed progress badly; second, about midday when they
were searching for cover in order to check position and eat lunch, they
were sighted by an Italian reconnaissance aeroplane, a Gibli, a small,
slow, unarmoured but manoeuvrable aircraft which carried one machine gun and two bombs. It was L.R.D.G. practice to fire on and try
to bring down the Giblis, the sharpness of whose sting lay, not in their
armament, but in their ability to report. They therefore opened fire,
but with no more effect than the Gibli's two bombs which fell wide of
the trucks. Holliman instantly decided that they must make for cover
since more aircraft would be coming. They therefore drove back about
two miles where some scrubby country afforded them a measure of
concealment. Sure enough three bombers appeared and proceeded to
strafe and bomb the area where they were hidden, fortunately causing
no damage either to men or trucks. They remained to eat and then
moved on. By about half past four in the afternoon they were some
forty miles from Sirte and, although it was not customary for L.R.D.G.
patrols to get too close to the enemy coastline by day, they pressed on
in order to get Stirling's party to a position about three miles from
both the coast road and Sirte airfield. But then another Gibli appeared,
this time too high to be fired at, but not too high to see them. Surprise,
that indispensable ingredient of all Stirling's ideas, had been lost before
he could do anything. Nonetheless, they continued until they were so
near the coast road that they heard enemy patrols talking and moving
up and down in their vehicles. Stirling concluded that the Gibli's
report had alerted the enemy to the possibility of a raid and decided
at once that they must do all they could to avoid another failure. So
much depended on their being successful this time. As it appeared
likely that there would be a reception committee at Sirte airfield, they
would divide the raiding party into two. Sergeant Brough and he
would have a try at Sirte, while Mayne and the rest of the men would
go to Tamet, some thirty miles west of Sirte, where there was a new
landing ground. There it should still be possible to surprise the enemy.
In any event, one of the two parties might be lucky. The chances were
doubled, and herein was revealed the great strength of the S.A.S. - its
crucial ability to operate in very small groups, the very reverse of that
prime principle of war, concentration.

The plan therefore was for Stirling and Sergeant Brough to walk
beyond the Sirte Airfield to some higher ground where they could get
a good look next day with a view to raiding at eleven o'clock that
night; at that same time Mayne and his party would attack Tamet.
Holliman's trucks would pick up the two groups after the raids and

they would then make their way separately to a rendezvous some eighty miles out in the desert. Having arranged with Holliman where to meet him after his raid and what recognition signs would be used, Stirling moved off with all the vehicles and men so that enemy patrols might be persuaded into thinking that they were all going away; then he and Brough dropped off by themselves. Before they had walked far, they found themselves on the edge of the airfield with whole lines of aircraft appearing. At this point Stirling turned over in his mind whether to set about destroying some there and then, but almost at once rejected the idea as it would prejudice Mayne's chances on the following evening. They went on to reconnoitre further, but this time stumbled over some Italian sentries. The consequent shouting and shooting forced them to retire into the desert again. While firing continued – it seemed the enemy thought there was a Commando raid from the sea – they made their way to a point overlooking the airfield, where they found some scrubby cover and slept. In the morning they saw that they had a good view both of Sirte village and the landing ground. There was quite a lot of activity, aircraft taking off and landing, and there seemed to be about thirty Italian Caprioni bombers based there. Despite almost being disturbed by some Arab women tending a patch of cultivated land on the ridge, all appeared well as they perfected their plans. Then in the afternoon a terrible thing happened:

> They began observing the airfield again. After an hour Brough noticed that the aircraft were taking off in twos and threes and none seemed to be returning. The two men watched with growing dismay. There was no doubt about it, the landing ground was being evacuated. By dusk it was empty ... now there was nothing to do but kill time until the rendezvous.

To start with, they became even more worried. Stirling and Brough, having got to the coast road about half past ten, some two hours before they were to meet Holliman's trucks, were hoping to hear soon some signs of activity from Tamet. Eleven o'clock, the time for Mayne's attack, came; half past eleven, still no explosions from Tamet. It was beginning to look like total failure again, triumph for the gilded staff sceptics, disbandment for the S.A.S. But suddenly all doubts and fears were swept away. A great flash glowed in the west, followed by explosion after explosion. Stirling had never heard 'so musical a discord, such sweet thunder'.

Shortly afterwards Holliman's trucks arrived to pick them up. Before they left Stirling mined the road and had the satisfaction of seeing an Italian truck blow up on it and crash. Then off they went to the rendezvous, where at about eleven o'clock that morning they were joined by Mayne's party. They had had a wonderful success – twenty-four enemy aircraft destroyed and no casualties of their own at all. Their first action on Tamet airfield had been to disturb what seemed to be a party going on in the officers' mess hut by spraying the inside of it with bullets and shooting the lights out. Mayne then told four of his men to continue this little battle by keeping the survivors quiet, while he and five others got on with planting bombs on the aircraft. When Mayne found there was one bomb short, he proceeded to climb into the cockpit of the remaining aircraft and tear out the instrument panel. Mayne was not a large and tough Ulsterman for nothing. One of his men, Corporal Seekings, tells us what happened on the journey back:

We had not gone fifty yards when the first plane went up. We stopped to look but the second one went up near us and we began to run. After a while we felt fairly safe and stopped to take another glance. What a sight! Planes exploding all over, and the terrific roar of petrol and bombs going up.

We got cracking again. The L.R.D.G. were flashing lights at few minute intervals. We packed our compass away. Next thing we knew we were off our course. A light flashed to our right, we turned towards it but it was soon obvious that the enemy were flashing lights as well. We had an alternative signal – blasts on a whistle. We blew it and were answered nearby, much to our relief.

I was gasping for a drink. We had no water with us and Paddy had set a cracking pace. Sergeant Jacko [Jackson, a Rhodesian] gave me a water-bottle – one of the big type the Rhodesians had. I took a long drink from it. As I took it from my lips I could not get my wind. I realised too late it was neat rum. In a matter of minutes I was three-parts in the blind. I staggered to my truck and fell off to sleep in spite of the rough going. I awoke to the sound of hammering and cursing – the steering had broken and the fitter was doing his best to put it right. Jacko had got a fire going and a brew on. I think it was Mike Sadler, the navigator, trying to tell him we were only a few miles from Sirte, to which Jacko replied he did not give a hell if we were only a few yards he intended to have a brew.

It was Mike's first patrol as navigator. We had to rendezvous many miles out into the desert with the other half of the patrol [ie. with the Stirling and Holliman group]. In spite of the rough going and darkness he made it dead on. A marvellous performance which he was to repeat often. In mending the truck we had been forced to dismantle the brakes and therefore couldn't stop. When we sighted the other patrol we had to coast

on towards them. They started firing everything. We almost died of shock,
thinking they had mistaken us for the enemy, but luckily they were firing
into the air, giving us a royal welcome – they had seen the fires and
explosions in the distance.

Stirling's ill-luck and Mayne's success were matched by the other two
raids by Lewis and Fraser, one a disappointment, the other a triumph.
Lewis found no aircraft at Agheila, which was being used as a staging
airfield. As an alternative he had intended to raid a roadhouse at Mersa
Brega which was often used as a meeting place for enemy generals and
their staffs. The idea was to capture them. But enemy sentries gave
the alarm before his party could strike, so they consoled themselves by
blowing up some enemy transport. Any disappointment that Stirling
and his comrades might have felt about Agheila, however, was more
than cleared away by Fraser's report when he returned to Jalo. They
had had a spectacular success at Agedabia, where their training, stealth
and courage were fully put to the test by having to dodge airfield
guards, lie doggo for an hour or so while surrounded by enemy and
then plant bombs on no fewer than thirty-seven aircraft. The confusion
once explosions began made their withdrawal a much easier affair.
Brigadier Reid, whose own operations were so much assisted by
Fraser's success, summed the whole thing up in his diary after meeting
Fraser:

> At first light there was a certain amount of excitement amongst the forward
> troops, and recognition signals by Very light were fired. I drove forward
> to see what was the matter and met Fraser of Stirling's L Detachment,
> whom I eagerly asked how he had got on. He said 'Very sorry, sir, I had
> to leave two aircraft on the ground as I ran out of explosive, but we
> destroyed 37'. This indeed was a wonderful achievement by one officer and
> three men. Incidentally, we heard later that Rommel had been in Agedabia
> that night. He must have had a bit of a headache.

Encouraged by these successes, Stirling determined to give Rommel
a few more headaches and he embarked almost at once on a further
series of raids. To reinforce success was, after all, a cardinal rule of
sound strategy. Although it was a rule to which neither Hitler nor
Churchill paid much attention, Stirling did. On 23 December he set
off again with S Patrol of the L.R.D.G. This time the idea was that
Mayne with five men would again attack Tamet, while Stirling with
four men would have another shot at Sirte. It was, not only in design,
but in result, the mixture as before. Stirling found Sirte airfield well
guarded, with a lot of German armoured vehicles about. There would

not be time to get through the airfield defences, deal with the aircraft and reach the agreed rendezvous on time. He therefore contented himself with blowing up twelve supply trucks, and shooting up a lot more while racing along the road with the L.R.D.G. trucks. It was all very exhilarating and Holliman greatly approved. Meanwhile Mayne again succeeded in walking into Tamet airfield and again scored very high marks by destroying twenty-seven aircraft. He and his party then joined Stirling and on their way back to Jalo enjoyed a delicious Christmas luncheon of gazelle, pudding and beer. There was a certain amount of good-natured chaff at Stirling's expense in that for the second time he had failed to do anything about Sirte airfield, compared with Mayne's second triumph at Tamet. He conceded that, with such hot competition, he would have to pull his socks up.

Two other operations had not fared well. Lewis's raid on Nofilia ended in his death. One of his men, Sergeant Lilly, tells us what happened:

> We reached Nofilia before dawn [26 December] and found a place to hide up where we could watch the aerodrome. There were not many aircraft in the field and the few that were there were very widely dispersed, but we noted the positions of them. As soon as it was dark we moved on to the landing ground and put a bomb on the first plane. We had just put one on the second when the first one went off – we were only using half-hour time pencils then. After that the airfield became alive with troops and we came very near to getting caught as we beat a retreat. It was a big disappointment to all of us that we had only destroyed two planes.

Much worse was to come. After returning to the rendezvous and making for Marble Arch, they were spotted by a low-flying Savoia, which circled round firing at them. They fired back without effect, then abandoned the trucks to get cover, but on another run by the Savoia Lewis was hit and died almost at once. So was lost the man whom David Lloyd Owen described as the finest David Stirling was ever likely to have serving with him. It had been Lewis's great capacity for reason and practicality which had so perfectly complemented Stirling's own breadth and imagination. Lilley and his companions, despite all the destruction wrought by enemy fighters, managed to get one of the damaged trucks going, went to the pre-arranged rendezvous with Fraser and his party, saw nothing of them and made for Jalo.

Later it transpired that there had been some misunderstanding about where they were to meet, for Fraser, having found no aircraft at his target, Marble Arch, went with his four men to the rendezvous, waited there fruitlessly for six days, then with some food but very little water, began a long walk, some two hundred miles, back to the British positions. They had all sorts of adventures and showed again what spirit, what resolution and what resourcefulness they were made of. Water was their principal worry, and one of the men, Sergeant Duvivier, has explained how they hit on various ways of keeping thirst at bay. He would take a sip from the half-pint in his water bottle – merely to hear it lapping about in the bottle helped him – moisten his mouth and spit it back in. He sucked small, smooth pebbles to prevent saliva drying up. They ate little, as swallowing became difficult. Then, after seeing what looked like an inland lake, they discovered on reaching it that the water was salt. So they hit upon a method to distil it, by heating the water and condensing the steam. It was slow and exhausting work, so they decided to try and raid an enemy truck. They succeeded and the raiding party of three came back with two jerry-cans of cool clear water. Tea, bully stew, cheese and dates made an unforgettable feast.

During the next three days Fraser and his four men marched on. Then they came across an Italian convoy, somewhere in the Wadi Faregh, and, being once more desperate for water, they surprised the crew of a truck somewhat apart from the others. They succeeded in frightening the Italian soldiers, but found no water, except what was in the radiator and this was quite undrinkable. Having persuaded the Italian soldiers that, if they stayed quiet, they would be taken prisoner by the British next day, Fraser and his companions moved on. By that evening they had been marching for six days and judged their position to be half-way between El Agheila and Mersa el-Brega. By this time they were so tired, weak and thirsty that they resolved to walk to the track and try seizing a vehicle, so that they could drive back to the British lines. They were lucky and surprised a small Mercedes car with two Germans in it. With a revolver suitably held at the German driver's head and somehow all packed into the car, off they went, and sure enough came to the Mersa rest house which they had previously planned to raid. Their German prisoners behaved, in spite of passing vehicles, and they motored on to a position some ten miles south of the road where the car bogged down in a salt marsh. After exchanging views with the two Germans, they parted company, the Germans walking north to the road, Fraser and his men further to the east. Two days later they met a British armoured car patrol and were safe. Their long walk had taken eight days. Such were some of Stirling's men.

Stirling, however, although he felt secure enough that L Detachment had so vindicated itself that he could now show himself once more, was concerned with getting more men and more supplies so that he could do more. After returning to Kabrit early in January, he therefore sought another interview with General Auchinleck. He had a new idea to put to the Commander-in-Chief. The Commander-in-Chief was, as usual, willing to listen. This sort of willingness is perhaps one of the marks of a great commander. For Auchinleck was in the same sort of position as Macbeth after Duncan's murder. He had scotch'd the snake, not kill'd it. And shortly the snake, or more properly the Desert Fox, was going to make some moves which would overcome Auchinleck like a summer's cloud.

5

SHARPENING THE STING

Force and fraud are in war the two cardinal virtues.

Hobbes

As *Crusader* drew to a close, Auchinleck might have been excused if he found some satisfaction in what had been done. Despite having to sack 8th Army's commander and appoint his own protégé instead; despite heavy losses and administrative exhaustion; despite his failure to prevent Rommel's orderly withdrawal or the Desert Air Force's total inability to punish the Afrika Korps in its Gazala position – despite all these things, there was some cause for comfort. Tobruk was relieved, Cyrenaica retaken and Rommel obliged to retire. These were no mean achievements. Yet, before his withdrawal, Rommel's Afrika Korps had received two unlooked-for bonuses to reinforce what he had described as the core of the army on which everything else turned – the panzer force. Before withdrawing from Benghazi the Axis forces had been able to welcome the safe arrival of a merchant ship, *Ankara*, which brought among other things twenty-two precious tanks for the 15th Panzer Division. This, together with a similar number delivered to Tripoli, greatly strengthened the core of the army. The panzer regiments were about to show once again what they could do in following Rommel's maxim that troops must be able to carry out operations at top speed with complete coordination. It was a maxim the British never understood or adhered to. 'To be satisfied with norms,' Rommel subsequently wrote, 'is fatal.' It was this that was the trouble with the British way of waging war in the desert. They were satisfied with norms. They could not seem to concentrate their forces under the right sort of leadership to go for and realize their principal objectives. The gift of a few extra panzers to Rommel was to enable him once more to shock the British into a kind of numbed inactivity, saved only

1 Lieut-Colonel David Stirling, DSO, founder of 'L' Detachment, SAS Brigade and CO 1 SAS Regiment. (*Imperial War Museum*)

2 Major Paddy Mayne, DSO and 3 bars, who took over 1 SAS from Stirling.

3 An LRDG patrol leaving Siwa Oasis, May, 1942. (*Imperial War Museum*)

4 Lieut-Colonel Stirling with Lieut McDonald's patrol, 1942. (*Imperial War Museum*)

5 Lieut Edward McDonald, DCM, Cameron Highlanders. (*Imperial War Museum*)

6 Corporal James McDiarmid, Black Watch. (*Imperial War Museum*)

7 Corporal Bill Kennedy,
Royal Scots Greys.
(*Imperial War
Museum*)

8 Some of the 'old hands'
who took part in most
of the early desert raids,
Kabrit, July, 1942. Front:
Sgt Dave Kershaw, MM;
Sgt Reg Seekings, DCM.
In jeep: left-RSM Riley
DCM; behind –
Sgt Richardson; right –
Sgt Ted Badger, MM.
On bonnet: Sgt Bob
Tait, MM: Sgt
Johnny Cooper,
DCM.

9 Parachute training at Kabrit, November, 1941. (*Imperial War Museum*)

10 A Patrol of the Free French SAS Squadron in the Gabes area of Tunisia, February, 1943. (*Imperial War Museum*)

Corporal Sillitoe, the sole survivor of a patrol which set out to destroy the railway west of Alamein. He is seen here recovering in the base camp after walking 100 miles without food or water. (*Imperial War Museum*)

12 An aircraft was used on the ground to familiarize the men with jumping out of the door. (*Imperial War Museum*)

Major Anders Lassen, VC, MC and 2 bars.

14 Men of the SBS at one of the caique bases on the Turkish coast, 1943. (*AFPU Ministry of Defence*)

15 Lieut-Colonel Ian Lapraik (centre) on the beach at Polonia, Milos, November, 1944. (*Imperial War Museum*)

6 Major Roy Farran, DSO, MC.

17 Sir Fitzroy Maclean, Bt. (*Jonathan Cape Ltd and Studio Briggs*)

18 Major Sandy Scratchley, DSO, MC, (left) with a group of the SAS who took part in the capture of Termoli, October, 1943. (*Imperial War Museum*)

19 Captain McDonald (standing in car), a Canadian serving with 3 Squadron, 2 SAS, setting out on a patrol behind the enemy lines with Italian partisans on Operation Gallia, near Alba, N. Italy, February, 1945. (*Imperial War Museum*)

20 Northern Italy, March, 1945; Operation Tombola. A jeep patrol of 3 Squadron, 2 SAS behind German lines at Vallestri, near Modena.

by the personal intervention of the rock-like Auchinleck. There was, however, one man in 8th Army who was not satisfied with norms – David Stirling. He understood the crucial importance and vulnerability of ports like Benghazi and was about to bring his own particular brand of activity to stir such places up.

Shortly before Benghazi fell to the British for the second time, Stirling had another interview with Auchinleck. This time he put to the Commander-in-Chief a proposal that L Detachment should strike, not at airfields, but at the ports through which Rommel's supplies came, and in particular at the port of Bouerat. He pointed out to Auchinleck that as Benghazi would shortly be in British hands, Rommel's supply ships would be obliged to divert to Bouerat, some 350 miles further west. This port would become an important base for fuel tankers and other supply vessels. Therefore, argued Stirling, both ships and fuel depots could and should be blown up. One of Auchinleck's great qualities as a commander was calm, and he received Stirling's new suggestion as calmly as he had dealt with the *Crusader* crises and as he was in the future to take command of 8th Army at a time when calm above all things was called for. Even the news that Stirling required more men did not ruffle him. He simply asked how many. When these discussions ended, Stirling had got the Commander-in-Chief's permission to recruit a further six officers and thirty to forty men, some of whom would come from the Special Boat Section* and who would clearly be of especial value in what he was now proposing to do. He informed Auchinleck that his raid on Bouerat would take place in mid-January when there was no moon. As he left, Auchinleck, whose satisfaction in the S.A.S.'s great success had put him into a giving vein, told Stirling that from now on he was a major. As there now were but ten days or so before the raid was to be mounted, he then got on with preparing it, initially from a temporary headquarters at his brother Peter's flat in Garden City.

There followed a furious week of organizing and planning, but, before Stirling returned to Jalo to start the operation, he had succeeded in acquiring two more invaluable assets – one a band of exceptionally able and aggressive Free Frenchmen, the other a symbol for the S.A.S. which has lasted to this day. One reason for enrolling the French was the difficulty of recruiting more British. Not only was there opposition

---

* No 8 Commando of Layforce had developed a special section with this name for carrying out beach and harbour reconnaissance with canoes. It continued to operate after Layforce's disbandment and came under Stirling's command in the spring of 1942. The S.B.S. is now part of the Royal Marines.

from the unimaginative staff of GHQ, but no fighting regiment was anxious to give up its best men. But Stirling heard that a squadron of Free French parachutists had arrived in Alexandria from Syria, and after some argument obtained agreement that they should join his unit. As there were about fifty of them, this was a major reinforcement. First they had to be trained in the use of explosives, and Stirling found the ideal man, a sapper officer called Cumper, whose lively sense of humour and Cockneyisms seemed to suit the French, and Kabrit resounded with encouraging bangs as they learned this part of their trade.

The symbol was, of course, the S.A.S. badge, the so-called Winged Dagger, although it was not really meant to be a dagger at all, but King Arthur's Excalibur, the freedom-winning sword. The wings were taken from a fresco in Shepheard's Hotel. They were, in fact, the wings of an ibis; the sacred white ibis was venerated by the ancient Egyptians and is still common in the Nile basin. The colours of the wings, Oxford and Cambridge blue, were selected because in the original L Detachment Lewis had rowed for Oxford and Langton for Cambridge. Wings awarded for seven parachute jumps were worn on the right arm, but after conducting himself well in action, a man could be given operational wings, that is the right to wear them on his left breast. The badge itself was worn in berets, at first white, later sand-coloured, which it still is. As Auchinleck himself happened to see and like the badge, staff disapproval and opposition dissolved.

As with all operations of war, good intelligence was needed for the Bouerat raid. Stirling wanted proper air photographs of Bouerat, and Peter Oldfield of the Air Reconnaissance unit proceeded to supply them. Stirling also discussed the whole operation with the Royal Air Force, who, during the moonless period of the planned raid, would in the normal way be doing a lot of bombing. It was agreed between them that the raid would be completed by the night 23/24 January, so that the R.A.F. could bomb on 24/25 January. One piece of information about Bouerat supplied by Oldfield was that oil tankers seldom spent long in harbour. Within a day or two of arrival they would have discharged their cargo and be off again. But there was more to Bouerat than simply being a port for delivery. Reconnaissances had revealed that it was also an area where oil was stored in bulk, either in depots or in vehicles. As things turned out, this was significant to the way in which the raid was eventually conducted.

Before going to mount the raid Stirling had a disagreeable duty to perform – to tell his most trusted subordinate that he would not be taking part in it. Someone had to train the new S.A.S. volunteers at

Kabrit. Only Paddy Mayne could do it. So David Stirling told him. With the utmost reluctance, bordering on insubordination, Mayne complied. On 11 January, 1942, Stirling left Cairo once more for Jalo. He was soon joined by two members of the Special Boat Section, including Captain Duncan, who brought with them the necessary kit for blowing up ships – a portable canoe, limpets and explosives – and also by two R.A.F. intelligence men. On 17 January the raiders, escorted as usual by the L.R.D.G., set off. Like some previous raids and those still to come, things did not go precisely as planned. Yet despite difficulties, disappointments and dangers, Stirling's coalition of imagination and improvisation once more yielded large dividends.

The patrol was heading for familiar country, as Bouerat is not far from either Sirte or Tamet. Navigation was in the experienced hands of Sadler, while Antony Hunter was the L.R.D.G. commander. Keeping well to the south as usual in order to evade enemy air reconnaissance, the patrol reached the edge of Wadi Tamet after five days. It was already 22 January and the plan was to have finished the operation by the 24th. There was no time to lose. Yet Stirling had still had no reports from Oldfield about air photographs of Bouerat. He was therefore obliged to break wireless silence, with the accompanying risk of interception and detection, by signalling to Siwa for information. Next morning it was clear that the enemy had been alerted, for, despite attempting to hide themselves in the Wadi, their presence was revealed to Italian air reconnaissance, quickly to be followed by an all-day bombing and strafing operation by the Italians. Most of the patrol survived, but when they reassembled that evening it was discovered that the radio truck and operators were missing. They were never seen or heard of again. This meant that there would be no information about oil tankers or dumps at Bouerat. They would have to find out for themselves. After moving to a rendezvous some thirty miles west of Wadi Tamet and sixty from their target, Stirling's sixteen men, plus canoe, weapons and explosives, were driven in one truck by Hunter and three others to within a mile of Bouerat. On the way the truck jolted into a hole and smashed the already assembled canoe. Still undaunted, Stirling and Duncan agreed that they would go respectively for the oil and the radio station. Although there were no ships to be seen at the port, Stirling's parties found storage depots, petrol bowsers and supply trucks and succeeded in blowing them all up. Duncan's group destroyed the radio station. And, despite running into an ambush on the way back to the main rendezvous, there were no more losses. What at one time had looked like being a failure had turned into a triumphant success.

The same could hardly be said of 8th Army's operations. Before long it became clear why Rommel had not been making more use of Bouerat as a supply port. He had been planning to use Benghazi again and he soon had it. On 18 January, just after Stirling had set off from Jalo, Rommel issued orders for his Army to advance three days later. There were no specific objectives or time-tables. He would simply advance and bring about a pell-mell battle. In what later became known as the Msus Stakes, Rommel's pursuit of the British, as von Mellenthin recalled, 'attained a speed of fifteen miles an hour and the British fled madly over the desert in one of the most extraordinary routs of the war'. Much of the Afrika Korps' success was because of their newly developed method of attack. Groups of anti-tank guns and panzers would leap-frog from position to position, each giving the other covering fire, and all done with such speed and sureness that the British seemed to have no answer to it. They constantly gave ground, sustaining losses as they did so. When the Germans began to be worried about petrol supplies and told Rommel so, he told them to go and get it from the British. By 6 February 8th Army was back on the Gazala line, the position which Rommel's *Panzerarmee* had abandoned two months earlier. All this obviously made a great difference to the S.A.S. On their way back from the Bouerat raid Stirling and his men had heard about 8th Army's retreat from a BBC report which Hunter picked up on his ordinary wireless set. They therefore approached Jalo with great care, found it evacuated by the L.R.D.G. and made their way instead back to Siwa. From there Stirling returned to the main S.A.S. base at Kabrit.

At the time of his return Stirling found that Paddy Mayne, disappointed and resentful at having been left out of the last raids and further disillusioned by the news of Rommel's successful counter-attacks, which made it seem as if all their previous work had been for nothing, had more or less given up trying to attend to the administration of training. But after a furious row, during which each was able to appreciate the true qualities of the other – Stirling as the imaginative planner and leader, Mayne as the born and brilliant man of action – they were reconciled. Sergeant-Major Riley, who had been a leading member of the Bouerat raid, took over supervision of training, including the French squadron. When Stirling found that Cumper, the expert in sabotage and explosives, had been posted away, he got him back, to become a permanent member of the S.A.S. Now began the planning for further raids, not only on the airfields near Benghazi, but on Benghazi harbour itself.

In his repeated attempts to attack enemy shipping in Benghazi harbour or elsewhere, Stirling had grasped the supremely important point that the battle for North Africa was a battle of supplies. Rob Rommel of substantial amounts of petrol, ammunition and the tanks which used them and his practice of blitzkrieg in the desert would soon come to an end. The final battles conducted by Rommel were, of course, dominated by the logistic starvation suffered by the *Panzerarmee* and by the material abundance enjoyed by Montgomery. But a lot was to happen before that. Hand in hand with supplies themselves went the lines of communication, the fuel and ammunition depots, the bases for repair and all the paraphernalia of modern, mechanized warfare. It was here that Stirling wished to strike, and had he had his way, his whole idea would have been expanded into a much larger organization – but still operating in small groups – which would have kept up an unceasing harassment of the enemy's supply lines up and down the coast. As it was he had to be content with small numbers of men. But this did not diminish the breadth and boldness of his plans. In the Benghazi area raids on airfields proved to be more profitable than those aimed at shipping. Nonetheless Stirling's expeditions into Benghazi itself were noteworthy both in illustrating what sheer audacity could accomplish, particularly when exercised by experienced S.A.S. men and a few extras who brought an almost comical aspect to a coalition of colossal fraud and negligible force.

For his first 'visit' to Benghazi Stirling collected some additional raiders – Gordon Alston, two officers from the Special Boat Section, Lieutenant Sutherland and Captain Allot, and Bob Melot, a Belgian who was helping British intelligence, spoke Arabic expertly and suggested taking two Senussi soldiers along with them to reconnoitre when they got near the town. The operation was to be mounted from the L.R.D.G. base at Siwa, the large oasis on the edge of the Qattara Depression. Siwa had been a stronghold of the Senussi Arabs, who had resisted former Italian conquest and at this time had allied themselves to the British in fighting Italians both in Egypt and Libya. To one observer, who was subsequently to visit Benghazi in Stirling's company, Siwa was all that the romantic stories he had heard about it had led him to expect:

Ever since I was a child I have been brought up on stories of Siwa. In the years before 1914 a cousin of mine had been one of the relatively few Europeans to enter the oasis, and he and my father had played their part in the operations which led to its capture. Now, it did not fall short of my expectations. Under the palm trees were pools of clear fresh water bubbling up from a great depth. Round one of them was an ancient stone parapet.

I remembered my father telling me what a joy it was to plunge into these pools after long weeks in the desert, and now, at an interval of a quarter of a century, I followed his example. The water was deliciously refreshing and gushed up with such force that it was like bathing in soda water.

In the middle of the oasis rose what was left of the fortress-town of the Senussi, built of mud and shaped like a beehive. The shells of 1917 had torn great breaches in its walls, revealing inside it the columns of the ancient Greek temple of Jupiter Ammon, whose oracle was famous in the time of Herodotus. Nearby, among the palm groves, were some older ruins, dating back to the ancient Egyptians. In the market place the Arabs clustered round us, friendly and curious, and soon I found myself being entertained to tea and mutton by several of the leading citizens. As in Central Asia, the food was placed in a large central dish, from which we helped ourselves with our fingers. An elaborate pipe was also passed round for each of us to take a pull at in turn as we squatted on the ground. Meanwhile the L.R.D.G. Medical Officer, who had accompanied me on this expedition, was fascinated by the disease from which my immediate neighbour was suffering. 'Very interesting,' he kept saying, 'and no doubt highly contagious.'*

From this oasis Stirling set out on 15 March, escorted by the Rhodesian Long Range patrol. He had with him in a Ford truck disguised to look like a German staff car Paddy Mayne and Melot, while Alston and Sutherland followed in an actual German staff car which had been captured. Other S.A.S. and S.B.S. men were with the patrol. On the 400-mile journey to Benghazi, they had to travel along the old caravan route, the Trigh el-Abd, which had been used by both sides in various desert advances and was extensively mined. Sure enough, the German staff car blew up on a Thermos mine, wounding Sutherland who had to return to Siwa with one of the Long Range patrol trucks. A more attractive feature of this country was the Djebel Akhdar, the great range of mountains in Western Cyrenaica, which overlooked the approaches to Benghazi and whose foothills provided excellent lying-up places for S.A.S. and L.R.D.G. patrols, particularly as the friendly Senussi would graze their sheep among the trees and wells and occasionally sell one for roasting.

A rendezvous was established in a ravine, Melot despatched his Senussi soldiers to reconnoitre and Mayne set out on an independent mission to attack an airfield south of Benghazi at Berka. When the Senussi soldiers returned next day, they reported that there were no

* In this passage from *Eastern Approaches* Fitzroy Maclean describes the beginning of his visit to Benghazi with David Stirling in May, 1942.

road blocks on the road between the escarpment town of Regima and Benghazi itself. It was by this road that Stirling intended to enter the city. The plan was that next day he would take six men in his Ford truck, including Alston, Allot, two S.B.S. and two of his old S.A.S. comrades, Cooper and Seekings, be guided by the L.R.D.G. to the road and then motor to Benghazi. They would rendezvous again on the following morning. As things turned out what had sounded like a desperate and dangerous adventure proved to be an uneventful reconnaissance. They drove into the town without incident, had a look round and assembled the canoe. Stirling himself walked about, meeting on the way a highly intoxicated, singing Italian, decided that the roughness of the sea put launching the canoe out of the question and drove away again. As a raid for destroying anything, it had been abortive. As a demonstration of what could be done, and what might yet be done, it had been invaluable. Moreover Mayne's raid on one of the Berka airfields destroyed fifteen aircraft. Indeed his description in a letter to his brother of what it had been like was one further illustration of the idea that fortune favours the brave:

At the moment I am about fifteen miles from Benghazi, so I won't be able to post this for some time. We did a raid on the local aerodrome three nights ago and one of the party hasn't returned yet so we are waiting for him. It's very pleasant country here, great change after the desert. Some of the people who know the South Downs say that it is very like it – low hills and valleys, lots of wild flowers and long grass. It is like a picnic – only annoying thing is the Jerry planes flying about, but we are well camouflaged. Luckily the Italians treat the Senussi very badly and so they will do anything to help us. The day and night after the raid we couldn't find our rendezvous. The maps are awful. We had been walking from 1.30 a.m. to seven o'clock the next night and couldn't find the damned place anywhere. We must have covered about fifty miles, first of all getting to the aerodrome and then coming away. It was no good walking round in circles in the dark. I more or less reconciled myself to a two hundred and fifty mile walk to Tobruk and so we (three of us, two corporals and myself) went to the nearest Senussi camp for some water and, if possible, a blanket.

Mayne went on to describe how the Senussis' initial suspicion soon disappeared once they realized their guests were *Inglese*, and then their hospitality knew no bounds. Blankets, a fire, boiled eggs, dates, a huge gourd of goat's milk, in fact a party which went on until everyone eventually retired to bed. Nor did Mayne's luck end there. As it happened the very men who were waiting for Mayne and his group at the rendezvous sent an English-speaking Arab to get a chicken cooked at the same little camp where Mayne and his men were. The long walk to Tobruk turned out not to be necessary after all.

Meanwhile Stirling was planning another go at Benghazi. The best account of this raid, which did little to discourage the enemy, but much to entertain the home side, is given to us by one of its participants, Fitzroy Maclean. He has described how David Stirling asked him to attend to the question of the right sort of boat. He chose a so-called 'Boat, Reconnaissance, Royal Engineers', a small, black, inflatable two-man affair, and with these boats they started training in the Great Bitter Lake. During this training they succeeded in planting some empty limpet mines on the hull of a tanker anchored off Suez, and having done so informed the unamused Port Authorities, asking for their limpets back. While training continued, the S.A.S. had acquired a new recruit, son of the Prime Minister, like his father an officer of the 4th Hussars, and now pining for some active service. Stirling was understandably reluctant to include him in the actual Benghazi raid, but was sufficiently susceptible to Randolph Churchill's pleadings to agree that he might be allowed to come as an observer up to the time when the L.R.D.G. released the S.A.S. raiding party. After intelligence briefings at Alexandria, they set out for Siwa, via Mersa Matruh, and at Siwa were as usual looked after by the L.R.D.G. This time they were to be escorted by the Guards Patrol, commanded by Robin Gurdon. With their preparations complete they left Siwa:

> The L.R.D.G. had provided us with the Arab head-dresses which they wore themselves. We were delighted with them. Apart from their romantic appearance, they were extremely practical articles of equipment. They were cool to wear and gave good protection against the sun, and, when you were not wearing them, you could use them as a towel or dish-cloth or spread them over your face and go to sleep, oblivious to sun, sand and flies.

For the first few days they drove by day and rested by night, and like all those who have served in the Western Desert experienced that astonishing change from the blazing heat of the sun to the cold night air of the desert, the change from bowling along in a truck with nothing on but shorts and sandals to the sudden need for every bit of warm clothing you could lay hands on and if possible what many of the L.R.D.G. had, a Hebron sheepskin coat.

Once they had passed through the wire they set a north-westerly course. The desert varied in colour, from reds and browns to greys and yellows, and in nature, at times flat and hard, at others soft and undulating. Desert creatures, like gazelles and snakes, were to be seen, sometimes at rather closer quarters than made for comfort. As they

passed a position opposite Gazala, they were parallel with the two
armies confronting each other, and from then on travelled by night,
concealing themselves by day in areas of rocks, or scrub or folds in the
ground. Sleep was not made easier by the pitiless attention of sun and
flies. Crossing the Trigh el-Abd and skirting round east of Msus,
where there were many signs of battle from the so-called Msus Stakes
of January, they drove on north-west to the Djebel Akhdar, which
Maclean found strangely like the Highlands of Scotland: 'brownish-
green hills and moorland thickly covered with scrub, with here and
there stunted trees'. There too they found again the Senussi, friendly
and courteous like all Arabs, willing to exchange eggs for cups of tea,
and ready to supply that all-important commodity, information. They
were now only a few hours' driving away from Benghazi and final
preparations had to be made. During these preparations the highly
experienced Corporal Seekings somehow damaged his hand with an
exploding detonator, and as he clearly could not go on to Benghazi,
Randolph Churchill, to his great delight, was allowed to take his place.

At ten o'clock on the evening of 21 May the patrol reached the
Barce-Benghazi road, parted company with the L.R.D.G. escort and
motored towards Benghazi in their truck – six of them, Stirling, Alston,
Maclean, Churchill and two NCOs*. Maclean spoke good Italian and
got them past a check-point, but a combination of events – being
chased by a car and rockets and sirens going off in the town – made
them suspicious that their presence was known about, so they planted
a detonator in the battle-wagon and went off into the Arab quarter.
But a member of the Carabinieri assured Maclean that it was only an
air raid, so back they went to rescue the truck in the nick of time from
exploding. Although there were clearly ships in the harbour, and Stirling attempted to inflate the boats, neither worked. Moreover Italian
sentries were beginning to be interested in their activities. Nothing
daunted, Maclean actually demanded an interview with the guard commander of the Docks Area, which succeeded in shaking off some
sentries and being awarded a present-arms by another. By the time
they returned to the truck it was getting light. It was hidden in the
lower part of a damaged house, and it was in the upper part of this
same house, fortunately empty, that they spent the day. Never ready
to give up easily, that evening they went out again:

As soon as it was dark, we left our temporary home and set out for a walk
round Benghazi, past the Cathedral and along the sea front, keeping a
sharp look out for anything that might be of interest on our next visit. For

* Corporals Rose and Cooper.

we were determined to return under, we hoped, more auspicious conditions. We walked down the middle of the street arm in arm, whistling and doing our best to give the impression that we had every right to be there. Nobody paid the slightest attention to us. On such occasions it's one's manner that counts. If only you can behave naturally, and avoid any appearance of furtiveness, it is worth any number of elaborate disguises and faked documents.* Our most interesting discovery was a couple of motor torpedo boats tied up to the quayside opposite a large square building, which, from the lights blazing in all the windows and the sentries on duty at the gate, seemed to be some kind of Headquarters. So interesting that we decided that it would be worth trying to blow them up on our way out of town.

Alas, it was not to be. The sentries were too vigilant, and Stirling decided to abandon any attempts at sabotage on this occasion. There would be plenty more opportunities. Not, however, for all those taking part in this raid. Although they all got back to the rendezvous on time and back to Siwa in good order, on the journey from Alexandria to Cairo soon afterwards, with Stirling as usual driving the truck, he hit one of a convoy of lorries and the truck overturned. Maclean and Churchill were both injured, as was Corporal Rose. The *Daily Telegraph* correspondent, Merton, was killed. Stirling himself suffered only a broken bone in the wrist, which prevented him from driving for a time. This was regarded as being not wholly unfortunate as Stirling's driving was often a good deal more dangerous, for both his companions and himself, than were his daring raids on the enemy.

Stirling was not the only man engaged in desert warfare with a knack of turning daring raids into significant victories. It was also the Desert Fox's stock-in-trade. And Rommel was about to indulge in one of his most successful demonstrations of how to shock the British into a kind of stunned immobility by speed and surprise alone. As a result, Stirling had to turn his attention away from shipping and ports. Once more the priority would be airfields and aircraft.

---

* A lesson not lost on the I.R.A. in, for example, their bombing attack at Chelsea Barracks in 1981.

6

BACKS TO THE WALL

There is no need for me to stress the vital importance of the safe arrival of our convoys at Malta and I am sure you will take all steps to enable the air escort ... to be operated from landing-grounds as far west as possible.

Churchill to Auchinleck 2 June, 1942

Stirling's next job confirmed the breadth and soundness of his whole strategic thinking. It was to assist with the re-supply of Malta. Throughout the North African campaign Malta admirably illustrated the interdependence of land, sea and air operations and underlined once more the point that if you could win and go on winning the battle of supplies, you could probably win the campaign itself. Malta was so obvious and painful a thorn in the flesh of the Axis lines of supply that it continues to astonish us that the only course of action to neutralize it which would be effective, its seizure and occupation by Axis forces, was never taken. It is true that the island was constantly harassed from the air and by sea. It is true too that many of the Axis High Command expressed the view time and again that its capture was an absolutely indispensable preliminary to a successful advance against Egypt. Admiral Raeder said it repeatedly; Mussolini recommended it in the strongest possible terms; Rommel himself, although he later allowed himself to be intoxicated by the logistic prize of Tobruk and put aside his conviction, maintained that the Axis powers had to have Malta unless they were to lose control of North Africa. But the 'greatest strategic genius of all time', Commander-in-Chief of the *Wehrmacht*, Führer of the Third Reich, would not, or could not, see it, and Malta remained in British hands.

So important was Malta to both sides in the seesaw of battles that many operations were mounted with the specific objectives of either suppressing or sustaining it. As the battle of supplies was the key to the campaign itself and as Malta seemed to be the key to the battle of supplies, Malta's influence on strategic events was unique. Indeed these events would often describe a classic circle. During the *Crusader* battles, for example, it was the offensive mounted by the Royal Navy and Royal Air Force from Malta against Axis shipping which weakened Rommel and assisted 8th Army in their advance. As they advanced the additional air support which the Desert Air Force was able to give Malta from landing fields further west enhanced Malta's capacity, not merely for survival, but, by virtue of further convoys arriving, for further offensive action against Axis shipping. Thus a revived Malta meant a more effective 8th Army and an effective 8th Army further revived Malta. On the other hand, if Malta were sufficiently weakened, Rommel would get more tanks, guns, petrol and ammunition, and so be able to push 8th Army back, robbing the Desert Air Force of the very airfields it needed to guarantee Malta's survival. In short Malta's dependence on 8th Army's success was matched by 8th Army's debt to Malta.

Now the whole strategic circle was to be described once again. Towards the end of April the Governor of Malta, General Dobbie, had signalled the Prime Minister to the effect that Malta's plight was more than critical. It had become a question of survival and without replenishment of their vital needs, particularly flour and ammunition, the very worst might happen. Bread consumption had been cut again and what was left would last only until mid-June. Churchill was always at his best when faced with supreme crisis, although he was perhaps inclined to over-burden his various Commanders-in-Chief with tele-grams which were at once too eloquent and too long. He was, more-over, prepared to take serious risks both at sea and in the desert to ensure the continued security of Malta, whose loss 'would be a disaster of first magnitude to the British Empire, and probably fatal in the long run to the defence of the Nile Valley'. He therefore sent Auchinleck what he described as definite orders 'which he must either obey or be relieved ... a most unusual procedure on our part towards a high military commander':

> The Chiefs of Staff, the Defence Committee, and the War Cabinet have again considered the whole position. We are determined that Malta shall not be allowed to fall without a battle being fought by your whole army for its retention. The starving out of this fortress would involve the sur-render of over 30,000 men, Army and Air Force, together with several hundred guns. Its possession would give the enemy a clear and sure bridge

to Africa ... it would compromise any offensive against Italy, and future plans such as *Acrobat* and *Gymnast** ...

We therefore reiterate the views we have expressed, with this qualification - that the very latest date for engaging the enemy which we could approve is one which provides a distraction in time to help the passage of the June dark-period convoy [to Malta] ...

Before we see how Stirling tried to help the June convoy reach Malta, we must understand why it was that Auchinleck did not do what the Prime Minister had ordered him to do. In the first place, after the beating it had taken during Rommel's spoiling attack of January and February, 8th Army simply was not ready to undertake large-scale operations. In the second place, Rommel was once again about to pre-empt the whole game by indulging in one more daring attack, this time one which nearly succeeded in spoiling the British position in Egypt altogether. That it did not quite do so was because of two things - Rommel's logistic starvation, despite the capture of Tobruk, since this prize persuaded him against insisting on Malta's capture too; *and* Auchinleck's steadfast generalship.

It was ironic that Rommel's initial and dramatic successes between 26 May, when the Gazala battle began, and 21 June, when he captured Tobruk, were partially due to the logistic abundance that he had enjoyed, because during April and May over 90 per cent of freight sent from Italy to Libya arrived safely. Even though Admiral Vian had succeeded in getting three merchantmen from Alexandria to Malta in March, much of their cargo had been destroyed in harbour by the Luftwaffe. Kesselring judged that by 10 May Malta had been neutralized and therefore released two fighter and two bomber groups from his *Luftflotte* at the very same moment that Malta received strong Spitfire reinforcements. So delicate was the balance of power which determined the battle for Malta that the seesaw swung once more in favour of the British. All this underlined the crucial importance of Malta. The Prime Minister had pressed his Commander-in-Chief to attack Rommel in order to help relieve Malta; instead Rommel had attacked 8th Army with success, but Malta had come to the rescue. Its reinforcement of Spitfires had enabled it to beat off renewed assaults, which were made with Luftwaffe squadrons withdrawn from Cyrenaica to attack Malta, thus giving 8th Army some degree of air superiority just when it was most needed. The loss of so much desert and airfields, although it made more difficult the replenishment of Malta

* *Acrobat* was the operation to take Tripolitania; *Gymnast*, later called *Torch*, was the plan to invade North-West Africa.

[only two out of seventeen freighters reached the island in June], nonetheless produced advantages for the British because of the extra space which Rommel now had to control.

Malta was saved from starvation and impotence at the very time when Rommel's advance, with its longer lines of supply, worsened by Malta's ability to hit back, was to cause his logistic position to deteriorate as never before. When Auchinleck stopped him at Alamein the turning point of the desert war had been reached, and the Germans were never again to mount a major offensive.

Now we must see how Stirling's activities assisted in all this. Stirling himself has summarized this period of his operations and he began by pointing out that he now had far more men. Not only had L Detachment been recruited back to its original size, but he also had the sixty Free French parachutists whom we have already met, and Captain Buck, who spoke German perfectly and recruited a small German-speaking unit, the Special Interrogation Group, made up of men who were prepared to pose as Afrika Korps soldiers with all the risks involved. As for the Malta convoy, Stirling wrote:

> Its safe arrival in Malta was vital. 'L' Detachment offered to attack on the same night the main landing grounds from which the Intelligence Branch reckoned the enemy would conduct their main efforts at strafing the convoy. The operation went reasonably well. We attacked nine landing grounds, two of which were in Crete and seven in Cyrenaica, destroying a total of about 75 aircraft and grounding a good many more over the vital period.
>
> The two sub-units covering Crete were landed by submarine and folboat, whereas those in Cyrenaica were dropped by the L.R.D.G. and picked up by them after the operation – that is all except one party of French who arrived at their aerodrome as a party of P.O.Ws. under German escort, the German escort being made up of Buck's Germans.
>
> By the end of June 'L' Detachment had raided all the more important German and Italian aerodromes within 300 miles of the forward area at least once or twice and a few of them even three or four times. Methods of defence were beginning to improve and although the advantage still lay with 'L' Detachment the time had come to alter our own methods. Therefore we developed the jeep with two sets of twin Vickers K guns and one Browning .5. The astonishing agility of the jeep enabled us to approach a target at night over almost any country. The technique turned out to be most successful and enabled the unit to be very much more flexible in its methods of operation.
>
> By the end of July, the unit was entirely motorised – our transport

consisting of jeeps and four-wheeled drive 3-tonners. The L.R.D.G. had given us tremendous assistance in training a cadre of navigators and in many other ways we were now self-supporting.

We must now complement this unemotional summary with an account of what the first jeep attack was like.

Like so many of Stirling's other ideas, it came from a sort of inspired improvisation during the course of an actual operation. The whole thing began during 8th Army's withdrawal to the defensive line of El Alamein at the end of June, 1942. Stirling determined to assemble his whole force, some hundred highly trained, experienced men, to take the offensive against the enemy's lines of communications in their forward areas. He somehow put his hands on twenty 3-ton trucks and fifteen jeeps, some of which were then fitted with Vickers K guns. Being completely mobile with their own transport would mean that they could take a lot of supplies and equipment, enabling them to raid for several weeks at a time without returning to base. The plan this time was to drive out with the L.R.D.G. to a rendezvous some 150 miles away, meet a further L.R.D.G. patrol there, and then try to raid airfields in the area Daba, Fuka, Bagush, Matruh and Sollum. They moved off on 4 July, escorted by Gurdon and drove to the rendezvous north of Qattara. Waiting for them there was Lieutenant Timpson of the L.R.D.G. who described the meeting and some of those involved in memorable language:

> In the afternoon a great cloud of dust could be seen approaching from the east. The country here is full of escarpments and clefts, and one could see the dust and hear the sound of vehicles long before they hove into view. Robin [Gurdon] was in the lead with his patrol. We directed them to a hide-out next to our own. Then came truck after truck of S.A.S., first swarms of jeeps, then three-tonners, and David in his famous staff car, known as his 'blitz-wagon', Corporal Cooper, his inseparable gunner, beside him and Corporal Seekings behind. Mayne, Fraser, Jellicoe, Mather and Scratchley were all there; Rawnsley was wearing a virgin-blue veil and azure pyjamas. Here was the counterpart of Glubb's Arab Legion in the west. Trucks raced to and fro churning up the powdery ground, until most of them came to roost after a while in a hollow half a mile away which we had recommended to them. As aircraft had been flying about we did not quite approve of all this crowded activity. Yet they had gone through the Alamein Line undetected; an M.E. 110 which now flew over took no notice; and the reckless cheerfulness of our companions was at least stimulating.

Having to rely chiefly on L.R.D.G. wireless communications – and on our navigators – David kept our operators busy sending and receiving messages for the whole party. We had a conference that evening and again the next morning, in which he revealed his plans and gave his orders.

The orders were that five or six raids would take place on the next night. These raids were to be made in support of 8th Army's counter-offensive against Rommel's successful advance. The counter-offensive came to little. Stirling's raids amounted to a good deal. The general idea was that a large group of S.A.S. would move to the Bagush-Fuka area, escorted by the gallant Robin Gurdon, and would then split up into a number of smaller patrols to attack airfields in these areas, three of them aiming for Fuka, one – led by Stirling and Mayne – against Bagush. At the same time two other patrols would make for Sidi Barrani and El Daba.

It was the Bagush raid which led to the birth of a new technique. Mayne had placed charges on forty aircraft, and when his men had withdrawn to witness the pleasing spectacle of forty explosions, they were puzzled when only twenty-two bangs took place. This disappointment was explained when they realized that some of the primers were damp. Stirling, as usual, thought of a remedy, at once appealing in its simplicity and amenability to instant execution. His idea this time was that with their vehicles – a truck, staff car and jeep – they would drive on to the airfield and shoot up the remaining aircraft with the eight Vickers guns they had between them. As with so many of Stirling's ideas, the combination of speed, simplicity and surprise worked wonders. The whole thing was over in about five minutes, and an extra twelve aircraft were destroyed. Members of the S.A.S. further away at Fuka, who saw what was going on at Bagush, commented as they saw all these additional explosions and fires that with 'Major Stirling and Captain Mayne – you bet there's some fun over there!' With this particular success the total number of enemy aeroplanes destroyed by the S.A.S. was now 180. What is more a new raiding technique had been born, and Stirling was not one to wait long before putting it into effect again.

It was at about this time that Stirling acquired the title of the 'Phantom Major', which subsequently was used by Virginia Cowles in her admirable account of Stirling's activities. It was the Germans who gave him this accolade, and he even began to make an appearance in Rommel's renowned diaries. The Desert Fox referred to Commandos operating under Stirling's command which, operating from the Qattara Depression and Kufra, mounted raids into Cyrenaica 'where they caused considerable havoc and seriously disquieted the Italians'. Tributes to Stirling's originality, courage and dash have come from many quarters. We have seen some of Fitzroy Maclean's already. David Lloyd Owen, who himself was a great leader, described Stirling's power over his men as something he had never seen before. The confidence he somehow induced in his subordinates was such that no matter what deed of daring he had demanded of them, they would have done it, knowing that he would have found a way despite all odds to dismay and subdue the enemy and once more emerge victorious. The renowned Popski, Lieutenant-Colonel Peniakoff, who knew all about the desert, was a brilliant linguist and ran his own private army of Arabs against the Axis forces, described Stirling as the 'romantic figure' of the Middle East war: 'With a light heart and cool courage he inspired in his men a passionate devotion and led them to thrilling adventures. Where we plodded, he pranced'. Even the French, never the first to admire British military qualities, were entranced by his combination of mild manners and restrained voice with unimaginable tenacity and toughness in action. They particularly admired and appreciated the gentle and kindly way in which he confided his enjoyment of shooting the enemy. Clemenceau observed once that a man who has to be persuaded to act before he acts is *not* a man of action: 'You must act as you breathe'. This was Stirling's secret and one he imparted to his men.

Such a way of going about their business was just right for the operation they now undertook against Landing Ground 12 at Sidi Haneish, one of the Fuka aerodromes which was usually crammed with Ju 52 transports. Stirling's idea this time was that eighteen of his new jeeps should carry out the attack with a view to destroying every aircraft on the field. Once again the priceless element of surprise would be theirs. The method which he outlined to his men was this. They would approach the airfield formed in line abreast and from this formation they would dismay the enemy defences by opening up with every gun they had, then re-deploy into two columns led by Stirling himself, with all guns, except those in front, pointing outwards, so that they could move rapidly between lines of aircraft, shooting them up as they went. The navigator, who would be positioned immediately behind Stirling, would not be able to use his guns, but the other seventeen jeeps, each with four Vickers, would all be able to fire simultaneously, a total of sixty-eight guns.

Navigating the way to the airfield was, as so often before, in the hands of Sadler. After some four hours driving from their hide at the edge of the escarpment, Sadler announced that they were only a mile from their target, which was straight ahead. Everything was so quiet

that this seemed rather unlikely, but Sadler was nearly always right,
so they formed up in line abreast and moved off. The accuracy of
Sadler's calculations was suddenly and alarmingly demonstrated to
them when the whole aerodrome half a mile in front of them was
illuminated. But it was not because their presence had been discovered.
It was the runway lights going on for a returning aeroplane. What
might have been a disabling loss of surprise instead made the job a bit
easier. Stirling made straight for the lighted runway as the aircraft
landed and opened fire, followed instantly by all the others. The roar
of machine-guns and the brilliance of tracer bullets added up to a fine
theatrical effect, although the airfield lights were quickly switched off.
Now Stirling put the practised drill into operation. A green Very light
gave the order and the eighteen jeeps got into their arrowhead formation, then motored fast between rows of Junkers 52, Messer-
schmitts and Stukas. The deafening noise of machine-guns was
equalled only by the searing heat of burning aeroplanes, which was so
intense that the hair and eyebrows of some of the S.A.S. men were
scorched. After changing jeeps, as his own had been hit by either
enemy mortar or machine-gun fire, Stirling gave further orders and
led the columns round in a circle, destroying more Ju 52s at the edge
of the airfield. Then they made off into the desert, split up into smaller
groups and returned to the rendezvous independently. One of Stirling's own group, Hastings, recalled that, after losing their way, they
felt thoroughly naked on a stretch of flat stony desert which offered
absolutely no refuge from the expected enemy aircraft:

> Then the desert became our friend. The fog cleared away and we found
> ourselves on the edge of a small escarpment dropping about fifteen feet.
> Before us lay what appeared to be a large bowl-shaped depression about a
> quarter of a mile broad, the walls were cut by fairly deep wadis with thick
> greenish-brown scrub up to three or four feet high. A few minutes before,
> our position had seemed very grave; now suddenly we had been shown
> exactly the place we were looking for.

Soon they were hidden away in the thickest patches of scrub and
undetectable from fifty yards away:

> Then only did relief set in. Since the vehicles were hidden it would be
> comparatively easy for each of us to run to cover on the noise of an
> approaching aircraft. We looked round at each other – we were indeed a
> ragged-looking bunch. Faces, hair and beards were covered in a thick
> yellow-grey film of dust, eyes were red and strained. Our dirty open-
> necked battle dress and loose overcoats hung upon us as upon scarecrows

and they fitted well into the background of the desert. One officer was trying to scrape large dried and sand-caked bloodstains off his trousers with a stick; the blood of the dead soldier who was lying on his back under a bush with a dirty blanket over the top of his body. Our mouths were dry and ill-tasting and there was a burning behind the eyes rather like the symptoms of a hangover – but for the moment we were safe or at least comparatively so.

But Corporal Seekings produced some tea and before long little groups of men were chatting and smoking and talking over their successful raid. The dead soldier was buried and they all went to pay their last respects to him:

> The officers got up, moved away into the scrub and stood gathered round the pathetic little heap of sand and stones. There was no cross, some of the men were trying to make one from the scrub and a piece of old ration box, but it was not yet ready. We stood bareheaded, looking at the grave, each with our own thoughts. Most of us had not even known this man, who was one of the more recent arrivals; he was just a name to us or perhaps a cheery red face and a shock of black hair. It was indeed a curious burial, just a two minutes' silence with a handful of tired, dirty comrades. Yet for this short fraction of time, lost in the middle of nowhere, there was dignity.

Despite the success of this operation – for on that single night, together with another raid elsewhere, the S.A.S had destroyed between forty and fifty aircraft, bringing their total so far, after roughly a year of activity, to some 250 – Stirling made it clear to his men that fire discipline had not been good: there was no need to fire off *all* the ammunition, only what was necessary to destroy their targets. At the same time the mobility which they now possessed had brought solid advantages – versatility in choosing targets, greater flexibility in attack and sheer speed of operations. They could now operate on any night of any month and not have to wait for especially dark periods.

As Stirling was planning another jeep operation in early August, he was blown for by GHQ Cairo, as they put it, to take part in a newly planned attack based on one of his own ideas. His reaction was unfavourable. S.A.S. operations were his affair. As at present deployed, provided only that he could be properly supplied, he could do real damage to Rommel's lines of communication. Besides, the last thing he wanted was for S.A.S. planning and actual operations to be subjected to someone else's ideas. On this occasion, however, he was not allowed to have his way. His whole command was to return to Kabrit and he would get his instructions at GHQ. It was a change at once unwelcome to him and, as it transpired, unfortunate for all. Yet it had to be recognized that a change was coming over the whole of the North African campaign, and this change was symbolized by the advent of Montgomery. 'No more manoeuvre – fight a battle' was Montgomery's message and his method for all the campaigns which he conducted. The S.A.S., on the other hand, represented and practised strategic manoeuvre at its most economical and effective. There was therefore bound to be a conflict of ideas and a sort of decline in the contribution which the S.A.S. would make during the final battles which 8th Army fought in North Africa. Yet Stirling never ran out of ideas and never stopped harassing the enemy until he himself was put out of action. And then others took over.

7

DECLINE, BUT NOT FALL

'I intend the next offensive to be the last offensive. What's the
matter with you, Colonel Stirling? Why are you smiling?'

'Nothing, sir, it's just that we heard the same thing from the
last general – and the one before.'

Montgomery and Stirling, October, 1942

David Stirling has recorded how much more difficult operations became after the El Alamein position had hardened into an organized
line. To start with, when 8th Army had been back on the Alamein
defences in July, 1942, the S.A.S. base established between Siwa Oasis
and Mersa Matruh had been kept in supplies simply by infiltrating
across the Alamein line itself. But later, as we have seen, because this
line became so tightly controlled, their supply route went through the
Qattara Depression. When this route was mined and patrolled by the
enemy, it was necessary to divert once again. 'Our supplies and reinforcements came up the Nile and across the desert via El Kharga to
the Kufra Oasis and then north through the Great Sand Sea to our
forward base near Siwa. Thus patrols had to detour nearly 1,800 miles
to deal with an objective which might be only forty miles from 8th
Army's forward positions'. Yet despite these formidable logistic constraints, Stirling's operational activities did not flag. Between stalemate
at Alamein and the final joining up of 1st and 8th Armies in April,
1943, the S.A.S. concentrated on four types of raid: further attacks on
Rommel's supplies and resources, special operations to assist the
British offensive itself, then during Montgomery's methodical advance
from there, attacks on enemy lines of communications, including railways, and finally raids in Tunisia.

It will be remembered that Montgomery took over command of 8th
Army during the second week of August, 1942. He at once set about

putting right what he regarded as wrong, notably training and morale. He then prepared for the enemy attack which he knew, by virtue of the Ultra intelligence system, that Rommel was going to launch at the end of the month. Having successfully repulsed Rommel's last fling, he turned his attention to his own offensive which was set for the last week in October. During this preparatory period, while strengthening and training 8th Army proceeded, it was important further to interfere with Rommel's supplies. In the end it was his logistic starvation which turned the scales against him, for Alamein was essentially a battle, not of tactical manoeuvre at which the Germans consistently excelled, but of attrition, an expensive push made by an Army under the tight control of its commander and with the resources to stand heavy casualties and losses, which the *Panzerarmee* could not. What Montgomery had been charged with was the achievement of a major victory, victory no matter what the cost, and he had the determination and hardness to see through such a battle. Despite doubts and even despair on the part of some others, he was able to gain a victory which was so important to the Allied cause. For a battle which depended, therefore, on pounding Rommel's Army to a point where it could stand the pounding no more, and would have neither the tanks, guns, ammunition, petrol nor men to continue to conduct such a battle, anything that could contribute to Rommel's shortage of the sinews of war was to be welcomed. And this is where Stirling came in once more, although, as he himself admitted, 'the most important and least successful operation undertaken in this period was a large scale raid on the harbour installations and shipping at Benghazi which took place late in September'. The planning for this raid began in August when Stirling was recalled to Cairo. What he heard about it there made him dislike the plan even more than when the notion of being directed by other people had first been put to him.

The basic plan was to interfere with Rommel's supply depots and harbour facilities at Benghazi and Tobruk. What Stirling himself was required to do by GHQ was to attack Benghazi harbour with forty lorries, forty jeeps and 220 men in order to destroy as much as possible. At the same time a force of some eighty men under command of Colonel Haselden was to drive into and attack Tobruk, supported by a naval bombardment and Commandos raiding from the sea. Meanwhile two smaller attacks were to be made – one to try and seize Jalo back from the Italians; the other, which was a mere diversion, a raid by the L.R.D.G. on Barce airfield. Stirling thoroughly disapproved of his part in it all. 'The whole plan,' he later recorded, 'sinned against every principle on which the S.A.S. was founded.' It was to be carried out by men, many of whom had no special S.A.S. training at all; it was far too large to be compatible with a key element of his operations – surprise; nor was it sensible to be tied to specific timings in conjunction with other, far distant and uncoordinated attacks. Seizing opportunity was what he and his men had thrived on in the past, not sticking to hard and fast timetables. But Stirling allowed himself to be persuaded to lead the operation against Benghazi, an operation in which he did not believe, by a seductive promise by the GHQ staff that it would be the turning of the tide in the whole North African campaign, that his own command would be expanded, that all those taking part in the various parts of the operations would come under his direction in the future for a series of raids on all enemy supply depots in Cyrenaica. With such glittering prizes held out to him, Stirling eventually agreed to raid Benghazi.

He once again got hold of Fitzroy Maclean, who was convalescing in Alexandria. Maclean recalled that one day David appeared, having just returned from the desert with his head full of plans for further large-scale raids. As he wanted him to come back to Cairo there and then, they persuaded the doctors to give him a medical certificate pronouncing an A1 state of health and then set off to make preparations. During their time in Cairo they both dined at the Embassy on an evening when the company included Churchill, the C.I.G.S., General Sir Alan Brooke, Field-Marshal Smuts and the new Commander-in-Chief, General Alexander. Stirling and Maclean could not resist the opportunity of saying something about the S.A.S., including, despite their misgivings, mention of the planned raid on Benghazi. Churchill, with his customary taste for the unorthodox and daring, approved. He also, as was his way, made some memorable comments, pointing out to Smuts that Maclean had used the Mother of Parliaments as a public convenience*, while Stirling, whose gentle ways and bold deeds instantly endeared him to the Prime Minister, he described as 'the mildest manner'd man that ever scuttled ship or cut a throat'. It was not only this couplet from *Don Juan* which fitted Stirling. The following one, as to his having such true breeding of a gentleman that you never could discern his real thoughts, would have been equally apt.

The four operations, Benghazi, Tobruk, Jalo and Barce, were to take place about the middle of September, and by the 7th Stirling's force had been assembled at Kufra. During their time in Cairo there

---

*Fitzroy Maclean became a Member of Parliament in order to escape from the Foreign Office and so be able to take part in the war.

had been some worrying indications that security about these forthcoming raids had not been good. They all knew what it would mean
if the enemy did get to hear of their intentions and make appropriate
reception arrangements, but there was nothing firm to go on and plans
could not be altered simply because of rumoured breaches of security.
The plan for raiding Benghazi was nothing if not bold. The idea was
to rush in, surprise the garrison, destroy everything in sight, and then
either hold on to it as long as possible or make it unusable by the
enemy. There was a good deal of enthusiasm for the general idea,
particularly as there were some sailors in the party whose job it would
be to seize any ships they could and sink them at the harbour mouth,
also two light tanks borrowed from a Hussar regiment which would be
used to help blast their way into Benghazi.

Fitzroy Maclean and Paddy Mayne were part of the advance party
and set off three days ahead of Stirling with the main body. They were
to make for the Djebel and meet Stirling there. This would mean
crossing the Great Sand Sea, which Maclean has described as something of an ordeal:

> With increasing frequency the leading truck would suddenly plunge and
> flounder and then come to an ominous standstill, sinking up to its axles in
> the soft white sand. Once you were stuck it was no good racing the engine.
> The wheels only spun round aimlessly and buried themselves deeper than
> ever. There was nothing for it but to dig yourself out with a spade and
> then, with the help of sand mats back precariously on to the firm ground
> you had so unwisely left. Then the whole convoy would wait while someone
> went cautiously on ahead to prospect for a safe way out of our difficulties.
>
> Or else we would find our way barred by a sand dune, or succession of
> sand dunes. These were best negotiated by rush tactics. If you could only
> keep moving you were less likely to stick. The jeeps, making full use of
> their extra range of gears, would lead the way, with the three-tonners
> thundering along after them like stampeding elephants. Very rarely we all
> got through safely.

But despite all their difficulties – there were some thermos bombs
lying about which blew up one truck, and they had to skirt the Italian
garrison of Jalo – they reached the Djebel and its welcome cover after
several days. 800 miles, motoring and 600 miles behind the enemy
lines without being discovered by enemy aircraft was not a bad
achievement.

Mayne and Maclean quickly got in touch with Bob Melot, the
Belgian cotton merchant, who lived with the Bedouin and gained valuable information for the British Army. What Melot had to say was far

from reassuring. From the enemy's greater alertness and presence it seemed likely that the rumours about their being expected to raid Benghazi were well founded. All this was confirmed by one of Melot's men, an Arab formerly employed by the Italians. Quite apart from reinforcements to the Benghazi garrison, there were minefields and machine-gun emplacements in position to protect the town and harbour. Even the date of the impending attack, 14 September, seemed to be known in the bazaar. When, therefore, they joined up with Stirling's party, all this was discussed, and Stirling felt it necessary to signal GHQ in order to discover whether they wished to change the timing of the attack. But GHQ were firm that bazaar gossip was to be ignored and the attack was to be made as planned. So they carried on, only to have their fears confirmed:

> We were almost on top of the road block before we saw it. This time there was no red light and no sentry. Only a bar across the road. Beyond it, in the shadows, something was flapping in the wind. The leading vehicles stopped and word was passed back for the rest of the column to halt, while we investigated matters further. On either side of the road there was wire and in places the soil seemed to have been dug up. This looked unpleasantly like the minefield we had heard about. If so, it meant that our only line of approach lay along the road through the road blocks. David summoned Bill Cumper, as the expert on mines, and invited him to give his opinion of this somewhat disquieting discovery.

Bill Cumper as usual did his stuff and it seemed as if there were indeed mines either side of the road. He then succeeded in dealing with the road block and the bar went up to allow vehicles to pass. Cumper actually prefaced what then happened by imitating Stanley Holloway with his renowned comment: 'Let battle commence'. It did:

> The words were hardly out of his mouth when pandemonium broke loose. From the other side of the road block a dozen machine-guns opened up at us at point-blank range; then a couple of 20mm Bredas joined in, and then some heavy mortars, while sniper's bullets pinged viciously through the trees on either side of the road.

Although they returned the fire as best they could and two of the leading jeeps gallantly charged the enemy, it was clear that all surprise was lost; and so, with the enemy able to call up reinforcements and quite outnumbered as they were and unwilling to be caught by daylight in the open, Stirling decided to withdraw, and away they went for the cover of the Djebel. Next morning, although they were concealed as best they could in the ravines at the foot of the escarpment, they were treated to endless attention by a host of enemy aircraft; bombing and machine-gunning destroyed several trucks, including the one with all their explosives. All day long their tormentors persisted, and even when night brought some respite, their position was far from enviable – 800 miles from their base, nothing but waterless desert in between, the enemy, who knew roughly where they were, able to attack from the air or with armoured forces, a lot of ammunition and food lost, and a number of wounded men from Bob Melot's party who had to be got to a doctor as quickly as possible. They drove in the dark to the wadi they had left only a day and a half before and again camouflaged all vehicles, but during the day one S.A.S. jeep, which was driving round, completely gave away their positions to an enemy aircraft. The result: more and more bombing and strafing, more vehicles lost, radio destroyed, more killed and wounded, less food and water. So it went on:

It was 17 September. At nightfall we ate our rations and started off again. We kept going all that night and all the following day. It was a risk driving by day, but, with our supplies of food and water as low as they were, it was one that had to be taken. It was very hot and the soft sand swirled up at us, as though a sand storm were threatening. With seven or eight of us to a jeep, it was not easy to relax, even when one was not actually driving. The sun blazed down relentlessly from a brazen sky. Occasionally someone would go to sleep and fall off, and we had to stop, waiting irritably, while he picked himself up and climbed back on again. The tyres too were beginning to feel the strain after so many hundreds of miles of rough going under a hot sun, and punctures came with increasing frequency. Changing a wheel, or digging the jeep out of soft sand began to seem more and more arduous as we grew weaker. Our throats were dry and it required an effort to speak. We counted the hours and minutes which separated us from the blissful moment when we could next allow ourselves to take a pull at the rapidly dwindling supply of warm, dirty, brackish water in our water-bottles.

The next real problem was what would happen when they got to Jalo, which had been the Sudan Defence Force's target as part of the same group of raids, for they were still between 400 and 500 miles from Kufra. Jalo was still in enemy hands, but they succeeded in making contact with the S.D.F. who, having been repulsed once, as they too had been expected by the enemy, were preparing to have another go. But a signal from GHQ told them to return to base. As the S.A.S. party set out to do the same, they were heartened by the news that, despite the failure of their raid on Benghazi, and as it transpired all the other raids except that on Barce airfield, they had succeeded in diverting considerable enemy air and ground forces, so that strategically their mission had been accomplished. Back at Kufra, they learned that the Tobruk raid, which had also clearly been expected by the enemy, was a total failure. The Royal Navy had lost two destroyers and four M.T.Bs., the troops who succeeded in getting ashore were all taken prisoner, while those taking part in the land raid under Haselden, who was killed, were mostly captured. All David Stirling's misgivings had been justified. But he himself was already full of new ideas for more operations in the desert and for other attacks as far apart as Europe and Persia.

There was another reason for looking on the bright side. The new Commander-in-Chief, Middle East, was General Alexander, who had been at the memorable dinner party in which Stirling and Maclean took part before the Benghazi raid, and Alexander had recommended that the S.A.S. should be expanded to make a proper regiment. Apart from making Stirling a Lieutenant-Colonel, it completely vindicated all that he had been striving to prove, that there was a real and permanent place for a unit, which, employing the tactics he had worked out and practised, could have a profound effect on the general strategic conduct of the war. Moreover, he would now be allowed to recruit further officers and men in order to continue with his work. There was yet one more cause for satisfaction. The great Shan Hackett*, who had so distinguished himself in the desert fighting and was to do even greater things at Arnhem, was now the Colonel at GHQ in charge of raiding operations, and it would be one of his jobs to help Stirling to coordinate his activities. The two men instantly took to each other and a great partnership began. It was severely put to the test when they went together to see Montgomery to try and get his agreement to recruiting for the S.A.S. some of the best officers and NCOs in 8th Army. Stirling needed about 150 and his appeal fell on, not deaf, but unreceptive ears. Montgomery flatly refused, but Hackett and Stirling had better luck with Montgomery's Chief of Staff, Freddie de Guingand, who promised to help. Nonetheless, it would take time to muster and train more men, and what Stirling was now thinking about was a series of concentrated raids on Rommel's enormously long lines of communication. Meanwhile, having re-formed his experienced men into a squadron under Paddy Mayne who was to leave at once for Kufra to set up a base on the edge of the Sand Sea to carry out raids against

---

* General Sir John Hackett, GCB, CBE, DSO, MC, MA, BLitt, LLD, the greatest soldier-scholar of our time.

the railway line and coast road, Stirling himself got on with the job of recruiting and training reinforcements.

The battle of El Alamein lasted, as Montgomery had predicted, for about twelve days. The master plan of feinting in the south and breaking through in the north succeeded in the end because Montgomery either had or created sufficient reserves to go on pushing at Rommel's forces and subjecting them to an unceasing bombardment by artillery and air forces until they could not continue to conduct a defensive battle. It has been described as 'a horrid, muddled, messy killing match – in scorching heat, choking dust and, generally a foot of exhausting, powdery sand – in which sheer courage and tenacity, backed by superior resources, wore out an enemy no less brave or tenacious.'* But the pursuit which followed Rommel's withdrawal was a cautious and slow affair. Rommel halted his army at El Agheila on 24 November, roughly a month after Montgomery's offensive had started. It was not until mid-December that 8th Army launched another offensive designed to trap the Desert Fox. It did not, of course, do so, but this lengthy delay in resuming the advance gave the S.A.S. further opportunities to attack Rommel's lines of communication.

Not that they had been inactive during and before the Alamein battle itself. Inactivity was not Stirling's forte. Paddy Mayne had established his squadron about 150 miles south of the Mersa Matruh railway and some 200 miles west of the enemy's leading defensive positions at Alamein. From there he mounted a number of sorties against the railway line, blowing up trains. During one of them an S.A.S. party found itself more or less caught up in the opening phase of the Alamein battle itself. Lieutenant Scratchley had been instructed to raid El Daba and cut enemy communications there:

> I can't remember how many men or jeeps we had, or how many days we drove to reach our objective. All I do know was that the night of October 23rd was brilliant and clear with a full moon. We figured we were about thirty miles behind the German side of the Alamein line, and twenty miles from Daba. As we jogged along under a wonderful starlit sky, it seemed strange to be so close to the enemy and hear nothing.
>
> It may have been ten o'clock or midnight when the barrage that started the great battle which was to mark 'the beginning of the end'† of the African campaign broke the stillness. The effect was colossal. Every inch

* Fred Majdalany.
† 'This is not the end. It is not even the beginning of the end. But it is perhaps the end of the beginning'. Churchill, November, 1942.

of the distance between El Alamein and the Qattara Depression was lit up by the explosions of bursting twenty-five pounder shells. From our distance it struck us more as a magnificent sight than the horror it actually was.

On this occasion Scratchley was ordered back to base before he could do the enemy much damage beyond cutting the railway, but a week later he set off on another mission only to find himself and his men in the thick of things, one moment being observed by German tanks, another shot at by British armoured cars, then capturing some dejected German officers, and after that to their great surprise finding a Daimler armoured car manned, not by their own side, but by the enemy. While on this, also abortive, mission they heard about the Anglo-American landings in North-West Africa, which really was the beginning of the end.

Meanwhile Stirling was continuing to collect and train his command, including the French squadron, what was left of the Middle East Commando, the Special Boat Section and some Greek volunteers. What is more, Bill Stirling, his brother, had been charged with the task of raising a second S.A.S. regiment and bringing it to North Africa. It was this which prompted the celebrated comment that the Regiment's name clearly stood for 'Stirling and Stirling'.

Stirling now submitted a plan to GHQ which proposed a series of raids on the 400-mile stretch of road between Rommel's position at Agheila and Tripoli. In all some 200 men with jeeps and trucks, and divided into sixteen different sections, would take part. Having got approval for the plan, Stirling instructed Mayne to take his squadron to a wadi called Bir Zalten, some 150 miles south of El Agheila, where Stirling himself with another newly formed squadron would join him. He left Kufra on 20 November with ninety men, thirty jeeps and some lorries and joined Mayne at Bir Zalten nine days later.

After his initial disagreement with Stirling and after his own initial successes, Montgomery became rather more sympathetic to the S.A.S. He referred to 'the Boy Stirling' and his being 'quite, quite mad', but that there was a place for madness in war. About Stirling's plan for attacking the coast road on a front of several hundred miles, the Army Commander was enthusiastic and even went so far as to say that, if successful, it could have a decisive effect on his next offensive. The broad idea of Stirling's plan was to disrupt enemy road traffic with sixteen patrols operating from sixteen bases, each patrol being responsible for a stretch of some forty miles of road. 'A' Squadron, under Paddy Mayne, had some success on the road east of Bouerat, and was able to force much enemy transport off the road at night, leaving it to the Royal Air Force to deal with the matter by day. 'B' Squadron, under Stirling himself, was not so successful in the difficult area north of Zem Zem, as the enemy had taken more precautions, which meant of course that Rommel had to divert troops to counter-raids. Many of the S.A.S. patrols were captured, among them that led by the great Vivian Street, who has left an admirable account of what it was like:

> As we topped a rise, we saw the road about a quarter of a mile ahead of us running like a ribbon across the desert. It was a great moment for us all. For over two weeks we had been travelling and had covered several hundred miles. All the while our talk, our thoughts, and even our dreams had been about 'the road'. At times it had seemed nebulous and unobtainable, and we doubted if we would ever be there by the appointed day, or even reach it at all. And now as we lay there sweeping the road with our glasses, we realised excitedly that our efforts had not been in vain and that all along the road other parties like ourselves were stealing up to strike at the enemy's supply line nearly two hundred miles behind their front.

It was not long before they struck. They soon saw a group of lorries which had pulled off the road for the night, and as there appeared to be no sentries, up they crept, planted their incendiaries in the lorries which were filled with supplies of all sorts, stole away again, and then waited. It was with the greatest satisfaction that they observed some twenty lorries go up in flames, with resultant panic from the Italian drivers. Having mined the road and destroyed telephone poles, the S.A.S. patrol drove off to their hideout, which they reached just before dawn. Street recorded that it had been a great adventure, easier than had seemed possible, and they felt there was nothing to stop them walking into the main square of Tripoli and repeating the performance there. But in subsequent attempts to do more damage in the area near Zliten, Street found that there was an embarrassingly large number of Italian soldiers and sentries about, with whom they had more than one brush:

> Suddenly there was a burst of firing from behind, and on looking round we saw three groups of men advancing towards us, gesticulating and shouting wildly in true Italian style, stopping now and again to take erratic pot-shots at us with their rifles. The four of us paused a minute. What could we do with our miserable pistols against fifty rifles?

They decided to run for it and their luck held. Not only did the Italian shooting remain incredibly inaccurate, but some convenient and freshly dug holes in the desert in some dead ground suddenly made their appearance, and into them they dived. Undiscovered by their pursuers, they spent an uncomfortable and cramped day before returning to their hide-out. Vivian Street was to have his share of luck as well as adventure during the coming months – he even escaped from an enemy submarine when it was depth-charged by a British aircraft en route across the Mediterranean – but when his patrol was near its Bir Dufan rendezvous, after having to abandon their jeeps in concealed positions for lack of petrol, they were spotted by Arabs, who gave away their hide to Italian soldiers. The systematic search by the Italians gave them no hope of escape:

> Through my mind flashed the picture of five Englishmen fighting to the death against impossible odds in the true story-book manner, but a couple of hand-grenades landing near us soon banished these mock-heroics, and with the enemy only twenty yards away we were forced to accept the inevitable and held up our hands in surrender.

It was not long, however, before Vivian Street, having so miraculously escaped from the Italian submarine and the sea, was back with his regimental comrades. Only a few other members of 'B' Squadron were as lucky. All in all the operations designed to disrupt 'the road' had not met with the success which Stirling and others had hoped for. But a new year, 1943, was to bring new ideas, new horizons and one appalling blow to the S.A.S.

8

AN END AND A BEGINNING

A leader of quite exceptional resource and one of the most underdecorated soldiers of the war. More than once he would have won the highest military order that a Sovereign can bestow, were it not for the rule that a senior officer must be present to vouch for the circumstances of the citation – and senior officers were never well placed to witness Stirling's raids behind the lines.

Sir Robert Laycock

On 12 January, 1943, Montgomery announced that his Army would be in Tripoli in ten days and his offensive to achieve this was timed for the 15th. The S.A.S. were to have four tasks, two of which were directly related to Montgomery's forthcoming attack, while two were further afield. One group was to operate to the west of Tripoli in order to assist 8th Army's advance from the east and to try to persuade the enemy to leave Tripoli in haste, without damaging the port facilities too much; a second party would reconnoitre the area of Mareth, which was known to be a future defensive line, in order to discover what preparations were being made and what routes round it might be found; thirdly, there were to be raids on the enemy's supply lines between Sfax and Gabes; while Stirling himself would lead a party as far as northern Tunisia in order to link up with 1st Army, which had been advancing east from Algeria since the *Torch* landings in November.

Stirling has since explained that his idea was not simply to make contact with 1st Army, but to sow the seeds for the formation of an S.A.S. Brigade:

My plan was to bring in my brother Bill's 2nd S.A.S. Regiment, and to divide down my own regiment, which had grown beyond the official establishment of a full regiment into the nucleus of a third one. This would enable me to keep one regiment in each of the three main theatres – the eastern Mediterranean, the central Mediterranean–Italy area, and the future Second Front. I felt it was vital to get intervention and support from a more important formation than Middle East Headquarters. The first step in this plan seemed to be to acquire the sympathy of the 1st Army's top brass, and to consult my brother Bill, who had recently arrived on the 1st Army front, as to the state of the game at the War Office. I was conscious that the reputation of the S.A.S. would be greatly enhanced if it could claim to be the first fighting unit to establish contact between the 8th and 1st Armies.

Stirling set out on 10 January, taking with him the brilliant navigator, Sadler, Corporal Cooper and a man from Paddy Mayne's squadron, McDermott. In all he had some eight jeeps and twenty men. They were aiming at a rendezvous near Bir Guedaffia, where they would meet Captain Jordan and his French patrols and also three others, who had been involved in the 'road' operations – Thesiger, Alston and Martin. After joining together and discussing plans and routes, Stirling decided on a rendezvous in northern Tunisia near Bir Soltane, which was only about thirty miles from the Mareth Line. From this rendezvous Alston and Thesiger would be able to establish themselves for getting the necessary intelligence about Mareth's defences, while Jordan and his Frenchmen would be able to make for the Gabes gap on their way to harass the enemy's lines of communication. It would also make a suitable base for Stirling's own intended activities. They would therefore move to Bir Soltane in two parties, one under Jordan, the other under Stirling himself.

When they met again at Bir Soltane, Stirling had received information from 8th Army Headquarters which made both their missions more urgent, and more hazardous. Tripoli was in British hands [it was entered by the S.A.S. and the 11th Hussars on the morning of 23 January] and Gafsa, in west-central Tunisia, had been captured by the Allies. Rommel's position was becoming increasingly difficult, particularly supplies, so that speed in disrupting further his lines of communication was the order of the day. Therefore Jordan must get on with it at once. Stirling, too, would have to speed up his reconnaissance of the Mareth flank routes and get himself in a position where he could further disrupt Rommel's supplies by raiding near Sousse. Rather than use the safer and slower route to the south of Chott Djerid and then swing north, he would have to follow Jordan through the narrow Gabes gap between Chott Djerid and the coast. For both of them it proved to be a case of more haste, less speed.

Yet on the whole Jordan did not do badly. Although on the morning of 23 January he found himself travelling alongside a German armoured car patrol, and worse still actually looking into the eyes of an Afrika Korps navigator, he did not wait to be identified. Accelerating away, he was followed by the bulk of his patrol, but during the race away from the enemy some jeeps were separated from the others and Jordan found that he was down to six jeeps and the radio vehicle. Approaching the narrowest part of the Gabes gap, he encountered three lorries moving towards him, dealt with them appropriately by machine-guns and went on. By next morning they reached the Gabes-Gafsa road and hid themselves nearby, remaining in cover all day and successfully mining the railway track that night. After some further minings, Jordan decided to return to Allied lines, but on the way he ran straight into a trap which had been prepared as a result of all his activity. By this time he and his jeep crew were alone, separated from the other jeeps of his patrol, and he felt that one solitary jeep with its machine-gun out of action was no match for the entire Italian company surrounding him. He was obliged to surrender.

Meanwhile Stirling himself with five jeeps and fourteen men had completed his reconnaissance of the Mareth flank and had followed Jordan's route through the Gabes gap. On the way his party had been spotted by German reconnaissance aircraft, but they pressed on through the gap and then hid themselves in a wadi, with bushes, shallow caves and inlets, on the far side of the Gabes-Gafsa road. It was here that the special German company, sent to track down and deal with the S.A.S., found them. McDermott and Stirling were prisoners, and were told not to expect any food as the orders were to shoot all saboteurs. Stirling took heart from his knowledge that Rommel had vetoed any such idea and from its being clear that he was in the hands of inexperienced troops. Sure enough he escaped that night, only to be betrayed later by an Arab who offered him food and water. This time Stirling was in the grip of Italian troops, who were delighted that they had succeeded where their German colleagues had failed. Stirling's daring deeds, in spite of frequent escapes from an Italian punishment camp, which resulted in his being sent to Colditz, were for the time being over. But his aim of ensuring that the S.A.S. would link up with 1st Army was achieved, for this is precisely what Sadler did. He, Cooper and the Frenchman, Taxis, had various adventures on the way, including a clash with a party of Arabs who were not interested in betraying them to the enemy, but simply in robbing and murdering them. But once more quick decisions and quick action in making a bolt for it won the day and they found themselves first with the Free French and then with the Americans at Gafsa. After an exchange of signals between 1st and 8th Army, their story was verified. In fact Sadler re-traced his steps to outflank the Mareth Line, this time with the New Zealand Division under General Freyberg. 'It was good to know,' he wrote, 'that the original journey had not been in vain.'

Indeed the whole concept and all the remarkable manifestations of it that had been directed by Stirling during the eighteen months between July, 1941, and January, 1943, by which time the North African campaign was virtually over, had been the very reverse of in vain. Pleydell, the S.A.S. doctor, made the point in his book, *Born in the Desert*, that he served with such a fine lot of men that he found it difficult years afterwards not to daydream about all their astonishing experiences. And if the critic had a question as to exactly what the S.A.S. achieved in the desert, he had his answer ready:

> To those who love statistics, I can only quote the following figures: we destroyed a total of approximately four hundred enemy aircraft in the desert; 'A' Squadron, during the autumn of 1942, demolished the enemy railway line on seven occasions; while between September 1942 and February 1943 forty-three successful attacks were made against German key positions and communications. Our raids then were more than mere pinpricks; and there were occasions when we must have diverted enemy forces and upset their road convoy system considerably; while the steady drain on aircraft probably exercised an influence on the desert war.*

All these claims can be sustained and more. But it was not just the material results which mattered. It was the spirit of the thing, the idea that a few bold men, whether at the time in question the main British forces were up against it or were advancing triumphantly, could lend a new strategic dimension to the whole conduct of war, could demonstrate with startling results the benefits to be gained from exploiting imagination, boldness and surprise. Like the Nelson touch, it was new, it was simple, it was singular; it must succeed, and it did. 'Who dares wins' might have been Nelson's own watchword.

But now there were two new circumstances which had to be taken into account for the S.A.S.'s future. One was Stirling's capture and removal from the scene; the other was the end of the North African campaign. The idea was to survive and to flourish. Its execution was to be distributed between a number of organizations and leaders. The French S.A.S. went off to rejoin the Free French Army and was later used to form the nucleus of the French S.A.S. regiments which were

* For a summary of S.A.S. Operations in North Africa, see Appendix 2.

established in Britain prior to the invasion of Normandy. The Greek squadron returned to the Greek Army for operations in the eastern Mediterranean. Paddy Mayne took the remaining men of 1st S.A.S. Regiment back to bases in Palestine, and, with the 250 officers and men he had, formed the Special Raiding Force; George Jellicoe took command of a similar number of men to make up the Special Boat Squadron. While the Special Raiding Force was designed for operations in the Balkans, the S.B.S. was meant for raiding in the Dodecanese. At the same time 2nd S.A.S. Regiment, under command of Bill Stirling, was increasing its numbers and training at Philippeville in Algeria.

With these special raiding forces as well as Commandos at their disposal, the Allies would be able to consider how best to employ them in pursuing what became known as the Mediterranean strategy. As early as December 1941, with the British beginning to bog down in Operation *Crusader* and the *Wehrmacht* beginning to suffer checks and reverses to their attempts to overcome Soviet Russia in one gigantic manifestation of *blitzkrieg*, the C.I.G.S., General Sir Alan Brooke, had noted in his diary his conviction that, for both political and military reasons, the British conduct of war should be directed to conquering North Africa as quickly as possible. In this way the Mediterranean would be re-opened and offensive operations could be staged. Brooke made this note a few days before Japan launched its attack on Pearl Harbor, an event that transformed the strategic circumstances under which the war was to be conducted. With both the Soviet Union and the United States as allies, and with Japan as an enemy, Britain slowly worked towards acceptance by the United States of the 'Germany first' strategy, and, despite some American opinion favouring concentration against Japan, this strategy was adopted. But it soon became clear that it was going to be very difficult, if not impossible, to get at Germany even in 1943, let alone earlier. In the end a direct attack across the Channel could not be mounted before 1944. Meanwhile, although Churchill spoke of the 'flexible manoeuvres', that would become possible from North Africa, which was to be a 'springboard, not a sofa', in fact the Mediterranean strategy was far from flexible. It became a campaign of attrition, not of manoeuvre, in that the whole idea was that for Germany this southern theatre would become a huge distraction from their main effort in Russia, an obligation to an ally which could not be ignored. There was little thought then of invading central Europe through its soft under-belly. The British and Americans engaged the Axis armies in Africa and the Mediterranean not just because it was expedient to do so. In 1943 there was nowhere else for them to do it. To Sicily, therefore, they went; yet when they landed there on 10 July they had not yet decided where they were to go next. All this uncertainty notwithstanding, the S.A.S. had a part to play in Sicily and what immediately followed.

It had been at the Casablanca Conference in January, 1943, that the Allied Mediterranean strategy was, in Michael Howard's words, 'born and legitimized'. The problem with which the Joint Chiefs of Staff had wrestled at this conference was one based on the premise that there would be neither enough men nor enough material to mount a cross-Channel operation into northern France before the spring of 1944. How, therefore, were the Allies to make use of North Africa, all of which would be in their hands by May, 1943, to hasten Germany's defeat? Three objectives were chosen: to open the Mediterranean and thereby release shipping; to oblige Germany to divert some effort to reinforce southern Europe and so relieve pressure on the Red Army; and to force Italy to capitulate. These objectives were to be realized – by invading Sicily! Further than that Allied plans did not go.

The campaign in Sicily lasted thirty-eight days, but was not exactly a walk-over. Over 30,000 of the Allies were lost, killed, wounded or missing, while the Axis forces lost some 167,000 men, of whom nearly a quarter were Germans. The loss of Sicily itself was not of profound importance to Hitler. At the time of the invasion he had once more rung the bell for Mussolini and made it plain that there was nothing to be done but go on fighting on all fronts, in Russia, in Italy, everywhere. It was the unconquerable will to resist that mattered. As often before, in the face of such eloquence and hardness, Mussolini remained silent. Others, however, did not, and within two weeks Mussolini had been dismissed and the new Italian Government under Marshal Badoglio soon put out feelers for peace. It was at times like this that Hitler's political judgment was cold and clear and his military action rapid and decisive. While the Allies talked and dithered between the fall of Sicily and the invasion of Italy, sixteen German divisions tightened their hold on Italy, having disarmed and dispersed the Italian Army as well. The campaign in Italy was to drag on for a year and eight months, and was in general not a campaign which gave much rein to the S.A.S. In the desert they had been 'as broad and general as the casing air'. Now they were to be 'cabin'd, cribb'd, confin'd, bound in'. None the less, they lived up to their reputation for daring and winning both in Sicily and Italy.

One of those who took part in assisting the landings in Sicily was the legendary Roy Farran, who recorded so many of his adventures in his memorable book, *Winged Dagger*:

About a fortnight before the Allied landings in Sicily, Bill Stirling revealed the exact nature of our task in a lecture in the Operations Hut. We were to land a short time ahead of the Highland Division to seize a certain lighthouse which was suspected of housing some machine-guns so sited as to be able to sweep the beaches on which the landings were to take place. He showed us an air photograph of the island on which the lighthouse was situated and left us to work out our plan. He had a great knack of appreciating the crux of a problem and we readily agreed to his wise modifications. At the time most of the unit was much more concerned with large parachute operations in Northern Sicily, Sardinia and Italy, so that we were left very much to ourselves in our minor task.

Farran was able to rehearse the operation on a little island near Djelli. This was particularly useful as it was the first time he and his men had used the landing craft carried by their mother ship, *Royal Scotsman*. A week before the invasion they moved to an olive grove near Sousse, where they continued training, but soon they were hard hit by malaria, and their total of forty-five men reduced to thirteen in a few days. The squadron commander, Scratchley, was so ill that he had to hand over to Farran, who during the voyage to Sicily found that he too was suffering from malaria, but dosed himself with quinine, sleeping heavily until woken up at three o'clock on the morning of the attack by Boris Samarine, his Russian second-in-command. Into the landing barge they went and were lowered to the sea, which, although extremely rough, tossing the barge about, did not stop them getting to Lighthouse Island. Once aground, Farran and his men waded ashore and wriggled up the sloping beach towards the lighthouse itself. As they did so three figures slipped out of the building and disappeared behind it. Then Farran rushed forward with his men and kicked open the lighthouse door only to find it empty. Meanwhile firing on the main beach to their left confirmed that the Highlanders were landing. Tracer bullets and mortars enlivened the scene, and, as Farran fired his success signal, Boris reported that he had found three terrified Italians hiding in holes with the machine-gun abandoned. Suddenly a colossal roar sent them all diving for cover, until they realized that the rocket barges were firing salvoes at the shore. Randolph Churchill, who was acting as liaison between the S.A.S. and the Highlanders, appeared and told Farran to take his men back to Bizerta as soon as they could get a ship, and then be ready to reinforce other S.A.S. operations elsewhere on Sicily.

One of these other operations was an attack on a four-gun coastal battery at Capo Murro di Porco, on the east coast of Sicily north of

Syracuse. The attack was successful in so far as the guns were destroyed and some 500 prisoners taken. But it was a misuse of the S.A.S. or, as it should more properly be called at this time, the Special Raiding Squadron. This sort of task, which was essentially part of the tactical battle, was more for Commando or parachute forces than for the S.A.S., which should have been kept for strategic operations. It is true that a number of small parties from 2 S.A.S. were dropped in northern Sicily during the campaign, and they did cause some disruption and confusion to the enemy. But the great idea of maximum strategic benefit combined with extreme economy of effort, which had been so strikingly demonstrated in the desert, still needed to be applied to the mainland of Italy. And the way in which it was to be done depended on the conduct of the campaign itself there.

Churchill as usual was over-optimistic. As early as 16 July, with the fighting in Sicily but a week old and with a month to go before the island would be in Allied hands, he was writing to Smuts in high vein. Italy was on the verge of collapse, the Allies must not only take Rome [it was not taken until almost a year later], but they must march as far north as possible, and with their right hand 'give succour to the Balkan patriots'. It was not until mid-August, however, that Churchill persuaded the Americans to follow their success in Sicily by landing in Italy itself. And the price paid was such that it robbed the Allies of any chance to give real meaning to Churchill's ideas of finding some easy backstairs into Germany, instead of the direct assault and hard fighting from which his memories of slaughter on the Western front in the Great War so instinctively recoiled. The price was that *Overlord*, the invasion of Normandy in 1944, had absolute priority and that there should also be a landing in southern France. In any event, neither Churchill nor the Americans reckoned with Hitler's fanatical determination to defend every inch of Italian soil that he could, not for Italy's sake, but to provide further depth to his own defence of the Third Reich. Indeed Hitler treated the defection of Italy as an advantage, in that now Germany would be able to carry on the struggle 'free of all burdensome encumbrances ... Tactical necessity may compel us once and again to give up something on some front in this gigantic struggle, but it will never break the ring of steel that protects the Reich'. Moreover, in choosing Kesselring to command in Italy, Hitler chose a man who believed in hanging on to territory which could easily be defended. Kesselring may have been astonished at the Allies' lack of speed and boldness, but he was so successful in delaying their advance from landings made south of Naples that he was able to establish the Winter Line across the peninsula only just north of that city. The Italian campaign was a slow and slogging affair, and although it may have achieved some of its purpose in distracting German forces from the Russian front, it was unrelieved by many acts of imagination or daring – except, that is, for some executed by the S.A.S.

9

ITALY

A man who has not been to Italy is always conscious of an
inferiority.

Johnson

About a week *before* the invasion of Sicily, William Stirling, commanding 2nd S.A.S. Regiment, was trying to educate Headquarters
15th Army Group as to how his Regiment should be best employed in
order to wring maximum strategic advantages. In a memorandum
dated 1 July, 1943, he explained the scope of his command, how it
should be controlled and how it should operate:

> 2nd S.A.S. Regiment expects to operate in such numbers as are most
> suitable for the task in hand, and is specially trained to gain access by any
> means available. A loose organization by Squadron, Troop, Section or
> Group [by this latter expression he meant the 4-man patrol] make it
> possible to operate without notice or reorganization in small or large
> numbers. A very high degree of individual training will make it possible to
> work in far smaller parties than other troops where vital tasks exist which
> cannot conveniently or economically be tackled by regular formations, and
> more particularly which require action far behind the enemy's lines or
> present special difficulties of access ...

> The employment of S.A.S. troops, especially in the planning stage, will
> be more strategic than tactical. S.A.S. activities should therefore be an
> integral part, however small, of the main plan, rather than a diversionary
> role allotted at a later stage. A general directive would greatly facilitate
> future planning. An S.A.S. Regiment, unorthodox, fighting irregularly,
> depends upon the enthusiasm of the commander by whom it is employed.
> While the personality of a commander is positive, so the personality of a
> staff is invariably negative, and when the staff gets between the commander

and the S.A.S. Regiment, the latter has little prospect of useful employment ...

After a few months, should requirements appear for the disruption of Italian communications via Albania to Greece, a force of 300 men could work over hundreds of miles in up to 140 parties with shattering effect. In Italy, jeep patrols brought in by gliders could fight their way to vital objectives with explosives by the ton. In concert with a major operation, mountainous areas could be infested with small parties, which if sufficiently numerous will completely saturate local defences and paralyse communications. So far rough landings by parachute have not been accepted. 2nd S.A.S. Regiment is prepared to accept rough, unreconnoitred landings which can easily be undertaken with imperceptible increases in dropping casualties and advantages too obvious to mention.

All that William Stirling was saying had been said before by his brother David. Think strategically, try to see what huge benefits are to be gained by using my Regiment imaginatively, boldly and *as part of* the main idea. We're willing to go anywhere, do anything, he was saying, and all we ask is that you plan operations rationally, supply us adequately, give us proper training and recruiting support, and guarantee both security and continuity. Alas, as far as some of the first operations in Italy were concerned, his pleas fell on unreceptive ears.

The Italian campaign may be conveniently divided into four phases: the initial invasion including Salerno, and advance to the winter line; the fighting to capture Rome, embracing the battles of Cassino and Anzio; the advance from Rome to the Gothic Line and the battles there which bogged down during the autumn of 1944; finally the crossing of the Senio in the spring of 1945 and the rapid advance northwards, until the end in May. The S.A.S. had a part to play in all four. One role which had great promise right at the beginning, if only it had been carried out in the strength recommended by Bill Stirling, was Operation *Speedwell* in September, 1943, at the time of Italy's surrender, designed to reduce the rate of German reinforcements to the south. This really would have been a proper strategic use of the Regiment if only the idea had been matched by an appropriately generous allocation of resources in terms of aircraft and supplies.* But all that 15 Army Group would agree to was that two aircraft would be used to drop thirteen men in the mountains north of Spezia to attack

---

* It is interesting to note that Brigadier Shan Hackett, then commanding 4th Parachute Brigade, proposed a similar task for his Brigade. Colonel, then Captain, John Waddy prepared the maps for his plan, and has prepared all the maps for this book.

rail communications between Genoa and Spezia, Bologna and Pistoia, Bologna and Prato, Florence and Arezzo. The plan was that on 7 September at about midnight two sticks of S.A.S. men would be dropped. One under command of Captain Pinckney would drop south of Bologna, near Castiglione, and attack railways south of Bologna for two weeks, then make their way south to Allied lines. The other stick was to be commanded by Captain Dudgeon and would operate against the railway Genoa–Spezia.

In the event Captain Pinckney was lost, but two of his parties under Lieutenant Greville-Bell and Sergeant Robinson succeeded between them in derailing two trains in tunnels and two more on lines outside. Both of them reached 8th Army lines after several months and numerous adventures. Captain Dudgeon's stick also had mixed fortunes. He himself and Trooper Brunt, after killing a number of Germans, were captured and shot. Two others, Sergeant Forster and Corporal Shorthall, were never seen or heard of again, and were presumed also captured and executed. But Lieutenant Wedderburn and one of his men, Tanky Challenor, blew two trains up on the Spezia–Bologna line, and we shall see shortly how they got on. Even these relatively significant successes by a mere handful of men showed how enormous might have been the effect of a really bold and substantial operation, as Bill Stirling had advocated and was later on to draw once more to the attention of Allied Force headquarters. But first here is what Challenor had to say about the operation:

> We were to parachute into two areas of Italy and derail trains in tunnels by explosives ... It was to be no picnic. We were to be dropped by night on a tricky operation deep behind enemy lines in hostile mountain country. Nobody had any information as to conditions we were likely to encounter. The actual purpose of the raid was straightforward, but afterwards it was to be the age-old method of Shanks's pony, the hard footslog through enemy-held country towards the advancing Allied armies which had landed at Reggio, on the toe of Italy, three days before the launch of *Speedwell*. ...

> The sun was dipping low over the horizon as we took off from Kairouan. There was a great deal of aimless chatter about the respective merits of Italian wine and women. At least, they could not be any worse than the North African variety, particularly the wine ...

> By 11.30 pm we were nearly there. We met some flak in the Genoa/La Spezia area which ceased as we flew inland. I was No. 6 in the dropping order and last out. I saw that we were a nice tight stick. In the direction

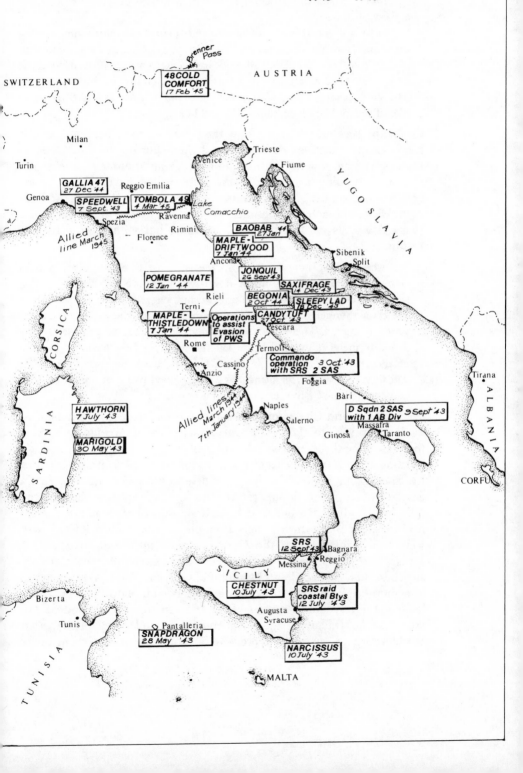

OPERATIONS IN CENTRAL MEDITERRANEAN

1943 — 1945

SWITZERLAND

AUSTRIA

48 COLD COMFORT
17 Feb '45

Brenner Pass

Milan

Turin

Venice

Trieste

Fiume

YUGOSLAVIA

GALLIA 47
27 Dec '44

Reggio Emilia

Genoa

SPEEDWELL
7 Sept '43

TOMBOLA 49
4 Mar '45

Lake Comacchio

Spezia

Ravenna

Rimini

Allied line March 1945

Florence

BAOBAB 44
27 Jan

MAPLE-DRIFTWOOD
7 Jan '44

Ancona

Sibenik

Split

POMEGRANATE
12 Jan '44

JONQUIL
26 Sept '43

Rieti

SAXIFRAGE
14 Dec '43

BEGONIA
2 Oct '44

SLEEPY LAD
18 Dec '43

Terni

MAPLE-THISTLEDOWN
7 Jan '44

CANDYTUFT
7 Oct '43

Operations to assist Evasion of PWS

Pescara

Rome

CORSICA

Cassino

Anzio

Termoli

Commando operation with SRS 2 SAS *3 Oct.'43*

Foggia

Tirana

Bàri

D Sqdn 2 SAS with 1 AB Div *9 Sept '43*

Allied lines March 1944 7th January 1944

Naples

Salerno

Massafra

Ginosa

Taranto

ALBANIA

HAWTHORN
7 July '43

SARDINIA

MARIGOLD
30 May '43

CORFU

Bizerta

Tunis

Pantalleria

SNAPDRAGON
28 May '43

SRS
12 Sept '43

Bagnara

Messina

Reggio

SICILY

CHESTNUT
10 July '43

SRS raid coastal Btys
12 July '43

Augusta

Syracuse

NARCISSUS
10 July '43

TUNISIA

MALTA

of Spezia we clearly heard the wail of an air raid siren. Down below the Apennines looked like hillocks. It had been a high drop, 7,000 feet, the highest I had been on.

Finally I plunged into a small tree and spent a frustrating time tearing the chute from the branches and then scraping a hole in the ground with my knife to bury the damn thing. I had landed in a small wooded copse on a scrub-filled mountainside. I began to walk on my line to link up with Mr. Wedderburn, using a low whistling sound as a pre-arranged means of identification. Within an hour we had all linked up.

Challenor goes on to explain how they checked their bearings, agreed a rendezvous for seven days later, and then split up, he and Wedderburn spending several nights climbing along mountain tracks and eventually finding a tunnel on the railway line long enough to lay charges, one on each line, at some distance from each other. At midnight they approached the tunnel, found it unguarded and placed their two charges, as it turned out just in time, but with most gratifying results:

We were making our way back to the entrance when we heard a train coming. It was travelling on the down-line where we had placed the first set of charges. Running and falling we just cleared the tunnel mouth as the train thundered in. With a rumbling BOOM the explosion echoed down the tunnel. There followed a crashing, smashing, banging, screeching sound of metal piling up. As we left the scene we both heard it – a train on the up-line. We listened in awe. BOOM! Again, more crashing noises and then an eerie, awful silence. We had claimed two trains and undoubtedly blocked the La Spezia-Bologna line as ordered.

Wedderburn and Challenor then climbed back into the mountains and made their way to the rendezvous. As had been previously agreed, they left after three nights, but they still had some explosives and, on learning from a friendly farmer that trains were still running between La Spezia and Pontremili, they decided to blow that up too. Again charges were placed, along came a train, 'the explosion echoed the hills, we laughed like hell and headed south'. There was not a great deal to laugh about during their attempts to reach Allied lines. There were near brushes with the Germans; they improved their use of Italian; friendly farmers sometimes gave them food and shelter, or they ate chestnuts washed down by mountain stream water. Weeks turned into months. Wedderburn began to have trouble with his feet; Challenor got a re-occurrence of malaria and, on top of it, jaundice. On arrival at an Italian village, Challenor, near collapsing point, asked Wedderburn to go on, as there was no point in both of them being caught and a farmer had told them that there were German soldiers about. But Wedderburn refused. 'There is something in the make-up of S.A.S. officers that make them like this.' They were hidden away by the Italians for several weeks, well aware of the risks that were being taken on their behalf. 'If two armed parachutists had been found in their home, the whole family would have been executed.' It is good to be able to record that despite being twice captured, Challenor escaped each time and at length reached 8th Army lines in April, 1944, some eight months after being dropped near La Spezia, the previous September.

Towards the end of 1943 Bill Stirling, still trying hard to get the Supreme Allied headquarters in Italy to see how S.A.S. troops should be employed, had some hard things to say about their refusal to mount operations of sufficient strength in September, 1943, when the unique yet fleeting opportunity presented to the Allies by Italy's changing sides was crying out for exploitation. He pointed out that instead of a mere handful of men, ill-equipped and inadequately supported, (Operation *Speedwell* had only thirteen men in five parties) there should have been anything up to a hundred parties properly mounted and supported. Had this been done, he claimed as he had repeatedly urged, the German supply and reinforcement to the Salerno bridgehead by rail from north and east would have been negligible. Telephone communications, power supplies, road transport – all would have been seriously disrupted:

> I submit that examination should be made into why, aircraft and personnel being available, an effective force was not sent against German L. of C. in northern Italy, so that when similar opportunity occurs in the future, advantage may be taken of it ... I submit that this paper merits consideration by the General Staff in relation to all future major operations, particularly where the hard necessity of seaborne assault allows the enemy with land communications a far quicker build-up than we can possibly attain by sea.

Stirling also pointed out how very economical S.A.S. operations were to mount. Six aircraft per night for ten nights could drop 600 men, organized into 250 self-contained parties. If two or three parties in Operation *Speedwell* could do what they had done, just imagine, Stirling asked, what might be the cumulative effect of 200 such parties. No type of operation, he concluded, paid a better dividend, either in personnel or material. It was because of the High Command's failure to see all this that Stirling was later, before the Normandy invasion, to resign his command. It was, however, not only in northern Italy that the S.A.S. contributed to the Italian campaign.

They also operated against both the toe and heel of Italy. The Special Raiding Squadron landed at Bagnara to interfere with the German communications and dissuade them from making a stand in the toe. In the event there was little German reaction and the S.A.S. men held on at Bagnara until other British units came up to take it over. Meanwhile some other detachments of 2nd S.A.S. had landed with 1st Airborne Division at Taranto on 10 September. Here their job was to push inland to find out what was happening, operate on the enemy's flanks and generally interfere with him. The War Diary of 'D' Squadron's detachment commanded by Roy Farran shows what their activities were like:

10th September. Disembarked at last light at port of Taranto. Reported to Para Bde HQ and ordered to advance along Massafra road. Fired on by Italian soldiers at road block, who mistook us for Germans. Sqn Leader narrowly missed by rifleman who was killed by S.S.M. Mitchell with a Bren gun. Contacted enemy post 2 miles south of Massafra and fire was exchanged in the dark. 3 prisoners taken, of whom one escaped, because the guard had his Tommy gun on safe. Relieved 2359 hrs by Airborne Recce, and ordered to patrol coast road. Contacted 'A' Sqn areas Palagiano, and laagered there for remainder of night.

On the following day Farran's squadron executed a most successful ambush of a German column near Ginosa:

I waved the jeeps into ambush position and the last vehicle was still backing into the trees when I saw the head of a large column approaching from the west. I threw myself into the ditch, pointing my tommy-gun up the road. I half suspected that they were Italians and the first vehicle was nearly on top of us before I noticed the German cockade on the front of the driver's cap. The squeezing of my tommy-gun trigger was the signal for the whole weight of our fire-power to cut into the trucks at practically nil range. Having once started such a colossal barrage of fire, it was very difficult to stop it in spite of the fact that the Germans were waving pathetic white flags from their bonnets. I remember screaming at a Frenchman called Durban to cease fire and making no impression on his tense excited face until the whole of his Browning belt was finished. At last the racket stopped and I walked down the road towards a tiny knot of Germans waving white flags from behind the last vehicle. All those in the front trucks were dead. Still panting from the excitement of the ambush, we screamed at them to come forward with their hands up. A totally demoralised group of Germans was led up the column by an officer, bleeding profusely from a wound in his arm and still shouting for mercy. It was plain that there would be no question of further resistance from any of them. In all we took about forty prisoners and four trucks. Eight other vehicles were destroyed and about ten Germans killed.

Such actions as these, tapping in with patrols, trying to discover the extent of German positions, harassing the enemy wherever possible, and helping the advancing 8th Army, had their value, although it may be questioned again whether these methods were really making proper strategic use of the S.A.S. Their real job should have been well behind the enemy lines, not arguing the toss with front line troops, and doing what normal reconnaissance units could do, however much better the S.A.S. might have done it. In October, however, 2nd S.A.S. and 1st S.R.S. became involved in the battle of Termoli, the Adriatic port.

Roy Farran has described how they became involved. In the first place they were being used to assist escaped British prisoners of war who were at large behind the German lines. Small parties of S.A.S. were either dropped by parachute or landed from the sea along the Adriatic coast between Ancona and Pescara. They would then make contact with the ex-prisoners and guide them back to the beach where they would be picked up periodically by landing craft or motor torpedo boats. Meanwhile Termoli itself had been seized by a combined force consisting of 3 Commando, 40 Marine Commando and 1st S.R.S. It was there that Farran joined them. By this time 78th Division had arrived and was beginning to take over from the Commandos. But a battle was just about to start as the German 1st Parachute Division attempted to retake Termoli. Again the War Diary succinctly records events:

5th October. Major Scratchley arrived from 8th Army and Sqn ordered into Bde reserve to assist in the defence of Termoli. Heavy shelling all day. Sqn took up position Albergo 1100 hrs. Sqn ordered to defend railway line to coast, one mile south of Termoli. Heavy mortaring, shelling and sniping, but Sqn took up good position and stayed there. Lt. Mackie with 10 men and three Bren guns on left of railway, and Lt. Jackson with 10 men and three Bren guns on right of railway down to sea. Sqn HQ in centre of railway line. 1st S.A.S. troop under Major Pope and 40 R.M. Commando on left. Germans advanced to within 600 yards of Sqn position in evening, and machine-gunned in obvious attempt to draw fire. Sqn held fire owing to (a) shortage of ammunition and (b) to conceal exact positions from enemy mortars. Heavy mortaring until last light. Sqn spent cold uncomfortable night in its positions.

6th October. Mortaring, machine-gunning and shelling of Sqn positions began at first light. Accurate sniping by enemy down line of railway.

1330 hrs. Lt. Mackie and troop advanced with 1 section of 40 Commandos to seize and hold a ridge 500 yards in front of old position.

1400 hrs. Lt. Mackie's troop obliged to withdraw from new position, owing to shelling from Sherman tank on left.

1430 hrs. Sqn at last allowed to open fire on enemy positions, range 600 yards, as London Irish advanced on left. A good shoot had by all, with visible effects, casualties inflicted on enemy.

1700 hrs. It was very great to see large numbers of German infantry withdrawing in confusion from their positions, unfortunately just out of range of small arms fire.

1800 hrs. Sqn relieved by London Irish and withdraw to Billets. Total casualties, 3 wounded.

Thus was the hour to hour activity unemotionally recorded, and the Diary went on to say that they then moved to more comfortable billets, were issued with new clothes, cleaned up, well fed, and on 11 October were inspected and addressed by General Montgomery. This was followed by a Squadron feast of tomato soup, roast turkey, Welsh rarebit and fruit. In his own account of the battle Roy Farran brings more colour to it all by remembering that, when walking along with Sandy Scratchley and Brian Franks, he felt obliged to duck as each shell crashed home, while his companions ignored them. He was equally concerned when he discovered that a railway engine and truck in the middle of their position had been loaded with high explosive, which might easily be detonated by a mortar. Despite their success, Farran noted that it was the only pure infantry battle that he ever fought in the war and that he never wanted to fight another. The fact was that it misused the S.A.S. Farran's last operation in 1943 was more to his liking, however, and was in keeping with the true concept of destroying enemy communications well behind the line. He took sixteen men to land in rubber boats from a motor torpedo boat between Ancona and Pescara to blow up the railway line. It was an uncomfortable affair: heavy rain, appalling going, near misses at being discovered by German patrols, including a cavalry one, uncertain encounters with Italian peasants, most of whom in fact were friendly and gave Farran's party food, wine and shelter, the loss of two men – all this notwithstanding, they blew up the railway line in sixteen places, destroyed electric pylons and telegraph poles, and altogether so much pleased 8th Army with the trouble they had caused the Germans that General Montgomery sent them what Farran described as 'his usual good boy

gift of newspapers and cigarettes'. It was to be some time before
Farran returned to Italy. But other members of the S.A.S. continued
to do their best to help the main armies forward.

In December, 1943, with the Anzio landings already planned to take
place on about 22 January, 2nd S.A.S. was told to prepare plans for
disrupting rail communications which might be used by the enemy to
counter the Allies' efforts at Anzio. They selected two areas – one forty
miles north of Rome, near Terni and Orte, and the other on the east
coast near Ancona. Both operations were to be launched by parachute,
and, although widely separated in space, would be coordinated in time.
At first it was hoped to mount both attacks on the night of 15 December, but bad weather combined with the state of the moon forced a
postponement until 7 January. On this night two parties each of four
men dropped about twenty miles west of Ancona, in order to blow up
the Rimini–Ancona railway line. They reported some successes, but
failed to return by the planned coastal pick-up. Some were captured,
some believed drowned. But we will follow in more detail the adventures of the group which dropped near Terni; about 100 miles behind
enemy lines.

At about midnight on 7 January Lieutenant Worcester with sixteen
others, officers, NCOs and troopers, organized into four parties,
jumped from two Dakota aircraft of the United States from a height
of only 800 feet in bright moonlight on to a DZ, which was thirty or
forty miles to the east of their targets. The DZ was covered in four
feet of snow and, because the two aircraft dropped their groups in
different places, the party did not rendezvous on the DZ. Instead they
made their way separately to their targets, some thirty-five miles away
across snow-covered mountains. The idea was that four groups should
blow up the railway in four places on the night 13/14 January and
cause as much disruption as possible. Two of the groups, led by
Lieutenant Parker and Sergeant Hill, did lay their charges on that
night, while Squadron Sergeant-Major Lloyd laid his on 16 January.
The commander of the entire party, Lieutenant Worcester, found that
his target had already been destroyed by Allied bombing, and so moved
on to attack the Terni–Rieli railway. Reports which were received later
showed that the attacks achieved their aim in stopping all rail movement in that area for some days.

Now came the business of getting to Allied lines by moving south
in the hope that their advancing friends would make this relatively
easy. It was a forlorn hope. For a number of reasons – partisan activity,
the attempted escape of Allied prisoners, the Anzio landing itself – the
enemy's vigilance and sheer presence in large numbers resulted in the

eventual capture of every single man of Lieutenant Worcester's total
of seventeen. But some of them evaded capture right up until the
beginning of June. Worcester himself made contact with the local
Italian partisans after finishing his job and immediately set about organizing them into teams to carry out further sabotage. He still had
60 lbs of explosive left and hit upon the agreeable notion of tossing
home-made bombs into the back of lorries as they moved slowly along
the snow-covered roads. In this manner he succeeded in destroying
twenty-five trucks and disposing of a good many German soldiers. One
of his men, Trooper Helier, with a pistol in each hand, even took on
a German staff car as it drove along the road and killed the two
German officers who were in it.

By 1 March Worcester had collected an additional five escaped
prisoners, who included a South African soldier and an American pilot.
But their inevitable unfitness was making it difficult for the S.A.S. to
move quickly south, so Worcester split his group into three, hoping
thereby to give each the best chance of getting through. His own party
of himself, Helier and Cobley was short of food, but they marched
hard, covering twenty-five miles a day for three days before their good
fortune ran out. After an encounter with a German patrol, they were
obliged to stop for the night, and early next morning were surprised
and captured. As will be seen, the S.A.S. did not give up lightly.
Before dawn on the following morning, they attacked their guards, but
alas did not get the best of it. Worcester recalled:

> Helier, Cobley and I were left in a room with five Germans to guard us.
> At 6 a.m. I noticed that the enemy were becoming drowsy so I asked for
> some water. A bottle of wine and a glass were produced and I threw these
> at the first two Germans. We then made an attempt to escape. I was hit
> in the leg by Schmeisser fire early in the scrap and I saw Cobley go down
> with two Germans on him. Helier was hit twice in the arm and leg, but
> kept fighting, and eventually a German stood over him and emptied his
> magazine as he lay on the floor. My leg was useless and I thought Helier
> was dying. I managed to give him a shot of morphia which made him lose
> consciousness. In the afternoon we were moved out and carried on ladders
> to Santa Maria, where all the inhabitants turned out to see us. We were
> taken by ambulance to Caisoli where we stayed for sixteen days, thence by
> varying stages we were moved northwards to Germany.

Similar adventures befell all the others who had parachuted into the
area on the night on 7 January. After attacking their targets, they
moved off into the hills before starting their long and hazardous march
south towards the British lines over 100 miles away, often encumbered

with former prisoners-of-war of great variety – Australians, New Zealanders, Americans and British. Like Worcester, Sergeant-Major Lloyd split his men into smaller groups to improve their chances. He himself headed for Rome, joined up with partisans and mounted attacks on German vehicles and troops. On 22 April he neared the British positions at Anzio and was actually fired on by his own side. Encountering a British patrol he fell in with them, and then, within sight of safety, they were all overpowered by a German patrol.

As for the others, Lieutenant Parker with seventeen escaped prisoners-of-war was surrounded and captured on 21 March. Sergeant Hill, heading south towards Anzio, was betrayed by an Italian farmer, and had the bitter sight of this same farmer being paid off by his German captors before being marched off. Lance-Corporal Lawrence, who had started the operation with Lieutenant Worcester, was the last to be captured. On 1 June, five months after he had parachuted into enemy territory, he suffered the same fate as Sergeant Hill and was given away to the Germans by an Italian farmer.

If we think about the brave efforts of these skilled and determined soldiers and attempt to gauge their results against what the main Allied armies were up to in their great struggles at Cassino and Anzio, we might be in danger of concluding that they did not amount to very much. Yet it must be conceded that, at a critical time in the battle for Rome, an important part of the Germans' rail supply line was put out of action for at least a week. Moreover, the Germans were obliged to divert many troops to hunt down the S.A.S. parties with their accompanying prisoners-of-war, troops which could otherwise have been deployed in the principal operational areas. Once again the S.A.S. had demonstrated their ability to use minimum force in imposing considerable annoyance and distraction on the enemy. At the same time these operations illustrated the difficulties of conducting such operations in the relatively restricted and controlled areas behind enemy lines in Italy. These difficulties underlined David Stirling's maxim that his men should be used whenever possible on broad strategic tasks rather than tighter, tactical ones.

It would be wrong, while still in Italy, not to mention Paddy Mayne's part in the earlier operations, when, while battling with the German 1st Parachute Division, he was seen to kill twelve Germans, and subsequently to go off by himself to try to exact some revenge for the deaths of a truck-load of British soldiers killed by an enemy shell. Philip Warner comments in his own book that the various accounts of Mayne's exploits were so extraordinary that they seemed to verge on exaggeration. He seemed to bear a charmed life, but those who knew him and fought with him claimed that, though he may have had an exceptional share of luck, it was rather his astonishing speed of reaction and decision, to say nothing of being a lionheart, that did much to account for his exceptional deeds. That the quality of the S.A.S. men was well understood by senior generals was made plain by the tributes paid to them by Montgomery and Dempsey, then commanding 13 Corps. Montgomery made it plain that wherever he went he liked to have with him those who had fought with him. And he indicated that before long he hoped to be going back to England. Dempsey's farewell speech to the Special Raiding Squadron was such that it demands inclusion in full:

> It is just three months since we landed in Sicily, and during that time you have carried out four successful operations. You were originally lent to me for the first one, Capo Murro di Porco. That was brilliantly planned and brilliantly carried out. Your orders were to capture and destroy a coastal battery, but you did more. I left it entirely to you what you did after that, and you went on to capture two more batteries, and a very large number of prisoners. An excellent piece of work. No one then could have foretold that things would have turned out as they have. You were to have returned to the Middle East after that operation, but you then went on to take Augusta. You had no time for careful planning; still you were highly successful.
>
> Then came Bagnara and finally Termoli. The landing at Termoli completely upset the Germans' schedule and the balance of their forces by introducing a threat to the north of Rome. They were obliged to bring to the east coast the 16th Panzer Division which was in reserve in the Naples area. They had orders, which have since come into our hands, to recapture Termoli at all costs and drive the British into the sea. These orders, thanks to you, they were unable to carry out. It had another effect, though. It eased pressure on the American Fifth Army and, as you have probably heard, they are now advancing.

Dempsey went on to say that, in all his military career and all his experience of units under his command, he had never come across one in which he had such confidence. He then gave six reasons why he thought they were so successful and added that he hoped they would bear these reasons in mind when training newcomers to their ranks. The reasons, which are very simple and as relevant now as they always were, should serve as a model for all those who hope to command:

> First of all, you take your training seriously. That is one thing that has always impressed me about you. Secondly, you are well disciplined. Unlike

some who undertake this specialized and highly dangerous job, you maintain a standard of discipline and cleanliness which is good to see. Thirdly,
you are physically fit, and I think I know you well enough to know you
will always keep that up. Fourthly, you are completely confident in your
abilities - yet not to the point of over-confidence. Fifthly, despite that
confidence, you plan carefully. Last of all, you have the right spirit, which
I hope you will pass on to those who may join you in the future.

It would have done David Stirling's heart good to hear this tribute,
and the S.A.S. has abided by these rules ever since. They were and
are exactly what Stirling had always had in mind. Dempsey then
outlined some principles which he intended should apply to his own
employment of the S.A.S. in future. Not all of these would have
enjoyed Stirling's support. While he would have accepted the first
principle of not using the S.A.S. unless the job was worthwhile, he
would not have agreed with Dempsey's idea that they should not be
used too far ahead of the main army. Dempsey actually said he must
be able to reach the S.A.S. in twelve to twenty-four hours of their
employment. This was quite contrary to what had gone before, and
fortunately did not inhibit their proper use in the future. His other
points - that proper time for careful planning, whilst not excluding
rapid seizure of opportunity, must be allowed, and that, once a job was
done, the S.A.S. must be extracted for further reorganization and the
next job - were sound enough. He finished by looking forward to
further association with them. As Dempsey was to be one of Montgomery's principal commanders in the great battles for France, there
was little doubt about its likelihood. It is to France that we must
shortly turn our attention. But it must be said here that there were to
be further operations in Italy* in support of the third and fourth
phases of the campaign, which were mentioned at the beginning of
this chapter. To preserve a chronological sequence, however, these will
be dealt with later. Before we leave the Mediterranean, however, we
will do well to take a look at what George Jellicoe and others had been
up to with the S.B.S.

* For a summary of S.A.S. operations in Italy and elsewhere in the Mediterranean
see Appendix 3.

10

IN BOATS

The S. B. S. was too hazardous a service to remain intact for long.
Philip Warner

This is not the place to deal fully with the Special Boat Service. Others, notably John Lodwick in *The Filibusters*, have already done so. But the association of the S.A.S. and the S.B.S. was very close, indeed the S.B.S. was actually part of the S.A.S. at one time. It is therefore important to understand their relationship, to say something of the S.B.S.'s story, the men who served with them and what it was they got up to. We have seen that, when the 1st S.A.S. Regiment was reorganized in 1943, part of it became the Special Raiding Squadron under Paddy Mayne, while the Special Boat Squadron was under command of Lord Jellicoe. Now we must go back to the S.B.S.'s origins.

In July, 1940, small sections of experienced canoeists were formed to work with the newly raised Commandos for such tasks as beach reconnaissance and to get information about enemy positions and fortifications. One of the leading lights in this was Lieutenant Roger Courtney, who with other enthusiasts had experimented with folboats and had convinced Combined Operations headquarters of their military potential. Courtney's section was attached to 8 Commando and did a good deal of training during the winter of 1940-41. Then in January, 1941, he and his Special Boat Section sailed to the Middle East with 8 Commando (Layforce). During the early part of that year Courtney's section carried out beach reconnaissance of Rhodes and also took part in a Commando raid on Bardia. Then, after the break-up of Layforce and the general deterioration in the British position in the Middle East, with the evacuation of Greece and Crete and withdrawal to Egypt's frontier in the desert, Courtney's section was attached to the R.N. submarine base to work with them. Although the S.B.S. was at this time independent, it had no official title or badge, but simply worked under HQ Combined Operations in the Middle East and was employed on such jobs as harassing raids and inserting agents ashore on hostile territory. The places visited for these purposes were varied and included Sicily, Albania, Crete and Italy. The S.B.S. also became involved in the abortive raid on Rommel's headquarters in November, 1941. In December Courtney returned to England to organize S.B.S. activities there, and Kealy took over in the Middle East.

Soon after this the S.B.S. began its association with the S.A.S., for in January, 1942, David Stirling took an S.B.S. team to raid Bouerat harbour, although, as we have already seen, the canoes got damaged and that part of the raid was not successful. Nonetheless they succeeded in blowing up many petrol lorries. A similar sort of raid on Benghazi in March with both S.A.S. and S.B.S. men was again frustrated by damage to the canoes. However, the S.B.S. carried out useful reconnaissances both at Gazala and in Syria in May and June, 1942. It was in this latter month that a major S.A.S. operation was mounted in support of the Malta convoy. We have already seen something of what happened on land in Chapter 6. Lord Jellicoe, at this time in the S.A.S., has left an admirable account of what it was like to take part in one of the raids on an airfield in Crete.

The attack on Cretan airfields was specifically in support of the west-bound convoy to Malta which was to leave Alexandria on 11 June, and the party of which Jellicoe was a member was commanded by the gallant French Commandant Berge, M.C., Croix de Guerre, and contained also three other men of the Fighting French forces and a Greek guide, Lieutenant Costi. Jellicoe himself was there to be as useful as he could and in particular to liaise with the Naval people. The plan was to attack the landing ground at Heraklion at midnight on the night of 12 June, at the same time as three other landing grounds in Crete would be raided by other members of the Special Boat Section. Jellicoe was given his orders on 4 June and was required to embark with the raiding party only two days later, having by then chosen the boats to use, done some training and assembled all the necessary equipment.

They duly embarked in a Greek submarine, *Triton*, and managed to do a little training in the mouth of Alexandria harbour, both with inflated rubber dinghies which were the preferred craft and with the ship's dinghy in case they had to land in the face of a stiff off-shore breeze. Both *Triton* and another Greek submarine, *Papa Nikolas*, left on the evening of 6 June, the latter carrying an S.B.S. group for the raid on Maleme, while *Triton* made for a position off the coast to the east of Heraklion. The voyage there took four days and then a daylight periscope reconnaissance was done so that the raiding commander could decide the best place to land. After that the submarine submerged and they spent the next day eating and sleeping. Then that night, 11 June, the submarine surfaced, the six raiders embarked in two rubber boats, with equipment in a third, and began the journey to the shore. It was dark and calm, and *Triton* towed the rubber boats to a position within about two miles from the shore, when they cut their tow because searchlights at Heraklion airfield had been switched on to counter an R.A.F. raid on it, and this produced too much light for the submarine's security. It took them about two and a half hours to paddle ashore, with a good deal of baling out necessary, as the boats leaked, one casualty of the baling being Jellicoe's best service dress cap. They disembarked at about 0115 hours on a most suitable beach some fourteen miles east of their objective. Then the boats were towed out to sea by Jellicoe and with difficulty sunk, having been filled with pebbles and then cutting the inflation chambers. The idea of sinking the boats was, of course, not to prejudice other suitable beaches for later landings.

They were now about three hours behind the time-table, but set off inland with Berge leading. They all had machine-carbines, twelve special bombs for the attack, food, water, maps, amounting in all to 50 lbs per man. After crossing the coast road, avoiding enemy patrols whose lighted cigarettes made this easy, they found themselves in precipitous country which made their progress very slow. They were in fact making their way up a valley which had already been identified from air photographs and maps, but once it was light they encountered numerous peasants and decided that even though well behind schedule, having covered only six miles out of the twenty to their objective, they would have to lie up for the rest of that day if they were to escape detection. They found a place beneath the crest of a hill, where it was very hot with the sun beating down, and some of them became so thirsty that a lot of their precious water was used up. About 6 o'clock that evening a shepherd came to talk to them and was undeceived by their talking German to him, speaking English himself. But he seemed friendly so they went to the nearest village to fill up with water. There, surrounded by friendly peasants, they decided to push on by the easiest route through the villages, pretending to be Germans after curfew time, but still rather unnerved by the racket of barking dogs as they approached each new village. By first light the next morning they were still not in a position to look down on the airfield itself, which is sheltered to the south by hills of up to 1,000 feet, intersected by narrow, deep valleys. But they found some excellent cover among caves in the rock of the gorge which they were crossing.

Once more they lay up all day [it was already 13 June and they were well behind their planned timings], but towards evening Berge and Costi, dressed in plain clothes, climbed up the hill beneath which they were hiding, and at last were able to see the landing ground and estimated that there were some sixty aircraft, mostly Ju.88s, on it. Later, leaving Costi with the heavy equipment and machine-carbines in the cave, which was to be the rendezvous after the operation, the party set off for the landing ground. As they drew near it, they had to avoid enemy positions, including an anti-aircraft battery at Prassas, and all this took time. At about half an hour before midnight, they realized that to get on to the airfield they would need to cross a steep and rocky ravine and, while attempting to do so, an enemy sentry heard and challenged them. They froze and the sentry lost interest. Trying again a bit further east, the same thing happened and they had to abandon the attempt that night, retiring to the hills again, during the day finding some shade and grapes in the vineyards. That evening they got some water and this time approached the airfield before it was dark in order to locate enemy defences. While waiting to get through these, they observed a number of Ju.88s taking off and returning in groups of eight and by their exuberant flying evidently celebrating some success.* As the aircraft landed, they taxied to blast-proof shelters around the airfield.

Soon after this Berge, Jellicoe and the others made their way through the wire fence, lay down there, and almost at once encountered a German patrol. One of the French corporals, Mouhot, gave such a drunken snore that the German sentry appeared satisfied and moved off, only to return shortly afterwards, but by this time the S.B.S. group had hidden in a bomb dump. Then the R.A.F. came to the rescue with a raid which dispersed the German patrol, and, as it ended, enabled Berge and the others to move into the shelters and place bomb charges on sixteen aircraft† on the southern side of the airfield. They then moved across to the northern dispersal area, only to find that most aircraft there were derelicts. However, they succeeded in putting more charges on aircraft engines under repair and on a number of trucks. As the first charges began to explode, there was only an hour or so of daylight left and they made their way through the main

* Indeed the raid was too late to stop successful attacks on the convoy.

† It was later confirmed that sixteen aircraft had been destroyed.

barrack area, mingling as they did so with the harassed occupants. As they moved away, they were disappointed to see that not many of the aircraft attacked actually caught fire. This was because the fuel tanks were, as a matter of deliberate policy, not filled. By eight o'clock that morning they were back at the rendezvous, where they found that Costi had managed to gather together a splendid meal of roast chicken, bread, soup and wine.

That evening off they went again, aiming to get as far south as possible, heading for Krotos, a village near Cape Martelos on the south coast. A wrong turning, however, took them in a half circle and next morning they were not much further from Heraklion than when they had started. However, a lucky meeting with one of Costi's friends, a Greek Army major, provided them with food and a guide. By the following morning they reached Karkadhiotissa, and there had a rest; it was the first sleep enjoyed by either Berge or Jellicoe, who had kept going on Benzedrine. They were further comforted by eating a sheep provided for them, but distressed at the news that sixty Greek hostages had been shot by the Germans as a reprisal for their Heraklion raid. They moved from Karkadhiotissa on 17 June, still going south, this time towards another village, Vali, which was reached next morning. They swam and refreshed themselves and moved on that night across the plain of Messaria. Then Costi and Berge visited the former's family, to return with the bad news that his brothers had been obliged to take to the hills, and with the slightly better tidings that, although food was short, his mother had given him two chickens.

The end of this adventure is perhaps best told in the gallant George Jellicoe's own words:

As always, it was found impossible the next day to avoid contact with the peasants who all appeared friendly. One, in particular, brought us some excellent wine and we questioned Lieutenant Costi about him, who said he was not only a personal acquaintance of his but an excellent man. That afternoon Commandant Berge and the French party rested in a small valley in the northern slopes of the hills to the south of the plain. I went forward with Lieutenant Costi as guide to get into contact with our agents in Krotos, whom I met that evening. Leaving Costi at Krotos, as he was tired, I went back with one of the agents to bring the main party to the rendezvous with the Special Boat Section. It was then dark, and although I searched the ground carefully where the party had been, I was unable to discover them. The agent was unwilling to stay there in daylight, so I sent him back to Krotos and searched further for evidence as to where the party was. Some young local peasants from the neighbouring village arrived in a great state of agitation, and from what was said and the signs used, I was led to understand that Commandant Berge had been betrayed and attacked by a party of Germans. After a resistance in which one of his party had been killed, he had surrendered and been led off. I had had suspicions that something had gone wrong owing to finding traces of the meal tidily arranged. From my knowledge of the French, I knew, firstly that nothing would have been left over and secondly, if it had, it would not have been tidily arranged. They told me that the German patrol was returning to search the area and advised me to flee.

This I did and contacted the agent in Krotos whom I was lucky enough to run into on the track. When I told him what had happened, he became incoherent with fear and I was forced to abandon all cooperation with him. I was wearing civilian clothes at that time and was unarmed. By pure chance that evening I met Lieutenant Costi with a local peasant at whose house he had spent the night. This man, Miroyannis, was fully aware of the situation and of the risks he was running in sheltering Lieutenant Costi. He immediately welcomed and fed me and showed me where the main rendezvous with the S.B.S. was, whom I contacted that evening. Miroyannis himself went back to the area where Commandant Berge had been captured to find out news of him. He confirmed the impression I had received from the peasants and stated that the German patrols were searching the area for Lieutenant Costi and myself and said that Commandant Berge and the remaining prisoners had been transferred to Heraklion. It was clearly impossible to do anything to help them.

Three days later we received word by local runner who told us that the boat which was to take us off would arrive that evening. I spent three days in some caves, and occupied my time swimming and attempting to combat the insects which swarmed round me, and in the contemplation of food. On 23 June, the small boat commanded by Lieutenant Campbell arrived and the party embarked along with some twenty miscellaneous refugees. Lieutenant Costi was with me and he had with him one of his brothers and sisters. The twenty miscellaneous refugees were mostly brigands, called patriots in that part of the world. There were approximately two hundred people waiting for the evacuation on the beach at the time and something approaching a free fight until the boat put off. Luckily these people were mainly not armed Those giving most trouble were a number of Cypriots, one of whom it was found necessary to submerge. The *Porcupine* arrived off Matruh two mornings later and we were gratified to witness a German air raid which meant the port was still in our hands. We landed from the *Porcupine* and arrived at Alexandria in a 10-ton lorry provided for us next morning.

The hall porter at the Cecil Hotel was somewhat surprised at my appearance as I was very curiously dressed. From what information that was available, it appeared that Commandant Berge and his French party captured with him were shot at Heraklion by the German authorities.

This was one example of how the S.A.S. and S.B.S. combined to do their dangerous work. There were to be many more and Crete was to be visited again. It is in connection with Crete that M Detachment, S.B.S. should be introduced, for it was planned that this detachment should raid Crete in the autumn of 1942. It was at this time commanded by Fitzroy Maclean, although it had been formed for a very different purpose, which had nothing to do with boats at all. It was designed for operations in Persia, and Maclean's actual task there turned out in the end to be a long way from the sea or any boats. It involved kidnapping a Persian general, known to be pro-Axis, in the ancient and beautiful city of Isfahan. With the authority of General Maitland Wilson, commanding Persia and Iraq, Maclean set about raising a force of 150 volunteers, to be trained in S.A.S. operational methods, and while engaged in this, he was instructed to report to Wilson's Chief of Staff, General Baillon, in Teheran. There was, it seemed, trouble brewing in southern Persia, where German agents were active among the tribes and, if this trouble got out of hand, the supply routes to the Persian Gulf might be threatened. Moreover, the Persian Army in the south might side with any rebellious tribesmen. Maclean's account of it all explains who was the dangerous figure behind it:

> A sinister part was being played in all this by a certain General Zahidi, who was in command of the Persian forces in the Isfahan area. Zahidi was known to be one of the worst grain-hoarders in the country. But there was also good reason to believe that he was acting in cooperation with the tribal leaders and, finally, that he was in touch with the German agents who were living in the hills, and through them with the German High Command in the Caucasus. Indeed, reports from secret sources showed that he was planning a general rising against the Allied occupation force, in which his troops and those of the Persian general in the Soviet-occupied northern zone would take part and which would coincide with a German airborne attack on Tenth Army, followed by a general German offensive on the Caucasus front. In short, General Zahidi appeared to be behind most of the trouble in south Persia.

He had therefore to be removed and this was the task Maclean was given. His plan broadly was to introduce himself into Zahidi's residence in Isfahan under the pretext of accompanying a British brigadier

who would be calling to pay his respects. A platoon of Seaforth Highlanders would be nearby in case of trouble; the sentry on duty at the
residence was to be distracted by a Persian-speaking member of R.A.F.
Intelligence; Maclean would have some of his men, including the
faithful Guardsman Duncan, in the vehicle with him, suitably armed,
and on getting into the Residence, they would simply abduct the
General. It all worked like a charm:

> When, a couple of minutes later, General Zahidi, a dapper figure in a
> tight-fitting grey uniform and highly polished boots, entered the room, he
> found himself looking down the barrel of my Colt automatic. There was
> no advantage in prolonging a scene which might easily become embarrass-
> ing. Without further ado, I invited the General to put his hands up and
> informed him that I had instructions to arrest him and that if he made any
> noise or attempt at resistance he would be shot. Then I took away his
> pistol and hustled him through the window into the car which was waiting
> outside with the engine running. To my relief there was no sign of the
> much-advertised bodyguard. As we passed the guardroom, the sentry once
> again interrupted his conversation to present arms, and the General, sitting
> bolt upright, with my pistol pressed against his ribs and Duncan breathing
> menacingly down his neck, duly returned the salute.

Away they went to the rendezvous for Zahidi to be flown out of Persia
for safekeeping in Palestine. Once again, who had dared had won.
After this Maclean got on with the job of training his detachment in
S.A.S. methods, with the help of Sandy Scratchley and Bill Cumper
and some new jeeps and weapons. But it soon became clear that, as
1942 drew to a close, with the *Wehrmacht* defeated at Stalingrad and
in North Africa, the centre of gravity of the war was moving westwards. There was no threat now to Persia, and as General Wilson was
moving to Cairo to become Commander-in-Chief, Middle East, with
the whole of the eastern Mediterranean under his operational command, Maclean persuaded him that M Detachment should move from
Persia. Before long they had joined up with George Jellicoe at Athlit,
where he was training his S.B.S. men with canoes and rubber dinghies. Shortly after that Maclean took his men to the Lebanon to continue training in mountain warfare high up behind Beirut. Plans to
raid Crete fell through because air photographs revealed that their target, another airfield, was no longer in use by the Germans. The next
idea was to drop into Greece, but this too fell through. Eventually,
Maclean was chosen to head a Military Mission to assist the Jugoslav
partisans led by Tito. It was there that he continued his unique and
courageous contributions to the Allied cause, as he has so modestly

and brilliantly recorded in *Eastern Approaches*. But this meant that he ceased to be part of the Special Air Service.

By April, 1943, with the campaign in Tunisia drawing to a close, Jellicoe's Special Boat Squadron was established at Athlit, south of Haifa. They were still very much part of the S.A.S., wearing S.A.S. uniform and badges. His force was about 250 strong, and the two main operational detachments were L under Langton and S under Sutherland. Langton had been involved in the abortive attack on Tobruk, which, as we saw in Chapter 7, David Stirling had so strongly deprecated, and during it, having gathered a few other S.A.S. men, including Sillitoe and Watler, paddled round the harbour in an assault boat to the consternation of the Germans shooting at them, and succeeded in landing on the other side of the bay. There he collected more men and, after splitting them up into smaller parties, sent them off to evade the enemy and make their way back to Allied lines. Most were captured. Langton and a few others eventually succeeded.

There is an agreeable recollection of the Athlit days by one of the S.B.S. men who was there. In it R.A.C. Summers gives exactly the feel of what it was like:

Of all the bases used by Special Boat Service, Athlit must surely be the one most suitable for training and remembered with nostalgia by all. Legend has it that Lord Jellicoe, our Squadron Commander, in looking for a S.B.S. base, flew over Athlit and decided that this was to be the place. 'Me Lud', as some disreputes called him, secured it. He usually got his way. It was a wonderful choice. Remote. The tented camp was on the shore between a rocky promontory and the old Crusader castle of Athlit. The Mediterranean more or less lapped our tents. Recruitment and training started and was pretty tough for all. We were a mixed bunch. Infantry, Tankies, Gunners, Engineers and a few Marines. A sprinkling of Greeks from the Sacred Squadron and a few Guards. A number of Commandos and Guards seemed to become the NCOs. The Guards were still keen on drill but it was not easy to stamp on the sand and 'bull' in many ways died the death.

Small boating came strange to many. Also the parachute course. Early on 'Me Lud' said that we only parachuted for the pay and prestige! In the end S.B.S. did a fair number of parachute ops. Boat training was varied. We had 'Jellicoe Intruders' to master. These were rubber boats that were leak proof - like hell. They all leaked and we never had a dry landing. Even wetter but much more fun were the Folboats. Great for paddling about the bay. Later on when we were landed wet through with a long slog up the mountains to hide away, not so funny. We cooperated with the

21 A Stirling bomber drops supplies over Northern France.

22 Captain Michael Blackman (centre) with his patrol of 1 SAS meets an advancing American tank destroyer unit, Normandy, July, 1944.

23 An officer of the French SAS liaising with the Polish Armoured Division during operations in N.E. Holland, April, 1945.

24 A group of 2 SAS at Modena, Italy, after Operation Tombola.

25 Brigadier Michael Calvert, DSO, Commander SAS Brigade, presents a posthumous DSO to the widow of Commandant Simon, second-in-command, 3rd French Parachute Battalion, 1945. (*Imperial War Museum*)

26 Major-General G. Surtees presents medals to the troops of the Belgian SAS in
the Grande Place, Brussels, 20 October, 1952. Behind General Surtees is Lieut-
Colonel Blondeel, the Commanding officer of the Belgian SAS. (*Imperial War
Museum*)

27 A jeep of D Squadron, 1 SAS, enters Kiel Harbour in May, 1945. (*Imperial War
Museum*)

After the Belum Valley operation, Malaya, February–March, 1952. Left to right: District Officer; Major Jeff Douglas; Lieut-Colonel Tod Sloane, CO 22 SAS; Major Alastair MacGregor.

S51, S55 and Sycamore helicopters about to embark SAS troops from a kampong in Malaya, 1954.

30 Major John Woodhouse demonstrating the SAS 14-day ration to men of the New Zealand SAS Squadron on their arrival in Malaya. Major Frank Rendle, the Squadron Commander, is on the right.

31 Men of A Squadron waiting to emplane before Operation Sword, Kedah, Malaya, January, 1954. Centre foreground: Major Dare Newell; right: Major John Painter, OC A Squadron.

32 Lieut-Colonel George Lea, CO 22 SAS, centre, with Major Johnnie
Cooper, left, and a Police Officer, Kuala Lumpur, 1956.

33 Some of 3 Troop, B Squadron, after a 14-day ambush in the Tasek Bera
area of Pahang, 1955.

34 Jungle parachuting. (*Imperial War Museum*)

35 Operation Beehive, April, 1955. Four men from A Squadron, 22 SAS, parachuting into primary jungle on the Selangor/Negri Sembilian border.

Navy ... and did some training at Beirut in a T Class submarine. On to the front and stern of the sub we clamped RE folding assault boats. The idea was that the sub would surface, we would rush along and release the boats and climb in with all our gear. The sub would descend and leave us to paddle away.

Fitness was ensured by a mad sadistic bunch of PT instructors. Marching with heavier and heavier rucksacks by day and night was the order. It was rightly assumed that we would operate behind the lines in mountainous country on foot. Gradually the Detachments became operational and quietly left Athlit.

S Detachment (Sutherland's) was first off. They had a nucleus of old S.A.S. hands and a few ex-Scottish Commandos. L Detachment (Langton's) had a few ex-S.A.S. but mostly new reinforcements. After the Sardinian and Sicily operations they required more reinforcements as only a handful came back. M Detachment (Maclean's) were mostly recruited by Captàin Fitzroy Maclean in Persia. They were largely Scots. Canny and surely the most loyal of the S.A.S. Association, as they turn up every year from their Highland Fortresses. M went off to the Dodecanese and captured a few islands.

From a historical point of view the Boat Squadron became the Special Boat Service. Detachments became Squadrons and the officers were promoted.

It was at this point really that the S.A.S. and the S.B.S. separated. But now we must go back to what Jellicoe's Squadron was doing in its operations from Athlit.

Almost a year after Jellicoe's previous raid on Crete, Sutherland commanded another one, taking with him three patrols, each of four men, under Lamonby, Rowe and Lassen. Anders Lassen, a Dane, was one of the most extraordinary men ever to serve in the S.B.S. He survived danger time and time again, but was eventually killed a month before the war ended, and for his last action near Lake Comacchio in northern Italy he was awarded the Victoria Cross posthumously. In the raid on Crete in June, 1943, he was aiming to destroy Stuka and Junker aircraft on Kastelli airfield. While he and another man made a diversion to the west side of the airfield, the two others laid their charges; then Lassen returned to lay a few more. The raid was successful, but, once the alarm had been given, he had to make his way into the mountains and lie up there for about four days without food. The other two raiding parties found no aircraft, and also had to go into hiding. It was not until 10 July that the party was taken off Crete by a motor launch and by that time Lamonby had been caught and killed by the Germans. Sutherland and Lassen, however, took two

German prisoners with them, and on their way through Cairo actually
took these prisoners into the famous Groppi's for a drink before handing them over to the authorities.

The next target was a much more serious one - Rhodes. It was all
tied up with the imminence of Italy's making an armistice with the
Allies. Rhodes and the Dodecanese Islands were garrisoned largely by
Italian troops, and the intention therefore was to persuade the Italian
commanders to hand over control before the Germans could interfere.
Churchill, eager as always to seize initiatives, turned his eye once again
on that will-o'-the-wisp. 'When the tremendous events of the Italian
surrender occurred,' he wrote later, 'my mind turned to the Aegean
islands, so long the object of strategic desire'. On 9 September, 1943,
he had sent a cable to General Maitland Wilson, telling him that this
was the time to play high. 'Improvise and dare.' Wilson was only too
eager to obey but his resources were limited. Shipping and troops were
both in short supply, and American pressure was all designed to switch
resources away from this theatre, either for *Overlord* or to the Far
East. Nonetheless the S.B.S. were available, 'composed,' Churchill
recorded, 'of soldiers of the highest quality, transformed into an amphibious unit, intending to reproduce on the sea the fame they had
won in the sand. On the night of 9 September, Major Lord Jellicoe,
son of the Admiral, who was a leading figure in this daring unit, landed
by parachute in Rhodes with a small mission to try to procure the
surrender of the island.'

The man whom Jellicoe would have to persuade was the Italian
commander there, Admiral Campioni. While Sutherland and his group
occupied the island of Castelrosso to the east of Rhodes, Jellicoe,
accompanied by an Italian interpreter, Major Dolbey, and a signaller,
Sergeant Kesterton, parachuted into Rhodes itself. Unfortunately Dolbey broke his leg on landing, and Jellicoe thought he was surrounded
by Germans and actually ate the letter from General Wilson to Campioni. When with Campioni, where he had been taken by the Italians,
Jellicoe failed to convince the Admiral that the possible arrival of
British troops in about a week's time was a sufficiently comforting
thought to counterbalance the presence of some 6,000 German soldiers.
Jellicoe had to leave and put it like this:

> I then agreed to embark that night in a Motor Anti-Submarine boat for
> Castelrosso. It seemed to me on reflection that if the Governor was genuine
> in his policy of temporisation my further presence in Rhodes might well
> be an embarrassment to him and that if he was not genuine there was in
> any case no point in staying further. Before leaving I asked that all the

available intelligence on the minefields in the Aegean and on the Italian defences in Rhodes should be put at my disposal and this was done. We accordingly left the Governor's Palace shortly after dark loaded with a curious assortment of kit which included our wireless gear, two bottles of Rhodes wine and an excellent picnic basket.

So Rhodes was gone, but the S.B.S. went on with the Dodecanese. Castelrosso, Cos, Leros and Samos were all occupied by Jellicoe and his men, and subsequently reinforced by British infantry. The S.B.S. used motor launches and caiques. Major Lapraik, who had replaced Fitzroy Maclean, together with Anders Lassen, took the island of Simi, north-west of Rhodes, and used it as a base for harassing German positions in Rhodes. But the Germans were not prepared at this stage to allow a British presence in the Dodecanese. Slowly but surely, using their air superiority, they took back island after island, all the time being harassed by the S.B.S. and others. In the end the Germans deployed about six divisions in the islands, and many were the adventures and successes of the raiding S.B.S. parties. Men like Lassen, Walter, O'Reilly and others had their fill of raiding and shooting up the enemy. Philip Warner summed up their activities by comparing them with hunters who would accept any risk in pursuing what they wanted to do: 'They were living on boats, were surrounded by highly trained and entirely trustworthy companions, and had considerable freedom, both in the adventures they undertook and the lives they led.' And even though the Germans may have controlled the islands, the dissipation of the *Wehrmacht's* strength in doing so paid huge dividends in ensuring that the crucial theatre of operations in the West could not enjoy reinforcement by the German divisions which were committed in the Aegean.

There is one other name which must be mentioned in relation to operations in boats in the Mediterranean, the name of John Verney, who in his honest and witty way recorded his own version in *Going to the Wars*. At the time of preparing for the invasion of Sicily it was decided to mount a diversionary attack on Sardinia, and Verney, who had taken over temporarily from Langton, who was ill, was in charge. He has recounted how his group of five officers and twenty-four men embarked in a submarine, H.M.S. *Tiber* – the sheer number of them made it a desperate squeeze – and set off for Sardinia. On arrival off the enemy coast, they reconnoitred the beaches for landing places, but it was clear that several days in the claustrophobic and airless conditions had not sharpened the awareness and attitude of the raiding party. The submarine captain, Grigson, noted in his report that 'the troops

displayed an unnatural dullness and had to be shepherded to their
boats ... they seemed to have small mental grip on the situation'.
Perhaps it was as well therefore that, before any positive action was
taken, Grigson was obliged to announce that the submarine itself was
on the point of breaking down and they had to return to port. But
Verney still got to Sardinia. A week or so later he and his men were
given the task of attacking a German airfield at Ottana, and on the
night of 9 July, 1943, he found himself in a Halifax aircraft:

> When I wasn't asleep, I sat huddled in a coma of sheer funk, wondering
> how I should find the strength, when the time came, to move myself down
> the plane to that hole ... I saw the light and the despatcher shouting 'Go'.
> A mighty rush of air, the sensation of a piece of fluff in a whirlwind, and
> then a great quietness and peace and exhilaration. It was always, for me,
> a wonderful feeling of relief to find that the chute had opened and that I
> was suspended safely, and apparently motionless over the earth. Many
> people at that moment break into song.

There was much still to be done, but they did get to the airfield and
they did plant their explosives:

> The first explosion went off at exactly 4 a.m. We felt the blast. We halted
> half-way up the hill and looked back. Another seven explosions followed
> in the next two or three minutes. The noise and flashes were terrific. The
> petrol tanks caught alight and went up with a sudden flare, illuminating
> the landscape for miles. We had to squat out of sight in the scrub. At least
> two big blazes and, besides the major explosions, the sound of ammunition
> crackling and a few minor bangs. A Very light shot into the sky. And then
> silence again.

Did all these side-shows make any difference? We may applaud the
imagination, the offensive spirit, the gallantry, the sheer mastery of
technical difficulties, and the inspiration with which officer and soldier
alike were imbued and somehow passed on to others, but did it all add
up to winning the war? Did it really affect those areas where the war
was being won at that time, in the gigantic battles between the *Wehrmacht* and the Red Army, and was to be won in the future, in
Normandy and the Ardennes? The answer is *yes*. The Mediterranean
strategy *was* effective, creating as it did a huge distraction to the
German armed forces, without which their ability to concentrate in
the crucial operational theatres would have been greatly enhanced. But
quite apart from this, the daring, the successes, the great romantic
touch which all these irregular operations gave to the slow, plodding,

bloody struggles between armies of ironmongery were in themselves a justification of all that David Stirling had ever striven for.

Leaving aside all that the S.A.S. Regiments themselves did during the last two years of the war – in Sicily, in Italy, in France, Belgium, Holland and Norway – the record of the S.B.S. since the formation of Lord Jellicoe's Squadron at Athlit after David Stirling's capture in 1943 was remarkable. They eventually became what amounted to a regiment of their own. In 1943 they carried out raids on Crete, Sardinia, Sicily and Rhodes, and cooperated with Army units in trying to prevent the Germans capturing the Dodecanese Islands. In 1944 the S.B.S. raided German garrisons in the Dodecanese, Cyclades, Sporades and Crete. They moved to Italy, Jugoslavia, Albania and Greece. At the end of that year they were involved in the troubles with E.L.A.S. in Athens. 1945 saw further operations under Sutherland in Italy and Jugoslavia. There were raids on German garrisons in the Dalmatian Islands and Istria. In April of that year operations in northern Italy included one at Lake Comacchio:

Few men have influenced the enemy and those under his command to the same marvellous extent as Lassen. A second recommendation for the Victoria Cross was put forward after Comacchio. It bore the name of Anders Lassen, and it was successful . . .

He had been ordered to make a diversion on the northern shore of Comacchio. He selected Turnball for the job, but at the last moment decided to accompany this officer himself. O'Reilly, Crouch, Sergeant Waite and his patrol made up the remainder of the party.

The patrol landed and advanced along a road. The road was defended by pill-boxes set in echelon. Presently, very heavy machine-gun fire was opened upon the patrol. O'Reilly was severely wounded. Crouch was killed. The survivors took cover, dragging O'Reilly with them. Lassen, however, continued to advance. He silenced the machine-gun and the first pill-box with grenades. He then silenced a second, a third, and a fourth pill-box in the same manner, disposing with his revolver of men who continued to resist him. A fifth and penultimate pill-box hung out a sheet in token of surrender. Lassen advanced to take the surrender and was shot at close quarters.

He did not die immediately. He crawled towards his own men who, inspired by his wonderful example, ran forward and completed the work which he had so nearly finished single-handed. When they returned, Lassen was still conscious. 'Leave me,' he ordered. 'I'm done for'. They nevertheless continued to carry him until, feeling his body grow inert, and being themselves under fire, they were obliged to leave him. This happened on 9th April 1945. Lassen was then twenty-five years of age.

Lassen is buried not very far from where he fell. The operation in which he died was the last undertaken by S.B.S.*

Lassen's photograph still honours the walls of Headquarters, Special Air Service in London.

John Verney has an amusing passage in his book where he tells us of a War Office General who told him that in his opinion 'all irregular formations and private armies like Bomfrey's Boys contributed precisely nothing to Allied victory. All they did was to offer a too-easy, because romanticized, form of gallantry to a few anti-social irresponsible individualists, who sought a more personal satisfaction from the war than of standing their chance, like proper soldiers, of being bayoneted in a slit-trench or burnt alive in a tank'. Verney went on to say that he never argued with Generals. Quite apart from this particular General's being entitled to his point of view, Verney felt that he might be right. We, however, can not only argue with Generals. We can with total confidence point to both the benefits of S.A.S.-type operations in a major war, and to their indispensability in what we shall be examining later – the savage wars of peace. Nonetheless there is perhaps something to be said for Fitzroy Maclean's point that

> with the end of the war in the desert, the S.A.S. had lost a medium ideally suited to their type of warfare. The desert had played a vital part in their operations. Now they would have to adapt themselves to completely new conditions, to use completely new methods, if they were to achieve the same successes on the continent of Europe. I wished that David, so quick to grasp the potentialities of the desert for irregular warfare, had been there to help evolve a new continental technique.

Even without David Stirling the S.A.S. and S.B.S. had done some remarkable things in Sicily, Sardinia, Italy and the Aegean. They had been used with success. And yet it might also be said that they had been misused. In France it was to be different.

* *The Filibusters*, by John Lodwick, Methuen, 1947.

11

DESCENT ON FRANCE

If only they would land half a million men, and then foul weather
and storms cut them off in the rear – then everything would be
all right.

Hitler, 30 December, 1943

Towards the end of 1943 it was clear that Germany had lost the war.
Even Hitler almost acknowledged as much. His War Directive No. 51,
dated 3 November, had this to say:

> These last two and a half years of tough and bloody struggle against
> bolshevism have strained our military strength and energy to the utmost.
> It was appropriate to the magnitude of the danger and the overall strategic
> situation. Now the danger in the east remains, but an even greater one is
> emerging in the west: the Anglo-American invasion! The sheer vastness of
> the eastern spaces allows us to countenance even a major loss of territory
> if the worse comes to the worst, without it striking fatally at Germany's
> vital arteries.
>
> Not so the West! Should the enemy succeed in breaching our defences
> on a wide front here, the immediate consequences would be unpredictable.
> Everything indicates that the enemy will launch an offensive against the
> Western front of Europe, at the latest in the spring, perhaps even earlier.
> I can therefore no longer tolerate the weakening of the West in favour of
> other theatres of war.

The truth was that Hitler's game, like Napoleon's one hundred and
thirty years earlier, was going wrong more or less everywhere. That
ever-to-be-shunned chimera, war on two fronts, was no longer a fan-
ciful thing. It was looming up in the shape of a dreadful reality. In
the east the Russians advanced and went on advancing. 'Where will it
ever end?' wrote Goebbels. 'The Soviets have reserves of which we

never dreamed in even our most pessimistic estimates.' Town after town, which earlier the *Wehrmacht* had taken with such consummate ease, now went down to the Red Army with appalling regularity. Orel and Kharkov, Poltava and Smolensk, Kiev, Zhitomir; even such crucial objectives like the Crimea and the Donetz basin were either lost or cut off. Yet Hitler would give up nothing unless obliged to do so, not the Crimea, nor Greece, nor Crete, nor Italy. It was true that the Germans were hanging on in the Mediterranean and the Balkans, but hanging on with divisions which therefore would not be available either on the Eastern or the Western front. And the Allies were planning more shocks to be delivered in the West. For while Hitler and his staff were wrestling with the problems of where and when the Allied invasion would take place, whether or not they could hold on to the Ukraine, regarded as vital for feeding the German people, and how the new submarines and flying bombs might be put to use in exacting revenge, the three Allied leaders, Churchill, Roosevelt and Stalin, were putting the finishing touches to their Teheran conference. They had agreed that partisans in Jugoslavia would be supported, that attempts would be made to bring Turkey into the war on their side, that their military staffs would keep in close touch with regard to future operations in Europe and, most important of all, that Operation *Overlord* would be launched during May, 1944, as well as operations against southern France. The Red Army would launch an offensive at about the same time in order to prevent the transfer of German forces from the Eastern to the Western front.

The forthcoming battles in Normandy were to see a further duel between two former antagonists, Rommel and Montgomery, and each had his own particular ideas as to what should be done. Rommel was quite clear that the invasion had to be defeated on the beaches for the simple reason that Allied air supremacy would never permit the free movement of mobile reserves held too far back. He made this plain to his Army Commanders:

> In the short time before the great offensive starts, we must succeed in bringing all defences to such a standard that they will hold up against the strongest attack. Never in history was there a defence of such an extent with such an obstacle as the sea. The enemy must be annihilated before he reaches our main battlefield. ... We must stop him in the water, not only delaying him but destroying all his equipment while it is still afloat.

Montgomery knew Rommel and knew too that his old opponent would try to indulge once more in his favourite tactic, the spoiling attack, and so disrupt the landings. He would not, Montgomery declared, fight

the armoured battle on ground of his own choosing, but avoid it
altogether by using his tanks well forward, try to force the Allies from
the beaches, while securing Caen, Bayeux and Carentan. Had Rommel
had his way and had Hitler backed to the full his astonishing intuition,
announced on 2 May, 1944, that the main Allied assault would be in
Normandy, Montgomery might have had a more difficult time. In
what way did the S.A.S. make things easier for him?

There was inevitably much controversy as to how they should be
used. Even after the S.A.S. had been active for nearly two and a half
years, there were few military men in positions of authority who understood how they should properly be employed. In a remarkable letter
written early in 1944, while this controversy was in train, Sandy
Scratchley introduced the subject by explaining what the S.A.S. had
done so far – more of this later – and then gave his view as to what
should now be done in the battle for France. He pointed out that
S.A.S. soldiers were trained to work in small parties behind the main
battle area and that the distance behind would vary according to the
wishes of the Army or Army Group Commander. This level of command at once made plain the strategic, rather than tactical, level of
their correct employment. They were trained, he went on, in all forms
of sabotage in order to disrupt the enemy's communications, such as
railways and transport, and to destroy aircraft on the ground. This
latter task had become less important because of Allied air supremacy.
At the same time the S.A.S., like any other unit in the Army, would
do what it was told. Up to this time, after all, orders had been obeyed
with results that had given satisfaction all round. In the present controversy, Scratchley added, no task had been turned down except those
which had been turned down by 21st Army Group, after presentation
to Lieutenant-General Browning and their own Brigade Commander.

Of course, the S.A.S. leaders had themselves been urging on senior
commanders the methods of operation which they believed would
obtain the best results. So strongly had Bill Stirling himself been doing
so that in the end, having failed altogether to get his way, he decided
to resign his command. Scratchley was at pains to differentiate between
soldiers of the S.A.S. and what he called the cloak and dagger merchants of the S.O.E.*:

> Since the Prime Minister sent a signal to Jumbo Wilson ordering the
> S.A.S. home, 'Nat' Gubbins of S.O.E. started putting his men into uni-
> form. You can bet your life that he did this because he was windy of the

* The Special Operations Executive recruited men and women to work with resistance movements. Like the S.A.S. it was fairly exclusive – membership by invitation
only, as Professor M. R. D. Foot put it.

potentialities of the S.A.S. Private wars ought to have been overruled and S.A.S. should have been used to bolster up S.O.E. in the execution of the huge assignments which Gubbins has undertaken for his men in OVER-LORD. It is not too late.

Scratchley then made the point that it was quite wrong for the S.A.S. to come under Airborne Forces, except for transport through the air when parachuting. The S.A.S. were not parachutists in the customary use of the word. They merely had to be able to reach their objectives by any means – land, ship, submarine or air – and therefore were required to be able to parachute. What was more, under good dropping conditions it was practically impossible for even a small number of men to parachute into the correct area of enemy-held territory without being observed. This might be all right for airborne forces being dropped en masse to seize and hold important ground for a time until main ground forces linked up with them, but was quite inappropriate if you wished a small group to be dropped somewhere when the success of their mission depended absolutely on their *not* being seen. Thus, Scratchley concluded, the tasks of the Airborne Forces and S.A.S. were widely different. Small wonder, therefore, that

> there has been a hell of a rumpus between S.A.S. and Airborne. ... No one on the Airborne planning staff has had any experience in our type of work. Bill Stirling's tactless criticism which boiled over after his genuine efforts to help had been turned down, ended in his dismissal and we were unemployed. Whether because 21st Army Group got fed up with us, or because they can use us later, I don't know. My hope is that the latter is correct. Genral F. de Guingand is obviously much too busy at the moment, but he has always seen the possibilities of S.A.S. and I hope will again. I am backing the fact that he will want us, even if we are the 'bonus' that the Airborne staff call us. Everyone needs a bonus every now and then. My views are that we should be used as a stiffener to S.O.E. and the Maquis – as soldiers. We did that kind of work well in Italy. I don't think that the question before you is whether S.A.S. troops are worth while or not, but under whose command they should come.

Fortunately much of Scratchley's advice was accepted. It was, of course, the advice that David Stirling himself would have given. In his own outline of the S.A.S.'s history, written in 1974, Stirling makes use of the summary of the S.A.S. activities in France, written by Colonel Brian Franks who succeeded Bill Stirling as Commanding Officer of the 2nd S.A.S. Regiment. In this summary Franks explains that when the 1st and 2nd Regiments returned to the United Kingdom at the beginning of 1944 they were reformed and were to be doubled in strength. In addition to that the force was to be further strengthened by two Free French battalions, a Belgian squadron and the GHQ Reconnaissance Regiment (Phantom) to provide communications. In all they would total some 2,500 troops, with Brigadier Roddy McLeod as their Commander.* It was very satisfactory that, although initial planning envisaged using the S.A.S. in a tactical role to delay movement of enemy reserves to the beaches (it was in fact the furious row over this proposed misuse which led to Bill Stirling's resignation), wiser counsels prevailed. In other words David Stirling's own philosophy won the day and the planners decided to use the force strategically. The idea was to form a number of suitable bases from which to harass enemy communications.

First a small reconnaissance party with radio would be dropped by parachute, sometimes blind, sometimes with the aid of French Resistance groups which would provide flares and torches. If this advance party reported favourably, it could quickly be reinforced and, once bases had been established, the S.A.S. would be able to carry out their tasks of providing the French Resistance movements with a hard core of disciplined troops, so enabling them to increase the scope of their operations, and also to mine roads, blow up railway lines, ambush soft transport targets, report suitable areas to the R.A.F. to bomb, and generally inflict damage, casualties and confusion. There was little time for all the planning and training necessary for these operations, but at least the command arrangements were now proper in that the S.A.S. were to be used under the strategic direction of Montgomery's 21st Army Group, and indeed Eisenhower's own Supreme Headquarters. The broad division of areas was to be that operations on behalf of 21st Army Group would be in a large circle drawn from Abbeville to include Paris and the River Loire, while those under S.H.A.E.F.'s direction would be in the rest of France and Belgium.

Bases were to be formed at the outset in Brittany, Forêt d'Orleans, Vienne, north of Poitiers and Nièvre, west of Dijon, so that if suitable, after reconnaissance, reinforcements could be landed to attack the enemy's lines of communication. Other areas would be selected according to the battle situation and progress of operations. There were certain limitations and uncertainties about how these operations were

* Mike Calvert has paid tribute to Roddy McLeod in this difficult task of welding these forces together and organizing a highly efficient administrative system as well as comprehensive communications, for the huge scale of operations carried out from D Day onwards. Few people, says Calvert, understand McLeod's astonishing achievements.

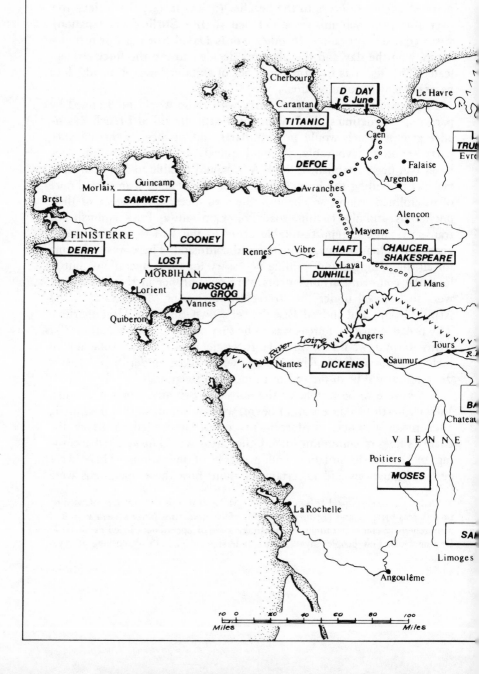

S.A.S. OPERATIONS IN FRANCE & BELGIUM 1944

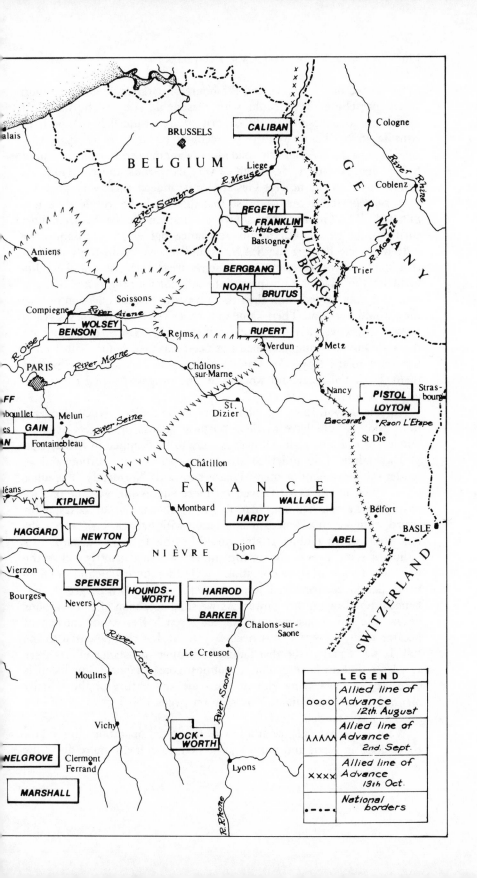

Cologne

BRUSSELS

B E L G I U M

CALIBAN

Liege

R. Meuse

River Sambre

River Rhine

Coblenz

G E R M A N Y

Amiens

REGENT

FRANKLIN

St. Hubert

Bastogne

R. Moselle

Trier

LUXEM-BOURG

Soissons

BERGBANG

NOAH

BRUTUS

Compiegne

River Aisne

WOLSEY

BENSON

R. Oise

Rejms

RUPERT

Verdun

Metz

PARIS

River Marne

Châlons-sur-Marne

FF

bouillet

es

Melun

River Seine

GAIN

Fontainebleau

St.
Dizier

Nancy

Baccarat

Raon L'Etape

St Die

PISTOL

LOYTON

Stras-bourg

Châtillon

F R A N C E

WALLACE

Béllort

BASLE

léans

KIPLING

Montbard

HARDY

ABEL

HAGGARD

NEWTON

N I È V R E

Dijon

Vierzon

Bourges

SPENSER

HOUNDS-WORTH

HARROD

BARKER

S W I T Z E R L A N D

Nevers

Chalons-sur-Saone

Le Creusot

River Loire

Moulins

River Saone

Vichy

JOCK-WORTH

Lyons

NELGROVE

Clermont
Ferrand

MARSHALL

R. Rhone

L E G E N D	
oooo	Allied line of Advance 12th August
ʌʌʌʌʌ	Allied line of Advance 2nd. Sept.
xxxx	Allied line of Advance 13th Oct.
-·-·-·	National borders

to be carried out. Distance and the hours of darkness would condition where parachute drops could with reasonable security be made. It would not be possible to do so east of longitude 4°E or south of latitude 46°N. There was the problem of reprisals on civilians who gave help to the S.A.S. Hitler had already announced that any captured S.A.S. men, whom he described as very dangerous, must instantly be handed over to the nearest Gestapo unit; indeed their very presence must be reported immediately, so that they could be 'ruthlessly exterminated'. The Germans had shown on frequent occasions what short shrift would be allowed to any resistance fighters. The Maquis, or indeed anyone helping the S.A.S., would receive comparably ruthless treatment. There were, moreover, some areas where it would be difficult for the Maquis to disperse into difficult country. Some of them were not even armed. And then there was the further question of how they would perform. Their value and effectiveness were not yet really known. Moreover, on the purely military side, S.A.S. operations on the scale now contemplated had not been executed before. Such ideas were new to the Royal Air Force which would play so large a part in them. Even the successful working of the proposed signal communications could not be guaranteed.

All this notwithstanding, plans were made for two types of operation. Some would have as their purpose attacks on targets at short notice, for example eighteen parties were to be dropped in Brittany on D Day minus 1 in order to attack lines of communication and so hinder the movement of enemy reserves towards Normandy. The other type, which in the event proved far more successful, was the one we have already touched on, that is the establishment of bases, after appropriate reconnaissance, in association with French Resistance fighters, from which raiding groups would be able to work outwards to a radius of some twenty-five to fifty miles. We shall shortly follow the fortunes of some of these operations, including those which most effectively employed armoured jeeps, thus giving the S.A.S. greatly enhanced mobility and fire power. As we shall see, soon after operations began, the enormous potential of the French Resistance movement became clear, so that it was necessary to exploit this potential to the full. It was equally true that failure to support resistance efforts were at a later time to have profound political consequences. But first it is necessary to have some idea of the scale and nature of the initially planned S.A.S. operations. The map on pages 124–5 gives us an idea of what was intended.

We may perhaps glance at a few of the initial operations to see how they varied in scope and purpose, and then examine in more detail the adventures of our old friends, Harrison and Farran. Operation *Hounds-worth* was typical of early successes. The first party was dropped on D Day minus 1 in the area of Dijon and, working in conjunction with a 'Jedburgh' team*, built up to a total of some eighty-four officers and men, who continued to do their work of destruction for three months. They succeeded in blowing up the railway line between Dijon, Lyons and Paris no fewer than twenty-two times, as well as the line from Le Creusot to Nevers. What is more, they were able to report many suitable bombing targets to the R.A.F., they killed or wounded more than 200 German soldiers and took well over a hundred prisoners.

A similar sort of operation, which, like *Houndsworth*, was carried out by 1st S.A.S., was *Bulbasket*, which also included men of the Phantom Regiment. Landing just prior to the main invasion, but in the area south of Châteauroux, they were able to cut the railway lines between Limoges, Vierzon, Poitiers and Tour a dozen times, besides inflicting some twenty casualties on the enemy. But treachery was the cause of heavy losses to themselves and at the beginning of August they were flown out again.

Operation *Gain*, which had some ten officers and fifty men using jeeps in the area Rambouillet, Orleans and Chartres, lasted from mid-June to mid-August. They moved about with great dash and boldness, driving jeeps down to the very railway lines they intended to destroy, mixing with German convoys, knocking out enemy trucks, petrol lorries, even trains, with their Vickers machine guns, and when, as often happened, surrounded by large numbers of enemy troops, somehow slipped through the rough country with the help of French Resistance workers.

They did not all get away with it. The commander, Major Ian Fenwick, heard on 8 August that three of his parties had been ringed by 600 Germans, and, as is the way with rumour, that most of them had been caught and killed with all jeeps lost. It was not so, but none the less Fenwick set out to find the facts for himself. Harrison has described what happened:

> Immediately Ian Fenwick set out in his jeep for the scene of the attack to verify the details himself. With him were Sergeant Dunkley, Corporal Duffy, Lance-Corporal Menginou of the 4th French S.A.S. and a sergeant of the F.F.I. He had not been long on the road when a German spotter aircraft located his jeep. The pilot passed the information back to the Germans at Chambon where they prepared an ambush for him. Unaware

* Jedburgh teams consisted of guides provided by Headquarters Special Forces. The teams organized local forces, armed them, arranged DZs.

of what lay ahead of him, Ian drove the avenging jeep on towards its appointment with the enemy. Then Fate played her last card. Into the road stepped the slight figure of a woman. As the jeep lurched to a halt she gasped out her breathless warning. The Germans were waiting in ambush further up the road. They must turn back.

But Ian's blood was up. 'Thank you, madame, but I intend to attack them.' He met the ambush at Chambon with all his guns firing. He was almost through the first body of Germans – there were others further back in the village – when a 20 mm cannon shell hit him in the head, killing him instantly. Out of control, the jeep careered wildly towards the woods and crashed. Menginou and the F.F.I. sergeant were killed.

It is pleasing to record that Corporal Duffy, after a series of adventures which included dressing up in German uniform when he was in a hospital ward with German and Russian wounded in a convent near Fontainebleau, walking past a sentry and courteously returning his salute, walking through woods in bare feet, bluffing German soldiers that he was a French farmer while mounted on a cart horse, found himself in an American-occupied town, Milly, where he was awarded the Purple Heart.

Another member of Fenwick's group, Wilson, had even more exciting experiences. When the car he was travelling in was fired at by German patrol vehicles, he regained consciousness after being hit over the eye and in the jaw to find himself alone in the car, surrounded by German soldiers. The other men of his group had escaped into the woods, except one American who was shot by the Germans as he began to crawl away. Then four of the enemy approached the car. Wilson waited until they were near and shot three of them. Next he was subjected to heavy machine-gun fire, hit again, lost consciousness, and came to tied to a tree. He received some unpleasant treatment from Gestapo men, was driven to Orleans for further interrogation, warned that the S.A.S., like the Maquis, were classed as terrorists and dealt with as such. A fellow prisoner was led out and shot. Eventually Wilson again awoke, this time in Orleans hospital. He was still there when the American troops arrived. With such men as these, 1st S.A.S. achieved great results in cutting communications, generally disrupting enemy movement and assisting the Resistance to resist. Paddy Mayne, who was also in the area, could be proud indeed of his men's achievements.

The map on p. 124, together with the summary in Appendix 4 of the operations in France, illustrate both the extent and the boldness of what was achieved. For our purposes here, however, examples of two

operations will be sufficient to show what it was like. The first is one
undertaken by Harrison, who had already taken part in S.A.S. raids in
both Sicily and Italy. On 13 August, 1944, he received his orders:

> There's been a change in your briefing. I want you to listen carefully. Your
> DZ has been changed. You will be dropping at a place called Les Placeaux.
> This is it here. Just on the edge of the Forêt de Merryvaux. Bob Melot will
> be waiting on the ground. When you get down you're to lie low until you
> hear from us. You can send for some more men if you need them. What-
> ever you do though, do not draw attention to yourself even if it means
> passing up big targets. There's a big airborne landing being planned. I
> can't tell you where. The rest of the squadron will be going down with
> them in gliders. As soon as you hear from us, you are to get through to
> wherever the landing has taken place. Never mind anything else. Your job
> is to get through as quickly as possible, gathering as much information on
> the way as you can about German defences and troop dispositions. You
> are to report with that information to Boy Browning.

With no more than that to go on, Harrison and his men dropped into
France. Harrison remembered that on the way down, while trying to
release his leg-bag, the rope jammed in the sheath and, when it finally
whipped free, wrapped itself round his hand and broke a finger. Having landed, there were soon voices, French voices fortunately, and
before long he and his party were with Bob Melot, some of the local
Maquis and some interested farmers. The parachutes and containers
were collected, Harrison's finger bandaged with a splint, and away
they went in a jeep. 'Here I was, bumping along narrow, dusty tracks
in the middle of enemy-occupied France in a British jeep, wondering
when I would get any breakfast and what I would get - if I got any.'
    They went to the camp of the Maquisard Chevrier, which was
complete with sleeping quarters made of branches and twigs covered
with groundsheets or tarpaulin, a dining area with tables and chairs,
again made from branches, lean-tos with arms and ammunition, all
concealed in the forest. There were guarded approaches to the camp,
sentries on duty; there were drilling and training areas; there was even
a store of fresh meat - live rabbits slung into a huge sheet. It took
Harrison some time to realize that this was not just a game, but a
deadly earnest group of men dedicated to a kill-or-be-killed contest
with the Germans. Having discussed things with Melot and decided
to send for more men and jeeps, they transmitted the proper signals
and by midnight were at the dropping zone to receive them, again
with the help of Chevrier and his men:

Five to two! We were quiet now. No more whisperings. All ears were strained for the drone of the approaching plane. The minutes ticked away slowly. Two o'clock! Still not a sound. One minute past, two minutes past, three. Faintly in the distance came the sound we had been waiting for. The steady rhythmic throbbing of a plane's engine. This was it. Or was it? It might be a German plane and, if we lit the fire, we were almost certain to be machine-gunned. All it had to do was run down the line of fires. It had happened before. My heart beat a little faster.

Such were the hazards of reinforcement. All was well on this occasion. The jeep came down in the thick of the wood, and took several hours to extract; most of the men landed safely, although a few, including Bill Fraser, were caught in the branches, and in the dark uncertain of how far from the ground they were. Fraser himself hung for two hours in darkness only to discover as dawn arrived that he was but three inches from the ground. After this success, Harrison sent for the rest of his troop, who parachuted in safely enough, despite some concern when a party of the F.F.I. travelling from a neighbouring village to help protect the landings was thought by the local Maquis to be White Russians, and who themselves thought they were running into a German ambush. Now that Harrison had his complete group, and was in close touch both with the local Maquis and the F.F.I. under its commander, Roger, he was ready for operations. The original idea of assisting the planned airborne landing in the Paris-Orleans gap had been cancelled, so he was free to start offensive activities in his general area. One of his most daring and dangerous attacks was at Les Ormes where, with two jeeps and their crews, he attacked a large number of German S.S. troops. As they drove into the village a German soldier carrying a pistol looked up at them in surprise. As Harrison put it – he died:

I took in the scene in an instant. The church in the middle of the square, a large truck, two German staff cars, the crowd of S.S. men in front of the church. The staff cars and the truck burst into flames as, standing up in my seat, I raked the square with fire from my twin machine-guns. The crowd of S.S. men stampeded for cover. Many of them died in those first few seconds in front of the church, lit by the flickering flames of the burning vehicles. Even as I fired I shouted to Hall to reverse ... the Germans who had escaped the first fury of our assault were now returning our fire. I turned to see why Hall had not got the jeep moving back. He lay slumped over the wheel. The tell-tale gouts of blood told their own story. Curly Hall was dead.

A series of extraordinary events followed. Harrison found that the

jeep's engine had been hit and rendered useless. All his machine-guns
had jammed, but the second jeep took over the job of keeping the
Germans' heads down, while with his carbine Harrison was able to
shoot a few more of them. He managed to reach a nearby orchard,
while Fauchois from the second jeep tried to drag Hall to the vehicle.
Lots of firing, lots of Germans, lots of confusion, but somehow the
second jeep was turned round, a last long burst of fire was directed at
the village square, while Harrison climbed aboard, and then off they
went at break-neck speed back to camp. It had been an astonishingly
successful affair. Harrison and his men had interrupted an S.S. execution party who were intending to shoot twenty French hostages.
Two had been shot before the S.A.S. intervened. In the resulting mêlée,
the other condemned men had got away. German losses were sixty
men killed and wounded and all three vehicles destroyed. Not a bad
score. It is all admirably recorded in Harrison's book *These Men Are
Dangerous*.

Equally dangerous, of course, was Roy Farran, and on 19 August
his squadron of some sixty men and twenty jeeps was loaded into
Dakota aircraft and flown to a strip on Rennes airfield. Twenty-four
hours later they were among the forest tracks north of Orleans ready
to deal with any German columns they could get to grips with. Among
his many exploits was his attack on Chatillon, where some 150 Germans were occupying the Château area. His plan was to seize the
road-junction Montbard-Dijon, and from there attack the north of the
Château. His right-hand man, Jim Mackie, occupied the cross-roads
with his party, while Farran's men with nine jeeps took up positions
at all junctions leading into the square. Then a bombardment of the
Château with mortars began, which caused a relieving column of German vehicles to drive straight into Mackie's ambush. Later Farran
himself was able to ambush eight German trucks loaded with troops.
The entire affair was a series of little pell-mell engagements with either
side constantly being surprised by the other. Farran himself recalls
how tired and uncertain he became:

After we had run along the tow-path to the lock, I led the party across
country to the east. We had just reached the cover of a thin hedge on a
skyline when two machine-guns picked us out. I had not realized that we
could be seen. We wriggled on our bellies along the furrows in a ploughed
field with the bullets kicking up great clots of earth all around. I have
never felt so tired. I knew that if we remained on that crest we would be
killed and yet I could not force myself to move any faster. Sergeant Robinson behind me was hit in the leg and still he moved faster than I. When

we reached a little dead ground I tried to help him, but I was too exhausted. Never have I been so frightened and so incapable of helping myself.

Jim Mackie appeared and we loaded Robinson into his jeep. At the friendly farmhouse, from which we had telephoned the mayor the day before, I dressed his wounds on the kitchen table, while all the women clucked and fussed around with kettles of hot water. After we had despatched him to the Maquis hospital at Aigny-le-Duc, we motored back slowly through the forest glades to our bases. The Battle of Chatillon was over. They say we killed a hundred Germans, wounded many more and destroyed nine trucks, four cars and a motor-cycle.

It is important to draw a distinction between what 1st S.A.S. were doing – cutting railways and generally disrupting communications south-west and south of Paris – and the role of the 4th French Parachute Battalion, which was to cut off Brittany. We have already seen how 1st S.A.S. got on in Operations *Bulbasket*, *Houndsworth* and *Gain*. Now we must turn to what the French S.A.S. did.

On the night of 5/6 June two parties of the 4th French Parachute Battalion dropped into Brittany, one at Morbihan, one at Côtes du Nord. They were among the first Allied troops to re-enter France, and were to establish bases in wooded, hilly areas which could later be reinforced as required. They would get in touch with local Resistance organizations in order to see how best to proceed. A few days later both parties reported being in contact with groups of several thousand F.F.I. At the same time they discovered that the Maquis were unarmed. More small parties were dropped two nights later all over Brittany. Their job was to harass the enemy's rail and signal communications. So successful were these S.A.S. parties from D Day onwards that there were almost no railway communications in Brittany. German reinforcements had to go to the battlefront by bicycle, with farm carts or on foot. Again on the night 9/10 June more parties of French S.A.S. troops, together with Allied officers of General Koenig's staff, were parachuted into Brittany. So began the adventures of a large group of some 300 French paratroops under the command of Commandant Bourgoin, whose men were dressed in full uniform and were very well armed.

Meanwhile the F.F.I. and F.T.P., numbering some 15,000, were being supplied by the night-time dropping of arms and ammunition. For this the S.A.S. parties and Allied officers coordinated the supply by sending messages as to the whereabouts and requirements of the F.F.I. and then directing Allied bombers containing supplies to appropriate dropping zones, where parties of men, whose numbers might vary from a handful to several hundred, waited to collect up the arms being dropped and then removed them. One night, when enemy patrols had dispersed and pursued the ground party, only four people were left on the DZ. A woman directed this small party and, by means of matches, succeeded in attracting the aircraft's attention and getting the supplies. On another night some people who had nothing whatever to do with the operation, but happened to be sitting in a forest round a charcoal fire, suddenly found containers dropping all about them. They collected the containers, hid the parachutes and delivered all the weapons to the local Maquis.

Both the French paratroops and the F.F.I. in Brittany had been instructed simply to build up their strength and sabotage enemy lines of communication, avoiding battle if possible. But it was not always possible, and they found themselves obliged to take on superior enemy forces which were hunting them down. One pitched battle lasted over thirty-six hours, the Germans using mortars and artillery and having to admit later to losses of more than 600. The Maquis and F.F.I. managed to escape at night with casualties of less than one hundred. They continued with their operations in small groups and completed many of their assigned tasks successfully. On the other side of the coin was the disagreeable fact that the enemy took brutal reprisals against these forces and against local civilians or farmers suspected of helping them. They tortured and executed captured paratroops, while the treatment inflicted on F.F.I. prisoners and local farmers was indescribable. The 'milice' and Russian troops with the *Wehrmacht* were the worst of all. One particularly gallant French officer, Lieutenant Marienne, together with his small base party, was executed in this way, as were many other officers and men who had distinguished themselves by their leadership and courage.

While the French S.A.S. troops helped local leaders to organize, train and arm all Resistance groups in central and western Brittany, specially selected Allied teams joined them in order to assist still further. One small party under a British officer did particularly well, and by late July over 15,000 F.F.I. men in central and western Brittany had been armed, with a further 5,000 also equipped in eastern Brittany. Cooperating with these large numbers were some four hundred French paratroops. Movement of enemy troops and supplies dwindled to a trickle, many locomotives and motor vehicles were destroyed, signal and telephone wires were constantly being cut. Enemy garrisons, which totalled some 70,000 troops, were compelled to remain in ports and towns, venturing out into the country only by daylight. It was all highly successful. Then another phase began. Shortly before the United States' armoured columns reached Brittany, having broken out from the Normandy bridgehead, General Koenig ordered the F.F.I. into overt action. This was at the beginning of August, 1944. They were instructed to harass the Germans to the utmost, to ambush and obstruct roads in Brittany, to prevent the blowing-up of bridges – in particular the viaduct at Morlaix. Those in Morbihan were told to occupy and hold the high ground above Vannes which controls the approaches to the ports of Lorient and Quiberon. They were also required to capture the Meucon/Vannes airfield. Some jeeps had already been delivered to these S.A.S.-led F.F.I. groups, but more were needed, and in one operation in daylight on 5 August a further supply of jeeps was landed within 600 yards of the enemy, the temporary landing field being successfully held against German attempts to take it until all the jeeps were off-loaded. Elsewhere, in the area of Finisterre, another ninety French soldiers from the 3rd Parachute Battalion were dropped in order to strengthen the Maquis there and to assist in the containment and discomfiture of the enemy garrison.

All these activities helped to make possible the speedy advance of the main Allied armies. It was in effect a classic use of S.A.S. troops – the distraction of enemy forces in such a manner that the strategic objectives sought by principal elements of Allied forces were gained so much more easily. The scope of operations was bound to change with circumstances. Whereas from D Day to July the idea was to harass and interdict enemy movement, as well as arm and train French Resistance fighters, once the Allies advanced from the bridgehead, these operations tailed off. Further and comparable activities over a much wider area than Brittany and Normandy were, of course, mounted, but also targets of opportunity were attacked, like Rommel's Headquarters, while once the enemy withdrawal from the Falaise pocket began, more harassing raids were made. Meanwhile, road-watching and information-gathering continued. During the period from July to October, 1944, the S.A.S. were active all over France – in Normandy, Brittany, the Rhone valley, eastern France, northern France and in the Ardennes [for detailed list of operations, see Appendix 4]. General Boy Browning commented in a report on all this at the end of August that the 'proved value which can be achieved by a comparatively small number of specially trained troops operating in small parties behind enemy lines is out of all proportion to the number of men employed, especially where assistance is given on such a complete and wholehearted scale by local inhabitants'. At the same time it had become clear that the S.A.S. needed to organize most carefully and thoroughly the bases in selected areas of operation, so that they could step up their activities to overt support for advancing Allied troops at the right moment. The jeep patrols had proved particularly valuable, and they were able to provide uniquely effective support during the advance of Patton's 3rd U.S. Army by watching and harassing the Germans' southern flank.

All in all their efforts thrived on opportunism and versatility. The S.A.S. obtained vital information, they notified targets for Allied bombing, they cut and disrupted enemy lines of communication, they killed, wounded or captured many enemy soldiers, they armed the local Resistance groups, and they obliged enemy forces to dissipate their own efforts in countermeasures. The scale of the thing was impressive. By the end of July nearly 800 S.A.S. troops were fighting the Germans from eighteen bases; during August another 1,100 troops were added and a further twenty-three bases established; nearly 500 air sorties had been flown by the end of August, no fewer than 8,000 panniers or containers had been dropped, together with sixty jeeps and some 2-pounder guns. The sheer complexity of some plans was remarkable. In one operation mounted on the night of 4/5 August forty-two aircraft took off from five different airfields in England, briefed to deliver troops and stores to twenty-two different DZs. Eleven gliders were also involved carrying eleven jeeps and forty-five trailers; these, together with the parachuting of 150 soldiers, four further jeeps and a hundred tons of stores, were all delivered. It was a triumph of good planning, excellent communications, admirable inter-service cooperation and a further demonstration that daring wins. Of course, daring also lost lives and an account of Operation LOYTON by 2nd S.A.S. – a number of whom did not live to tell the tale – is given in the next chapter.

12

LOYTON, TOMBOLA AND *ENDKAMPF*

Success generally depends upon knowing how long it takes to succeed.

Montesquieu

As the Allies broke out of the Normandy beachhead in August, 1944, and began to sweep through France, S.A.S. operations were mounted in northern France in order to disrupt enemy communications and gain information as to their dispositions, including the identification of air targets. One of these was Operation *Loyton*. At the beginning of August Lieutenant-Colonel Brian Franks, commanding 2nd S.A.S., was ordered to operate in the area between the Baccarat-St Die road and the French-German border. His instructions were to cause the greatest inconvenience to the enemy at all times by disrupting their lines of communication and supply. He was also required to report intelligence concerning enemy positions and movement, particularly headquarters and air targets. Franks thereupon made his plans after consulting various intelligence agencies such as S.O.E. and M.I.6. He was especially anxious for information about local contacts on the ground. The next step was for a reconnaissance party, under Captain Druce and Lieutenant Dill, to meet the Maquis there and prepare a dropping zone for Franks himself with his main body of S.A.S.

From the moment Druce and his team arrived in a meadow in northern France on the night of 12/13 August, he was at odds with the local Maquis commander, Colonel Maximum, whose guerrillas were far too noisy and indiscreet for Druce's liking. But as his own special radio had been smashed in the drop, he was obliged to cooperate temporarily with Maximum in order to use his radio to contact London. Ten days later the Maquis were betrayed by one of their own men and the radio was captured. Thereafter Druce kept his team to itself and succeeded by other communications in arranging for the

main party of 2nd S.A.S. to drop on the night of 31 August near St
Remy. It was not altogether an unexciting night as the S.A.S. report
shows:

> At 0300 on the morning of 1 September, Colonel Franks and his party
> jumped from 1,100 feet above the woodland prepared by Druce and lit by
> domestic flashlights. As they floated down, a burst of stengun fire sounded
> from the meadow.
> M. Fouche - suspected of being in the Germans' pay - had grabbed the
> weapon and was attempting to make good his escape. The excitable and
> virtually untrained Maquisards opened up in all directions. The clandestine
> arrival of the Commanding Officer and a large party of 2nd S.A.S. took on
> a nightmarish aspect as small-arms fire, crashing undergrowth and shouts
> in French, English and Russian - there were Russian deserters from the
> *Wehrmacht* among the Maquis - filled the air. But there was no word of
> German for there was not a German in sight, although this could not be
> ascertained amid such confusion. Captain Druce grabbed the erring M.
> Fouche and shot him through the heart.

Once Brian Franks and his main body had arrived, *Loyton* began in
earnest. His men began to blow up vehicles, kill enemy soldiers, ambush convoys and destroy railway lines. The enemy was surprised,
confused and very angry. Some of Franks' men were to suffer this
anger in Gestapo cells, torture in concentration camps and execution.
Franks had originally intended to use the local Maquis to help his
activities, but he soon came to the view that liaison with them would
jeopardize the whole thing and he thereafter operated independently
from the S.A.S.'s own, constantly shifting bases, secret and secure.
Typical of their actions was that of a raiding party under Lieutenant
Marx, which was reconnoitring country roads in the region of Celles-
Allamont:

> With a potent mix of fog-signal detonators and plastic explosive mines they
> blew up two *Wehrmacht* trucks on 8 September, killing the German soldiers
> in them. They then entered the tiny hamlet of La Chapellotte and found
> themselves face to face with a *Wehrmacht* patrol, some of whom, Marx
> reported later, were wearing Afrika Korps headgear. After a brisk gunfight
> at point blank range, the reports of which read like the script of a Wild
> West film, Marx's team obeyed the S.A.S. dictum of 'shoot and scoot' and,
> having shot it out long enough to send the Afrika Korps men diving for
> ditches and thick-walled cottage kitchens, they scooted.
> Four hours later, Marx and his patrol ambushed and shot up a *Wehr-
> macht* 5-ton truck. Returning from this to the 2nd S.A.S. base, hidden in

the nearby ridge of hills from Germans and Maquis alike, they were themselves engaged by a strong force of *Wehrmacht* who had taken exception to their day's activities. Marx managed to extricate all but three of his patrol [who] were last seen by their comrades running like hell up a track towards La Chapellotte, pursued by SS troops and Alsatian dogs.

In fact the three men got away. Meanwhile Franks was continuing with his three tasks – to harass the Germans, report intelligence and keep his bases secure. In order to achieve this security he had constantly to be moving. If an action resulted in men becoming scattered, trusted members of local Resistance groups would collect them from agreed rendezvous, and in this way a number of Maquisards – not of Maximum's group – rendered the S.A.S. great service. The S.A.S. operations during the first ten days of September were so successful that they obliged the Germans to send more and more troops to north-eastern France. Franks's idea was to make the Germans think that there were far more of his men there than the mere eighty-seven he actually had. The measure of his achievement is illustrated by the post-war report that two complete German divisions of exceptionally able fighting troops had been detached from the main battle to try and counter *Loyton*. However, simply because of the German strength detached to deal with him, Franks's job became more and more difficult. By 11 September his party was in danger of being pinned down by enemy forces. In his attempts to fight his way out of the trap, Franks had detached one group under Lieutenant Black to frustrate the German action to encircle his men. He succeeded in getting his main party away, but Black and his men were captured:

Cut off, in the heat of battle, from Franks' party, Lieutenant Black led the others towards Lac de la Maix, still the current emergency rendezvous. S.A.S. Intelligence learned that Black's party were sheltered for a few hours at the house of a Madame Yorg at Les Colins. There they brewed tea and moved on after sunset. By chance, Lieutenant Black approached the lake from the same side as had Terry-Hall, Iveson and Crozier, and he too decided to lie up in the sawmill house at La Turbine, unaware that Terry-Hall's guide, Gaston Matthieu, was a German collaborator and at that moment was informing on them to the Gestapo office at Raon L'Etape. . . .

Lieutenant Black, Sergeant Terry-Hall, Corporals Iveson and Winder, and Privates Crozier, Dowling, Lloyd and Salter soon became aware of the encircling Gestapo and *Wehrmacht* unit and, as birds sang in the woods around the sawmill and twigs snapped under the boots of cautiously approaching German soldiers, the eight S.A.S. men tried to slip away from

La Turbine. But it was too late. In a four hour gun-battle in and around the sawmill, Black was wounded in the leg, the S.A.S.'s ammunition ran out, and in the silence which descended, German soldiers approached and, after a fierce struggle, took them prisoner, one by one.

Before long they were in a Gestapo prison at Strasbourg, where they were interrogated and tortured. They gave away no information. Their fate, of course, was never in any doubt. Parachute troops captured outside the main fighting zone were always shot by the Germans, but only after the Gestapo had had their turn at trying to extract information. Lieutenant Black and his comrades, all of whose courage and dedication are beyond praise, were taken back to the St Die area and murdered in a wood nearby. Their graves, like those of other S.A.S. heroes, are in the War Cemetery at Duenbach.

Meanwhile Franks had received on the night of 19/20 September an air-drop of reinforcements and of six jeeps, which were equipped with both twin-barrelled Vickers K guns, always a favourite of the S.A.S., and with .5 Browning machine guns. Franks thereupon decided to use these jeeps in order to bring about gun battles with the Germans deep behind their lines, while other members of his group would continue with intelligence-gathering patrols on foot. The adventures of the jeep crews were numerous, but one story about each will give the flavour of their activities. On 23 September Jeeps 5 and 6 under Captain Druce and Lieutenant Manners went off to ambush the Senonnes-Moyenmoutier road. Despite betrayal by a French double-agent, they evaded a German trap and shot up what they thought was a Gestapo car. In fact it was the local mayor's, Monsieur Pi, who was unhurt and gracious enough to send the S.A.S. a message thanking them for the 'salvo in his honour', the message being even more graciously accompanied by two bottles of vintage champagne.

On the same day the other four jeeps, one commanded by Franks himself, were in the Celles valley. Numbers 3 and 4 joined a German convoy and destroyed the leading truck and three staff cars. Numbers 1 and 2, under Franks and Dill, drove across country towards Allarmont, coming under fire north-east of Celles. Franks's jeep overturned while manoeuvring to engage the enemy and Dill drove straight into an ambush. There followed a fierce engagement against no fewer than eighty S.S. and *Wehrmacht* troops, during which the S.A.S. men succeeded in fighting their way out on foot.

By now, the end of September, the pace of the main battle was slowing down. The Germans had succeeded in stabilizing the front line, aided by the bustling and brilliantly improvising General Model, and although the S.A.S. continued to harass the enemy, Franks was finding that he was too close behind the lines for comfort, besides having used up all his explosives and most of his ammunition. On 9 October he therefore ordered his teams to bring *Loyton* to an end, make their way to the west and contact the United States Army. An exfiltration rendezvous was laid down and was kept open until 12 October, by which time most of the known survivors had gone through. Sixty-three of Franks's 2nd S.A.S. men passed safely through the German lines to meet the U.S. 7th Army. But thirty-one did not return. Their contribution to the Allied success in bringing at last the battle to the very gates of Germany and their steadfastness in captivity can never be forgotten.

As it became clear that the battle for France had been lost by the Germans, a loss which cost them some twenty infantry divisions and over 2,000 tanks and assault guns, the Commander-in-Chief of the *Wehrmacht* made it plain to his generals that under all circumstances they would continue to fight the battle until 'as Frederick the Great said, one of our damned enemies gets too tired to fight any more'. There was no question of despair. The time had not yet come for a political decision. Tension between the Allies would grow, for all coalitions sooner or later lost cohesion. Meanwhile, it was his task not to lose his nerve. 'We'll fight until we get a peace which secures the life of the German nation for the next fifty or hundred years and which, above all, does not besmirch our honour a second time'. *Also sprach Hitler*. So by September, 1944, with the war already being fought on German soil – the Red Army was at the gates of East Prussia, the Anglo-American armies in the Rhineland – the Führer was directing a stubborn defence of the Fatherland which for a time kept his enemies at bay. But he was also preparing for the one thing which nearly all Allied opinion agreed was impossible – a counter-offensive by the *Wehrmacht*. The great question for Hitler was – where? There was a choice, although it was a limited one. East or West? It did not take Hitler long to reject the idea of squandering his last reserves in the East. The area of operations was too vast, the Red Army too resilient and inexhaustible, the objectives too vague and indeterminate to offer a prize of quick or dramatic victory. How different was the West! There he saw two Allied armies, British and American, not wholly in harmony, the opportunity of driving a great wedge between them, the capture of a great and militarily crucial port, Antwerp, and moreover the propitious circumstances of the Ardennes, scene of the great blitzkreig triumphs of 1940, to make use of. If it did not succeed, Hitler told Speer:

I no longer see any possibility for ending the war well. But we will come through. A single breakthrough on the Western front! You'll see! It will lead to collapse and panic among the Americans. Then they'll have lost their supply port. And a tremendous pocket will encircle the entire English army, with hundreds of thousands of prisoners. As we used to do in Russia.

The West, therefore, it would be, and as Hitler had succeeded in gathering some twenty-eight divisions together, he was bound to achieve some degree of surprise. The force included both 5th Panzer Army under von Manteuffel, the aristocratic cavalryman of drive, originality and courage, and 6th S.S. Panzer Army, commanded by the rough, hard-core S.S. but tactically dashing Sepp Dietrich. The attack was planned for mid-December, and four days before the battle Hitler once more harangued his long-suffering generals: 'If we can now deliver a few more heavy blows, then at any moment this artificially bolstered common front may collapse with a mighty clap of thunder. ... Wars are finally decided by one side or the other recognizing that they cannot be won. We must allow no moment to pass without showing the enemy that whatever he does, he can never reckon on capitulation. Never! Never!'

But the Allied front did not collapse. Despite some early German successes and advances, the Ardennes offensive was blocked and defeated – by the heroism of Bastogne's American defenders, by the sure grip which Montgomery established on the northern shoulders of the German penetration, by Patton's intervention in the south, and by the supreme omnipresence of Allied air power. The French and Belgian S.A.S. too played their part. It was, instead, the German front which was about to collapse, and just as the S.A.S. had greatly assisted in winning the battle for France, so they did the same in helping to win the battle for Germany.

With the Ardennes offensive an expensive failure – it cost the Germans some 120,000 men, 600 tanks, 1,600 aircraft and 6,000 vehicles – and his final reserves expended, Hitler now faced in the early months of 1945 a situation comparable with that of Napoleon in 1814. 'All the world,' wrote A. G. Macdonnell, 'except one man knew that the game was up'. France had no money, no army, no navy, no commerce, no industry, no munitions, no horses, and everywhere her frontiers were being invaded by her enemies' numerous armies. 'But the greatest brain of the age, alone among men, either could not or would not grasp the situation, and the struggle went on'. Whether in February, 1945, Hitler could be thought of as the greatest brain of the age, despite his self-portrait as the greatest strategic genius of all time, may be questioned, but his military position was equally unenviable and his determination to continue the struggle equally adamant.

While the *Wehrmacht*'s Supreme Commander continued to bellow crassly unrealistic instructions to his Chief of General Staff, the Allied leaders at Yalta, Roosevelt, Stalin and Churchill, were quietly arranging the partition of the Third Reich. It was high time to do so, for the Russians were threatening Vienna and Berlin, while soon afterwards American and British armies crossed the Rhine. By April Model's Army Group in the Ruhr had been surrounded, Alexander's armies in Italy had broken into the Po Valley, the Elbe was reached by American troops, and the Russians, who had taken Königsberg, breached the Oder defences, the last bastion before Berlin. Such a bad position could only worsen, as worsen it did. By 21 April Marshal Zhukov had reached Berlin's eastern suburbs, Koniev was at Dresden and Eisenhower was arranging for his armies to link up with Soviet forces on the general line of the Elbe and Mulde. Hitler's occupation, like Othello's, had gone, and all that remained for him to do was to do what Othello had done – put out the light, and then put out the light.

During these final months of March and April, 1945, the S.A.S. Brigade under Mike Calvert was busy helping the main British and Canadian armies cross the Rhine, advance to the Elbe and into Schleswig-Holstein. They were active in Italy, Holland, Belgium and Norway. Indeed in the last battles of the war – *Endkampf* – nearly all S.A.S. units were there at the kill either in north-west Germany or elsewhere in Europe. (See pp 263–4 of Appendix 4.) We may perhaps permit ourselves a glance at one more exploit, by Roy Farran, before we turn to what Sir Henry Maine, having pointed out that war appeared to be as old as mankind, described as a modern invention – peace.

Operation *Tombola* was mounted at the beginning of March, 1945, in the Tuscan Apennines north of the Allied lines. The whole idea of it was to harass and distract the enemy prior to the next main offensive by 15th Army Group. On his arrival in the area of Asta on 4 March Major Roy Farran's job was to organize the formation of a battalion of troops made up of 140 Italian partisans, 100 Russians and forty S.A.S. He described the first parade of the Italians as a picture of Wat Tyler's rebellion. As if this were not enough, Farran sent for a piper who was required to make his very first parachute descent in order to report for duty. 'Whether he jumped in kilts,' says the S.A.S. report, 'has not been recorded.' But he did accompany a most successful attack on a German Corps headquarters later in March with suitable noises from the bagpipes. This was one of Farran's major actions during

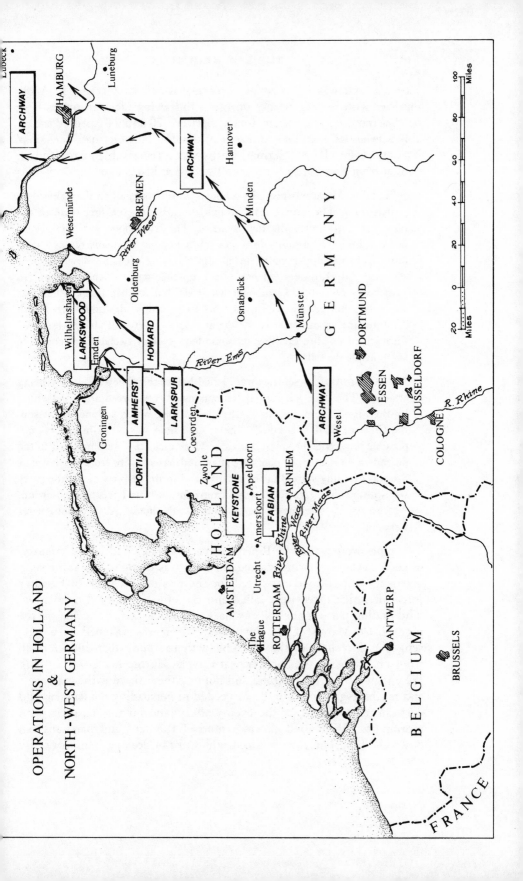

OPERATIONS IN HOLLAND
&
NORTH - WEST GERMANY

FRANCE

BELGIUM

BRUSSELS

ANTWERP

HOLLAND

The Hague

ROTTERDAM

Utrecht

Amsterdam

Amersfoort

Apeldoorn

Zwolle

Groningen

Emden

Coevorden

Oldenburg

Wilhelmshaven

Wesermünde

BREMEN

Lüneburg

HAMBURG

Hannover

Minden

Osnabrück

Münster

Wesel

DORTMUND

ESSEN

DUSSELDORF

COLOGNE

GERMANY

River Ems

River Weser

River Rhine

River Waal

River Maas

R. Rhine

ARNHEM

ARCHWAY

ARCHWAY

ARCHWAY

LARKSWOOD

HOWARD

AMHERST

LARKSPUR

PORTIA

KEYSTONE

FABIAN

Lübeck

Miles

100 80 60 40 20 0 20

Miles

Tombola, and was followed by a successful defensive action in April, together with further attacks on the withdrawing German forces later on that month. 'The actions fought between 20 and 24 April considerably accelerated the panic and rout of three or four German divisions.' The attack on HQ 51 German Corps was a remarkable affair, and an extract from Roy Farran's report tells us what it was like:

Villa Rossi. Alarm was given by a hooter on the roof and all the lights were switched on. The British ran through the machine-gun fire, through the main gate, and killed the four sentries. The front door was open. After fierce fighting the ground floor was taken but the Germans resisted furiously from the upper floors, firing and throwing grenades down a spiral staircase. Captain Lees led one attack up the stairs which was repulsed with heavy casualties. Lieutenant Riccomini led another attack which was similarly repulsed. Six Germans who attempted to descend were killed. ... After the 20 minutes set for the attack, the party withdrew westwards through intense fire carrying its wounded. At least twelve Germans were killed inside the villa.

Villa Calvi. All four sentries were killed before they knew they were being attacked. The door was locked but was eventually forced after weakening by Bren fire. There was furious fighting during which Colonel Lemelson, the Chief of Staff, was killed. The ground floor was taken but it was not possible to ascend the spiral staircase. More casualties were inflicted to the defenders on the upper floors by Bren and bazooka fire from the lawn. A fire was carefully started in the registry and in the map room. As the party was withdrawing Villa Calvi was burning furiously and eventually blew up. At least twenty Germans were killed inside the house. All telephone wires were cut.

The pipes were played by Piper Kirkpatrick, Highland Light Infantry, as soon as the first firing started. In all it was thought that some sixty German casualties were inflicted for the loss of seventeen of Farran's force, of which three were killed and the others wounded or missing. The raiding party made its way back across the River Secchia on the night 27/28 March. A few days later Farran was wakened by a messenger at 3 o'clock in the morning with the news that 200 German troops had crossed the Secchia near Cavola. Having made contact with the enemy at Cerre Marabino and holding them there with small arms and machine-gun fire, Farran succeeded in persuading his Russian and partisan troops to attack the enemy after some suitable barrages with mortar fire. 'With loud cheers a mob of Russians and partisans ran down the hill. The enemy took fright and ran, leaving behind twenty dead and twenty-five prisoners. It was all very exciting and we did not stop until we got to the River Secchia, across which the enemy troops had all fled by nightfall.' During the next three weeks Farran and his group fought more successful defensive actions and carried out a number of raids and ambushes, but his report shows that 22 April was the biggest day of the whole operation:

> It was obvious that the Germans were really on the run and owing to the fact that the American 1st Armoured Division was in the Modena area to the north, there were only two crossings over the river Secchia left open to the three German divisions – 232nd, 114th and 334th – which were withdrawing north-west towards the Po. At midday we noticed an enormous column of lorries and carts and a few tanks head to tail crossing the ford at Magreta. Our whole force with the guns took up a position on the last foothill overlooking the plain at Monte Petrone. Five hundred yards away from our most forward position was a German column resting for the day in Dinazzano, but they made no attempt to interfere with us.
>
> At 1430 hours we opened fire on the ford at Magreta, which was crammed full of carts and trucks. Aircraft overhead had previously taken no notice, presumably supposing it to be an Allied column. Many shells were fired into the target and ten trucks were set on fire. Horses and carts bolted or turned over. The aircraft noticed the smoke and dive-machine-gunned the column until twelve trucks were on fire, of which we claim three.

And so it went on. When the enemy's columns switched to the bridge at Sassuolo, Farran's fire was switched there too. The enemy also resumed crossing at Magreta and again received attention. It was altogether a very satisfactory finale to what had been a most successful operation. It was also just one more demonstration of how a few S.A.S. troops could raise and lead a force of local irregular troops, and with minimum distraction from the main Allied effort cause maximum disruption to the enemy. Two days later, on 24 April, Farran concentrated his force at Modena and then received orders to exfiltrate. The war in Italy had only two weeks to run.

When the war in Europe was over, Brigadier Mike Calvert, who had had a remarkable record with the Chindits in Burma and who in February, 1945, had taken over command of the S.A.S. Group from McLeod, was heard to say to Jakie Astor of the Phantom Regiment: 'Now for the Far East and a bit of action! I remember one splendid scrap we had when I was with Wingate's crowd; we ran into a bunch of Japs in a clearing in the jungle and there we were, hacking at each other with knives, swords, bayonets and the lot, just like an old-time battle'. Like Calvert, David Stirling, when released from being a prisoner of war, had some splendid ideas about operating once more in great spaces – think of the opportunities offered by China, he would say – but the end of hostilities with Japan put paid to such notions. It would not be very long, however, before the S.A.S. would be given their heads again to see what could be done in the great jungles of south-east Asia. For in that part of the world the British Army was to be engaged in two of the more or less continuous 'savage wars of peace'.

13

ENTR'ACTE

In order to have good soldiers, a nation must always be at war.

Bonaparte

The war was over. Everywhere peace was breaking out, and with peace would come two great problems for the S.A.S. – first, to assure survival, second, to adapt to a totally new role, which was to be almost the antithesis of what it had been in war. In war men of the S.A.S. had excelled at clandestine operations with minimum force in order to create maximum disruption; they had spent their time indulging in acts of stealth, sabotage and surprise; they had become expert at deeds which some people would now rather imprecisely classify under the heading of terrorism. With imagination, singlemindedness, determination, persistence and above all, daring, they had won countless little engagements, dismayed and distracted the enemy, raided, deterred, abducted, destroyed, implanted fear and apprehension, enforced the dissipation of security resources, and generally made a thorough nuisance of themselves. Now poacher was to turn gamekeeper, and although trouble would still be their business, it would be by deterrence or defeat of such violent acts, rather than their perpetration, that they would do it. This business would take them to the jungles of Malaya and Borneo, the burning rocks of Aden, the deserts and djebels of Oman, the bandit country of Armagh, the mean streets of Belfast and the elegant ones of London, Somalia, the Gambia, the Falkland Islands and a hundred other places around the world. In this process they would become the observed of all observers, the élite of all élites, the most admired and feared special force in all armies of all nations. But in this process of deterring and defeating insurgents, gunmen, terrorists and rebels, they would continue to produce maximum results with minimum force. They would continue to be specialists in many skills and qualities – physical and mental robustness, marksmanship, self-sufficiency and self-discipline, navigation, parachuting, languages, medicine, humility, humour. In short the regiment would continue to be the Man and the man would continue to be the Regiment. What is more the S.A.S. would undertake a uniquely important role in N.A.T.O.'s defence of the Central Front in Europe, and in this role the regular soldiers would be supported by two Territorial Army regiments.

Before we see how this came about we must briefly review their wartime activities and achievements. In doing so we can hardly do better than turn to Sandy Scratchley's short and rough account of what happened. In the letter already referred to he explained that L Detachment, S.A.S. Brigade, had been started in the Middle East by David Stirling and consisted of about sixty all ranks. Their first operation, undertaken in conjunction with the November, 1941, push, was by parachute and was not a success. The object had been to destroy aircraft on landing grounds and the reason for lack of success was the inability of pilots to drop the S.A.S. men anywhere near the correct DZ, aggravated on that occasion by strong winds. After this, the L.R.D.G. made themselves responsible for transporting L Detachment parties to and from their objectives, and this alliance achieved very good results. Then the Detachment expanded and became 1st S.A.S. Regiment, with its own transport, and in conjunction with the L.R.D.G. continued with its successful work. In July, 1942, a raid carried out with jeeps destroyed over thirty enemy aircraft at Bagush. The September raids on Benghazi, Tobruk and Jalo, however, when the line was established at El Alamein, were not successful. Not only had the operation been compromised by lack of security, but it represented, as David Stirling knew, a misuse of his people. Then, Scratchley goes on:

> Jeep patrols operating from the Sand Sea kept harassing enemy communications and blowing the railway before El Alamein. The railway was kept out of action by us and L.R.D.G. in one place or another between Tobruk and El Daba for thirteen of the twenty days immediately preceding Oct 23, 1942. [Authority for this – Shan Hackett, then G, MO III, GHQ MEF]. An abortive attempt to cut the signal communications from Rommel's HQ at El Daba and to blow up the main petrol dump of the Afrika Korps was undertaken by a party commanded by your old friend Scratch. About 40,000 Germans proved him wrong!
>
> Jeep patrols kept on operating with good results about 100 miles, or more, in front of 8th Army until Gabes, roughly Feb 1943. With the desert war drawing to a close, and David in the bag, 1st S.A.S. was split

into: (a) Special Raiding Squadron under Paddy Mayne, now commanding 1st S.A.S. (b) Special Boat Squadron under George Jellicoe, which operates in the Eastern Mediterranean.

Scratchley went on to explain that the S.A.S. in the desert had destroyed roughly 320 aircraft on the ground, adding that Paddy Mayne with his own hand was reckoned to have got about 100 of them. Besides this many dumps and trucks had been destroyed. He added that in his view without the help of L.R.D.G. they would have been unlikely to have got past the adolescent stage. In commenting on the value of all this, Scratchley quotes Montgomery as saying that the S.A.S. and L.R.D.G. were worth a division to him on his southern flank. The actual effects in terms of guarding airfields were remarkable. At the start of their raids about half a dozen Italian sentries might be wandering about an airfield smoking and talking. By July, 1942, there would normally be three sentries for every aircraft, one to each wing and one on the tail, so that the number of men diverted from other important business by the S.A.S. was considerable. What is more, many other enemy aircraft were kept away from the battle zone patrolling the desert in search of the S.A.S. These patrols were usually of three Stukas or three Macchis, both of which were very effective in combat. All these distractions had their influence on the main battle.

So much for the desert; Scratchley went on to show how the S.A.S. contributed to the assaults on Sicily and Italy, and the subsequent operations there and further east in the Mediterranean. We have also seen in the last chapter what happened during the supreme operation for 1944 – the invasion of France and blows aimed at the very heart of Germany. Some of the most telling tributes to the S.A.S.'s contribution here come from the commanders responsible for carrying out these operations. In a broadcast to the S.A.S. made in September, 1944, General Boy Browning gave it as his opinion that what these troops had done had had more effect in hastening the disintegration of the German 7th and 5th Armies than any other single effort in the British Army. No other troops in the world, he maintained, could have achieved with such small numbers so devastating an effect on the enemy. A comparable piece of praise came from the Supreme Allied Commander himself, General Eisenhower, who in a letter to the S.A.S. commander, Brigadier McLeod, wrote: 'The ruthlessness with which the enemy has attacked S.A.S. troops has been an indication of the injury which you were able to cause to the German armed forces both by your own efforts and by the information which you gave of German dispositions and movements.'

Yet we must ask again did they in the end make any difference, did their activities really matter? The answer is that even though the combined weight of the inexhaustible Red Army and Anglo-American ironmongery did not persuade the Führer actually to give up until the clock's hands were at five minutes past twelve, the S.A.S.'s contribution to the *Wehrmacht*'s defeat, by killing soldiers, destroying equipment, delaying movement and sapping morale, was very great. Moreover, by uplifting Allied spirit, by defiance and resolution, by fostering pride and hope, by daring and winning, the effect of what the S.A.S. did was incalculable. And since that time their successors, thriving on the imagination, resolution, courage and insistence on excellence of their creator, have in a manner at once inimitable and wholly to be admired left their mark with elegance and style on the world of terrorism and counter-terrorism. They have also added a new Regiment to the British Army, which none can contemplate without respect and awe.

'The British way in warfare,' wrote General Shan Hackett in his Foreword to David Lloyd Owen's book about the L.R.D.G., 'is not that of continental nations, whose natural tendency is generally towards massive frontal attack. It lies more in looking for the open flank and then making use of it. The British method lies predominantly in the oblique approach.' In commenting on this point, Michael Howard felt obliged to point out that it was a highly desirable method provided that there was a powerful continental ally able to take on the enemy's main forces and accept heavy losses while doing so. Great Britain certainly managed to shed a good deal of Austrian, Russian and Prussian blood in her struggle with Napoleon Bonaparte, and a good deal of French, American and Russian blood in her later struggles with the armies of Wilhelm II and Hitler. Yet we now seem to have abandoned the oblique approach in that the bulk of the British Army is permanently deployed on the continent of Europe to help deter, and if necessary take on, the enemy's main forces. Michael Howard also pointed out that this idea of employing troops on the flanks was also very useful when there was nothing else for them to do. And, as we have seen, there were times in the Second World War when the British Army was positively searching for areas and opportunities for engaging the German Army. Very effectively they did so, but we must agree with Professor Howard that at that time this was not a way that could by itself win wars. Times and methods change, and, as we shall see, the oblique approach can win wars after all. In seeing how the S.A.S. set about doing so we must turn to the so-called peace. For despite this peace, the S.A.S., once they had re-established themselves as an indispensable part of the British Army, were able to live up to Napoleon's maxim and be more or less continuously at war.

In October, 1945 – the same month that the wartime S.A.S. Regiments were being disbanded – Roy Farran was asked by Brigadier Mike Calvert* what he thought about the future of S.A.S.-type units in the peace-time British Army. In replying, Farran made a number of suggestions remarkable for their prescience. In the first place he gave it as his view that this type of warfare was only in very early stages of development. He thought that the whole principle of S.A.S. could be compared to the use of long-range cavalry patrols against enemy lines of communication, an example of this being the American Civil War. The essential difference was that air power had opened up the enemy's third flank, a flank which could be rendered invulnerable only by bad weather. 'Since it is now so easy to place troops across the enemy's lines of communication, I feel that it is important to have a unit of the Special Air Service type trained to operate individually with the minimum support and with the maximum amount of improvization'. Farran maintained that the arrival of nuclear weapons had positively increased the need for a unit whose adaptability would never tie it down to a particular area of operations. He went on to assume that any future war would of necessity be either a defensive or offensive one:

> In the former case a unit like the Special Air Service could inflict damage on the enemy and slow up his advance out of all proportion to its size. The most successful demonstration of this use of the Special Air Service was in the German offensive in the Ardennes last year. In an offensive war the S.A.S. would increase the speed of our advance by spreading panic and confusion in the enemy's rear.†

Farran went on to say that he did not believe that the success of an operation depended upon the friendly reception of a local population, although it obviously helped. 'I believe there will be great opportunities for guerrilla troops in the event of a war against Russia, which I suppose is the only possibility at the moment.' He went further, however, by anticipating what he referred to as that interim period between wars when we would be concerned with quelling risings in various parts of the Empire and pointed to the immense advantage of economy of force which the S.A.S. would be able to effect in such

* A copy of Mike Calvert's letter to Farran and other S.A.S. experts is at Appendix 5.

† As the Argentinians discovered to their discomfiture on the Falklands Islands.

affairs. 'If the principle of the S.A.S. does not continue, I cannot believe that the Army is thinking along progressive lines.' Air power had made an incalculable difference to warfare. Farran need not have worried. The lessons were not ignored.

There is perhaps no better way to introduce the S.A.S.'s role and deeds of daring during this so-called period of 'quelling riots', or what we might prefer to call keeping the peace, than referring to a paper produced some years ago by David Stirling, which contains a brief account written by the late Brian Franks of post-war S.A.S. activities and a comment on the Regiment in today's Army. He wrote:

> The present day S.A.S. is small – the smallest corps in the Regular Army – but they emulate their predecessors in their professionalism and work to the principles laid down in 1941 when David Stirling persuaded the Chiefs of Staff in the Western Desert that a force trained and selected specially for operations behind enemy lines should be formed. Surprise, deception and professional cunning are the effective weapons which enable them to produce results quite out of proportion to the numbers of S.A.S. involved in an operation.

The report goes on to say that after the pioneering of military free-fall parachuting, one example of their men's courage and cool, calculated initiative was given by Sergeant Reeves, who climbed the static line of a learner's parachute which became entangled in the aircraft's tail. Reeves cut the man free, dropped clear with him, pulled the novice's reserve parachute, and finally with but a few seconds in hand pulled the ripcord on his own parachute. For this feat Reeves was awarded the George Medal. But it is not just courage and initiative which matter. As David Stirling had always insisted, discipline too is of primary importance, discipline in selection and discipline in service. Only a small percentage of volunteers live up to the exacting standards required for further training, and the Commanding Officer has the right instantly to dismiss any officer or soldier whose performance should fall below what is expected. It is agreeable to be able to note that such a thing happens rarely indeed, simply because of the high demands the S.A.S. men make upon themselves.

The sheer versatility of the S.A.S. was shown not only by their actions in the end of Empire campaigns but in those which took place in the 'post-colonial' era. Ingenuity and intellect kept the Regiment to the very front of ways and means to employ military activity to solve problems which really demanded civil and social remedies:

> In one country of the Arab Middle East a group of S.A.S. parachuted at night, free fall, into a wadi basin 800 metres long where the surrounding

mountains stretched up to 1,000 metres above opening heights. In the subsequent operations the S.A.S. established schools and medical centres, plotted roads, built airstrips and mapped the whole area, in addition to attempting to seek out a small band of guerrilla infiltrators.

The report goes on to point out that in Malaya the S.A.S. did not merely help to defeat guerrilla action, but also to win control of the aboriginal inhabitants of the deep jungle areas from the Communist insurgents. It took eight years. In Malaya also the technique of parachuting troops into high jungle trees of sixty metres or more was developed. They would then lower themselves to the ground and make their way to the rendezvous. In another jungle area some years later the S.A.S. attacked the Indonesian infiltrators in Borneo along their lines of communication, and also raised, trained and supervised the activities of indigenous border surveillance troops. In the various campaigns designed to defeat attempts by neighbouring powers to overthrow legitimate governments, which turned to Great Britain for assistance, the S.A.S. spent many years too in Southern Arabia. One operation which was mounted in Oman in 1959 illustrated once more the S.A.S.'s astonishing versatility and adaptability. Insurgents were based on the plateau of the Djebel Akhdar and were successfully raiding down from there into the surrounding countryside. There were but two known routes to the top of the Djebel, which rises vertically up to 8,000 feet. Both these routes were so narrow that they could be climbed only in single file, and this meant that a mere handful of defenders was enough to deny access to any attacking force. Twice previously, normal infantry battalions had been repulsed. The troops involved had not been capable of scaling such heights in the face of accurate rifle fire. It therefore became necessary to ask a squadron of S.A.S. to undertake the task of suppressing the rebel bands. After some suitable reconnoitring which revealed some alternative routes to the summit, an attack was made. A deception plan drew the main body of enemy troops to the north of the plateau while the S.A.S. squadron climbed 8,000 feet during the hours of darkness at the southern side, using ropes for much of the climb, surprised the enemy piquets and overran the Djebel.

These are but a few instances of what had been done. Whether parachuting into the Atlantic to check on suspected bombs aboard the *QE II*, thwarting terrorist attempts to blackmail, subvert and destroy, rescuing hostages or assisting in the triumphs of British troops in South Georgia and the Falklands, there has never been any doubt about the victories of those who dared.

14

STENGAHS AND STEN GUNS

Take up the White Man's burden
The savage wars of peace –
Fill full the mouth of Famine
And bid the sickness cease . . .
The ports ye shall not enter,
The roads ye shall not tread,
Go make them with your living,
And mark them with your dead.

Rudyard Kipling

The first of the savage wars of peace which the S.A.S. took part in was the long campaign against Communist terrorists in Malaya. But before doing so the Regiment had to be re-born. In October, 1945, Roy Farran had had some perceptive things to say about the usefulness of an S.A.S. unit in peacetime. In the following year, 1946, the War Office completed a study of the role which S.A.S. troops had had during the Second World War. This study reached a number of conclusions that simply confirmed what S.A.S. people themselves, as well as those imaginative commanders who had successfully employed them, had long been saying. It was agreed that small parties of highly trained, disciplined troops operating behind enemy lines could achieve remarkable results, results quite out of proportion to the numbers used. This principle was reinforced by the view that future wars would be unlikely to feature massed formations locked in frontal struggles on petrified fronts as in the Great War, but would rather be conflicts of constantly changing and moving areas of close combat and powerful weapons. It had furthermore been made clear by experience gained between 1941 and 1945 that S.A.S. operations should be quite separate from the cloak and dagger merchants, whether S.O.E. or Secret Service, and that these operations should be directed from the highest level of command. Moreover, it was essential to distinguish between the S.A.S. and normal infantry, as their respective tasks were totally different. The normal infantryman was a member of a large team, dedicated to taking or holding ground in an orthodox military fashion. His job was to argue the toss with his conventional enemy in a conventional way. The S.A.S. man was the very kernel of the unconventional, an individualist, of exceptional mental and physical robustness, accustomed to live and survive alone or in small groups, busied in special skills of movement, of communication, of destruction and of killing, a man who could play the waiting game, a man who combined daring with deadliness.

It was hardly surprising, therefore, to find the War Office concluding that further development of the whole idea had to be encouraged and ensured. The great question in 1946 was – how? How was the thing to be kept going, with what precise purpose, designed to fulfil what part of British defence policy, represented by what sort of unit and run by whom? Fortunately for the S.A.S.'s future there were some strong men about who believed in the concept and were able to make others believe in it too. Among them were Mike Calvert, Brian Franks and L.E.O.T. Hart. It soon became clear to these men that the surest way to re-establish the S.A.S. was by creating a Territorial Army unit, and in 1947 a new regiment, 21 S.A.S. (Artists)* was born. Its first Commanding Officer was Brian Franks, the second-in-command, Major Hart. An account of this new regiment's activities comes later in the story. Here and now it is the reason for raising 22 S.A.S. and what they then got up to which must take up the running. It all started because the White Man's burden was about to be taken up again by the British in South-East Asia.

What became known in Malaya as The Emergency began in the middle of 1948. Chin Peng, who had fought with the British in Force 136 as part of the Malayan Peoples' Anti-Japanese Army, had been appointed Secretary-General of the Malayan Communist Party in the previous year, and he at once saw that the existing campaign of urban disruption by riots and strikes would not do. It was losing the Communists more ground than it was gaining. He therefore determined

* The number 21 was chosen arbitrarily, but led inevitably to the choice of 22 for the regular regiment and 23 for a second T.A. one. The Artists' Rifles, raised in 1859 as a volunteer corps and affiliated to the Rifle Brigade, had a long, gallant history and notably individualistic and imaginative members. Disbanded in 1945, reconstituted in 1947, it was a happy stroke which merged them with the S.A.S. to become 21 S.A.S. (Artists).

upon armed rebellion, in particular to take advantage of the discontent felt by half a million Chinese squatters in the rural areas, not far from the jungle's edge. The idea would be to mount a campaign of terror from a number of secure bases and then expand from them. This would mean a return to the jungle by the M.P.A.J.A., now renamed the Malayan Peoples' Anti-British Army. Chin Peng began his campaign with roughly 10,000 guerrillas, 3,000 of whom were organized into eight, later ten, regiments of actual fighting men based in the jungle, the rest a so-called Self-Protection Corps, operating outside the jungle with the tasks of providing information, recruits, food, weapons and money – in short an underground network of support for the active bands of what became known as Communist terrorists. Chin Peng's aim was to seize control of Malaya by a campaign of murder, coercion and economic disruption. The first wave of violence was set off by the murder of British planters in the area of Sungei Siput,* a town in Perak. So began the 'long, long war'.

From the British point of view the campaign may properly be thought of as having four broad phases. First from 1948 until 1950 the Army and the Police conducted their counter-insurgency operations under the direction of the Malay Federation's Commissioner of Police. As a holding operation, it was not unsuccessful, and various measures, such as compulsory registration, control of firearms and detention of suspects had had their effect. The Malayan Communist Party renamed its rebel forces the Malayan Races Liberation Army, broke up its regiments into platoons, which terrorized the local population, and abandoned the idea of establishing liberated bases. But their efforts to build up political support among the squatters continued to achieve some results. The second phase began in 1950 when General Briggs was apppointed Director of Operations. He established a Federal War Council, which was reflected in every State and District by proper machinery, consisting of police and military commanders under the senior officer of the Administration, to coordinate and supervise operations. But Briggs did not confine himself to organizing proper machinery. He struck blows at the Communist Party's organization by arresting and interning those outside the jungle and then interfering with the support which the terrorists had formerly enjoyed. His plan included the re-settling of all the half million squatters into new villages

---

* From time to time the terrorists would mine and ambush the railway line between Ipoh and Sungei Siput. In the early days of the Emergency, the author received an instruction from Major Loopy Kennard, not unlike Patton's telling his ADC to go down that track until you get blown up and then report back. 'Go down the railway line and report when ambushed!' I *was* ambushed and did report.

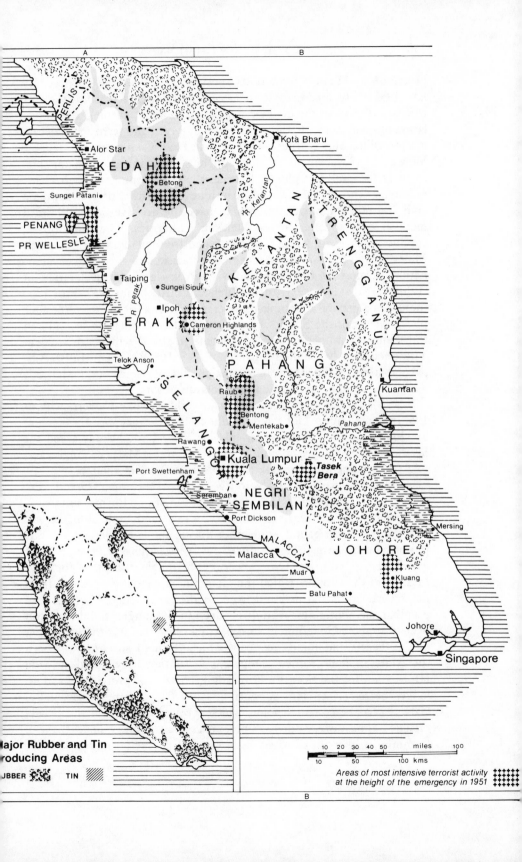

A

B

PERLIS

■ Alor Star

K E D A H

Sungei Patani ●

● Betong

● Kota Bharu

R. Kelantan

K E L A N T A N

T R E N G G A N U

PENANG

PR WELLESLEY

■ Taiping

● Sungei Siput

R Perak

● Ipoh

P E R A K

● Cameron Highlands

● Telok Anson

S E L A N G O R

P A H A N G

Raub ●

● Bentong

● Mentekab

■ Kuantan

Pahang

● Rawang

● Port Swettenham

■ Kuala Lumpur

Tasek Bera

A

● Seremban

N E G R I

S E M B I L A N

● Port Dickson

● Mersing

MALACCA

● Malacca

J O H O R E

● Muar

● Kluang

1

● Batu Pahat

● Johore

■ Singapore

Major Rubber and Tin Producing Areas

RUBBER ▦▦   TIN ▨

| 10 | 20 | 30 | 40 | 50 | miles | 100 |
| 10 | | 50 | | 100 kms | | |

Areas of most intensive terrorist activity at the height of the emergency in 1951 ▦▦

B

protected by Home Guard units specially raised for the purpose. By late 1951 these measures were having a serious effect on the Communists' ability to direct their insurgency without turning the population against them. At the same time, however, the terrorists' success in ambushing and murdering the British High Commissioner struck a blow at the Government's own confidence, and resulted in the appointment of General Templer in February, 1952, as the new High Commissioner who would not only combine in his own person supreme civil and military power, but would have the decisive gift of political independence to offer to the Malayan authorities. The third phase, conducted by Templer and others, lasted from 1952 until 1957, when Malaya received its independence, and consisted of the gradual elimination of most of the Communist guerrillas and the declaration of 'White' areas freed of terrorist influence. Finally, from 1957 until 1960 there was a general mopping-up operation. These, then, were the four phases. Most of the S.A.S. activities took place during the second and third phases, although there were some in the fourth phase as well. These activities led to the formation of 22 S.A.S. Regiment. But S.A.S. participation in the Malayan campaign did not start out under this name. At first they were called the Malayan Scouts.

The Malayan Scouts were the brain-child of Mike Calvert, who in 1950 was serving in Hong Kong. Blown for to Singapore by General Sir John Harding, Commander-in-Chief, Far East, he was asked for his views on fighting Communist terrorists in the Malayan jungle, and told to do something quickly to hit back at them in their base areas. Harding chose well, for Calvert was a remarkable man. Greatly experienced at fighting the Japanese in the jungles of Burma, renowned for his courage, his idealism, chivalry, loyalty and leadership, he was also the S.A.S. Brigade Commander during the latter part of the war in north-west Europe. He produced two very important ideas, both of which were acted upon. One concerned the jungle itself, the other had to do with the support which the Communist guerrillas received from the squatters who farmed and lived on the jungle edge. His first idea was that the aborigines, who dwelt deep in the jungle, should be won over to support Government forces – in a sense this was the beginning of the 'hearts and minds' concept which featured so largely in both the Malayan and Borneo campaigns – so that they could provide information for the Security Forces in exchange for protection, and no longer be terrorized into supporting Chin Peng's bandits. Secondly, Calvert saw the essential point, which formed the basis of the Briggs plan and almost every other counter-insurgency strategy since, that the Communist guerrillas had to be isolated from their sources of food, money, reinforcements and intelligence. Do this, he argued, and the guerrillas would be obliged to emerge from the jungle and so become vulnerable to detection and ambush. Such operations could, of course, be carried out by Police and Army units once the Briggs plan, which might more properly be called the Calvert plan, had separated the guerrillas from their support and obliged them to quit the jungle. Meanwhile it would be for the Malayan Scouts to operate deep in the jungle itself and take on the bandits on their home ground to find and destroy them in their deeply based jungle camps.

Thus Calvert formed the Malayan Scouts in 1950, and he used three main sources to establish them. *A* Squadron was formed from some one hundred volunteers from units in the Far East at that time; *B* Squadron came from the Territorial Army unit, 21 S.A.S.; and *C* Squadron was made up of volunteers in Rhodesia. The three squadrons were very different from each other. Whereas the Rhodesians were for the most part sensible, disciplined and at this time reasonably orthodox soldiers, and *B* Squadron, with all the training, experience and high standards of selection and dedication that Brian Franks had been able to imbue his men with, was well-knit, skilled and disciplined, *A* Squadron, which had been rapidly assembled without the proper selection processes so crucial to ensuring that the right type of man was recruited, contained some controversial figures. It has always been the case in the British Army that those soldiers who are constantly volunteering for some specially dangerous service are usually not to be relied upon as sound members of a team. There were clearly some of these in *A* Squadron, as well as some good men too. The discipline, that had been at the core of David Stirling's idea and still is today, was lacking. There were some rough, tough characters about; there was too much drinking; there was carelessness with firearms. But, as Calvert has subsequently pointed out, he was a man in a hurry, eager to get to grips with operations, and the more leisurely methods of selection and training were not compatible with his requirement to deploy his men into the jungle with sufficient experience of conditions there to be able to fight and survive. In any event, having established his operational headquarters in Ipoh, Calvert sent off his first groups from *A* Squadron into the jungle of Perak, supported by Chinese liaison officers and police, to establish bases, explore the area and set up ambushes on known guerrilla routes. Meanwhile, the other squadrons were completing their jungle training in Johore. It was from these somewhat haphazard beginnings that 22 S.A.S. Regiment was born in 1951.

Operations in the whole of Malaya during the first of the four phases described already were themselves haphazard. There was – or certainly to someone like myself at the time, a squadron leader of the 4th Hussars, patrolling the jungles, plantations and tin mines of Perak, or responding to some terrorist attack or rumour of terrorist presence – no central theme, no central intelligence picture, no grand strategy for discovering the situation, deciding what to do, telling everyone what it was, and then doing it. At one moment there would be a stengah* in one's hand, a few hours later a sten-gun. In the first instance one would be sitting comfortably in a club or rubber planter's bungalow; in the second making one's way through the unfamiliar jungle, or squatters' dilapidated huts, or sitting in a scout car wending a slow passage along steep, winding tracks with thick jungle either side, concealing who knew what. Ambushes were the guerrillas' stock in trade, as they became also the security forces' most effective method of killing. One simply responded to orders from the senior administrator, policeman or soldier in the area: 'There are reports of a group of ten bandits at so-and-so; go and deal with them'; or 'A Gurkha patrol has been ambushed on the track to X's plantation; go and sort it out'; or 'The night train to Taiping has been shot up at Chemor, the line mined and a gang of terrorists is in the area – get the train moving again'. These various jobs were done, but the initiative seemed to rest firmly with the Communists. It was only after the institution of the Briggs plan, the beginning of successes to the security forces and the denial of intelligence and supplies to the guerrillas that the initiative began to swing back to those trying to keep the peace. The S.A.S.'s role in all this process was varied. Sometimes it was food denial, sometimes to further the hearts and minds campaign to win the aborigines' support, sometimes directly to locate and eliminate a terrorist camp in the jungle. Before we see what some of these operations were like, it is important to understand some of the changes that had taken place after the departure of Mike Calvert, who, after an intensely active war – he had been decorated a dozen times for gallantry and distinguished service – was a sick man, with malaria and dysentery, and towards the end of 1951 was invalided home. But he had done a very important thing. He had recreated a regular force of the Special Air Service.

As has so often happened in the past, it was the arrival of a far more orthodox soldier who was able to assist some of Calvert's best officers to return to a system in which proper selection, standards of excellence, whether in discipline, care of weapons or personal integrity, and sound administrative backing were all watchwords. The new Commanding

* Whisky and soda.

Officer was John Sloane (nicknamed 'Tod' by the S.A.S.), and with
the help of two other famous S.A.S. men, John Woodhouse* and Dare
Newell, he set about reorganizing the Regiment during a period when
it was withdrawn from the jungle. To operate successfully in the jungle
demanded special skills. You had to be able to find your way when
walking through dense undergrowth with very limited visibility; you
had to carry and cook your own food; to build a *basha* of branches
and leaves; to communicate under appalling atmospheric conditions; to
cope with leeches, hornets, mosquitoes, snakes, tigers, water buffaloes;
to be instantly alert and a deadly shot at fleeting targets. Just as in
the old days the desert had been a friend, so now the jungle must be,
not neutral, but an ally.

It may be doubted whether the S.A.S. who took part in the Belum
valley operation in February, 1952, thought of the jungle as a particularly friendly ally when they had to parachute into it, using the
technique that became known as tree-jumping. The operation was
designed to deal with about a hundred terrorists who had positioned
themselves in a remote valley near the Thai border, where they were
both growing their own crops and coercing local Malay villagers into
supplying them with food. This group of Communist bandits had
withdrawn to re-group and make further plans for the future because
of initial successes of the Briggs plan in denying them food, intelligence
and opportunity. It was a joint operation involving the Police Field
Force (who acted as normal infantry), some Gurkhas, Royal Marine
Commandos and the S.A.S. Some S.A.S. went with the main body on
foot, while some fifty parachuted into a small dropping zone near the
guerrillas' camp.

One of the S.A.S. foot patrols was led by John Woodhouse, a
remarkable leader, who was regarded as one of the finest squadron
commanders the Regiment ever had, and later commanded the Regiment itself† with great success and distinction. Woodhouse insisted on
relentless efficiency and absolute professionalism. He would punish
what he regarded as slipshod methods of handling weapons, and once
required a soldier to walk about with a grenade whose pin had been
removed because he had accidentally discharged his rifle. Underneath
this insistence on the highest standards of military efficiency, however,
was a man of humour, compassion and sympathy. His men combined

* For extracts from a recently written, most interesting letter by John Woodhouse
see Appendix 6.

† At a time when I was commanding my own Regiment and all troops in West
Sarawak, including an S.A.S. squadron. More of this later.

infinite admiration for his sheer professionalism with a touch of apprehension as to their own ability to live up to his exacting demands. Yet
even Woodhouse was surprised by one of his men during the Belum
valley operation. Despite having been ordered back to base by Woodhouse because his feet were wet with blood and the skin was coming
away with his socks, Lance-Corporal Moseley disobeyed the order and
went on with the exhausting march up and down the jungle hills until
he reached the guerrillas' suspected position, only to find them gone.
When Moseley's boots were cut off his feet, it was found that he had
been continuing the march on suppurating flesh. Some places revealed
that his flesh had decayed right down to the bone. Two of Moseley's
companions, also ordered back by Woodhouse, had accompanied him
to complete the mission. Such was the mental and physical robustness
of the S.A.S. men, and such the inspiration of their leadership. Yet
Calvert himself had been the first to admit that the S.A.S. were merely
playing their part with others. 'Be under no illusion about this business,' he had told his men. 'We in this unit are not going to win the
war. All we can do is to play a particular part in it which other Army
units are not trained for or suited for.'

Certainly no other Army unit could have done what fifty-four members of the S.A.S. did in parachuting into the small DZ in the Belum
valley. In some ways the very success of this drop, in which there were
very few injuries among those who did land in the trees, was unfortunate in that tree-jumping became a recognized technique. Later, the
frequency of injuries caused the S.A.S. to abandon this method of
entering the jungle. In his admirable book, *Who Dares Wins*, Tony
Geraghty has reminded us of an article in the Malayan newspaper,
Straits Times, which described what it was like:

> They knew that if they landed in bamboo it would splinter and cut them
> deeply; rocky or boulder-strewn areas, bomb-blasted areas, spiky and weak-
> ened trees could smash their necks and bones. Aboard the aircraft, they
> joked and laughed for a few minutes after take-off. Then there was silence.
> Some slept; others read; a few glanced out of the windows, fixing their
> eyes on the jungle. All faces were stern. Ten minutes to go. They checked
> each other's gear. One man munched an apple; another sucked an orange.
> A voice said: 'Dropping Zone, two minutes to go'. Then: 'Stand up. Action
> stations'. A crew member stood near the door, tapping paratroopers on the
> shoulders, yelling: 'Right, right, right', as each approached him in turn and
> prepared to jump.

Geraghty also recalls the comments made by the second-in-command
of 22 S.A.S., Major Salmon, who admitted he felt scared when

standing in the doorway, but explained that it had to be conquered. There could be no turning back, so that when the tap on the shoulder came, there was no hesitation:

Next thing you know, you are floating through the air and it's one of the most wonderful feelings in the world; then you see the trees coming. You are coming down beautifully, steering for the middle of the trees. The hot air makes you swing violently, as if a giant had caught hold of you. You let the air spill out of the 'chute and look for a good, healthy tree. Sometimes you make that spot; often you don't. It's hard to tell until you're a few feet away. When you hit a tree you don't know whether you'll stay there or not. Often the branch snaps, you hurtle down, smashing into branches on the way, until you finally come to a halt. If it holds you, then you know you're safe.

There were certainly many injuries in subsequent parachuting operations. One of them was the commanding officer himself, by this time Lieutenant-Colonel Oliver Brooke, who at the time of his assuming command had quietly dealt with a prank by *B* Squadron, which involved setting off explosives near the Officers' Mess, by returning seventeen soldiers to their original units – the worst conceivable punishment for a member of the Regiment.

Yet there were sound reasons for continuing to parachute deep into the jungle, for this was where the S.A.S. needed to be used [see Appendix 7]. In the first place it was absurd to waste such specialists on normal infantry tasks, indeed to do this was to contravene a cardinal principle and purpose of their creation. Also, as the terrorists withdrew deeper and deeper into the jungle, so they had to be located, harried and eliminated. And just as Templer's campaign to win the hearts and minds of the Malayan peoples was largely won by the Administration and the Security Forces outside the jungle in the towns and villages and plantations, where these peoples lived and worked, where the rule of law, justice, political, economic and social reform, the promise of national independence, together with heavy odds on the Government's actually winning had their effect, so a comparable campaign in furtherance of Calvert's original aims was waged by the S.A.S. deep in the jungle, attacking terrorists, succouring the Sakai aboriginals and winning also their loyalty and alliance.

Between 1952 and 1958 the S.A.S. carried out many more operations. Two, which illustrated their variety, duration and results were Operations *Hive* and *Termite*. The first of these in late 1952 was conducted in the state of Negri Sembilan and was really an extension of the food denial policy. During the two months it lasted the S.A.S.

cooperated with Gurkha and Fijian infantry in patrolling and domi-
nating a large area of jungle at Seremban in order to disrupt the
Communist bandits' activities there and to remove them from their
supporters among the local people. By driving them away from other
sources of food, the guerrillas would be obliged to fall back on their
own dumps of supplies in the jungle. Then by further patrolling,
harassment and ambushing, it was planned to account for some of the
hundred terrorists thought to be in the area. Finding and stopping
Communist guerrillas in tracts of jungle hundreds of square miles in
dimension is no easy thing. In this respect the jungle was neutral
indeed, but perhaps more neutral for the few seeking to evade notice
than for the many trying to find needles in haystacks. Some sixteen of
the terrorists were accounted for eventually, not many out of a hundred
believed to be there, but on balance the operation was thoroughly
worth while. After all, during their nine years in Malaya the S.A.S.
caught or killed only about one hundred bandits, say ten per year, not
quite one per month. But it was enough. It would serve. The thousands of man-hours spent patrolling, searching, pursuing, shooting at
fleeting targets had their dividend.

Yet it must be admitted that Operation *Hive* was not the best way
to employ the S.A.S. In the end it became clear – and this point was
fully understood when it came to the next jungle war in Borneo – that
the S.A.S.'s greatest value, as it had been in the Second World War,
lay in the strategic, not the tactical, field. Give them the task of
clandestine surveillance, intelligence gathering, winning local sympathy
and support, and you were using them to your best advantage. They
could always be asked to deliver a deadly coup de grâce if necessary,
and in numerous counter-insurgency and counter-terrorist actions they
have done so. Indeed Operation *Termite*, which lasted for four months
towards the end of 1954 involved once more parachuting into the
jungle, into clearings created by Royal Air Force bombing, then con-
verting the aborigines to the British way of thinking and rounding
up Communist terrorists, of whom fifteen were removed from the
scene.

As always with the S.A.S. some extraordinary characters abounded
in these Malayan days. The brilliant John Woodhouse came back to
command a squadron. George Lea, who years later took over operational command in Borneo from the legendary Walter Walker, commanded the Regiment. Years later George Lea was persuaded to write
an article about taking command of the Regiment. Having been given
the news in December, 1954, while in England, he remembered meeting Mike Calvert in Singapore four years earlier –

while he was working on the establishment of a unit which was initially to be the Malayan Scouts and which was later to become 22nd Special Air Service Regiment. It certainly never entered my head at the time that I might one day become intimately concerned with this unit. ... I don't mind admitting now that I would have been genuinely alarmed.

I lowered myself gingerly into the Commanding Officer's chair for the first time on the morning of 26 January, 1955. ... My first important encounter that morning was with the RSM. He somewhat disconcertingly came straight to the point by saying: 'Sir, I would like to know your policy'. I must have been a grave disappointment to him because of all the things I may or may not have had at that moment I certainly had not got a policy. ... However, this was the beginning of a very happy partnership. ... I remember realizing almost at once that a combination of pure chance and good luck had steered me to what was without any doubt going to be one of my greatest experiences. The Regiment had got something. You could sense it from the moment you arrived. ... However, let us be quite honest. That something was not absolutely one hundred per cent good right through. The fact was that the Regiment was still growing up. ... Operationally the Regiment had achieved many successes but there was still room for improvement. Those lengthy operations lasting three months or more involved much that was really excellent, but at the same time cloaked much that was of very questionable value ... jungle marathons must have scared away all self-respecting Communist terrorists for miles around. But there were many in the Regiment who knew this was not the right way to do business and who were determined to improve techniques. ... I consider myself fortunate indeed to have commanded at a time when the Regiment could field five operational squadrons, and there is no doubt that the healthy competition provided by Frank Rennie's Kiwis and Dudley Coventry's chaps from the Parachute Regiment did the 22nd far more good than many of the old hands were prepared to admit at the time.

George Lea concluded that while taking command had not been easy, handing over was far more difficult. He had become very possessive after three years and, like all other commanding officers, hated leaving. But he did at least hand over to an old friend [Tony Deane-Drummond].

With George Lea were some other renowned S.A.S. characters. John Cooper, who had been a corporal with David Stirling in the desert, was there. Peter de la Billière, who subsequently commanded 22 S.A.S. and the whole S.A.S. Group, joined them at about this time. So did Harry Thompson, who was with me in Borneo and alas killed there in a helicopter accident. Rhodesians, New Zealanders, Fijians,

the Parachute Regiment, all played their part in the four squadrons
which the Regiment now had. The remarkable Sergeant Turnbull,
who was the very model of a modern S.A.S. man – linguist, jungle
tracker, marksman with a repeater shotgun, cool, infinitely tough,
patient and perseverant – on one occasion killed four terrorists
single-handed by tracking them to a jungle hut in which they took
shelter. Such individual acts of courage, initiative, endurance and sheer
perseverance characterized the whole idea that David Stirling had
founded a dozen years before.

Another example of such perseverance was the action by Harry
Thompson's squadron in finding and eliminating the group of terrorists led by Ah Hoi in the Telok Anson swamp, south-west of Ipoh.
Thirty-seven men of D Squadron parachuted into the swamp early in
1958. Then one troop under Peter de la Billière and another under
Sergeant Sandilands began their search. Eventually they made contact
on the Tengi River and closed round Ah Hoi's position, supported
further afield by police and military units. The long slog through the
marshes, with leeches, thorns which cut and ulcered legs, prickly heat
and other infections, had paid off. Ah Hoi and his group surrendered.
From this time forward the Malayan campaign was little more than a
mopping-up affair. It is doubtful whether any unit other than the
S.A.S. could have carried out an operation like the Telok Anson one.
Harry Thompson's own account of it is so full of interest and colour
that it deserves extensive inclusion here:

> The drop took place at 7 a.m. 9 February. The whole three troops and
> Squadron HQ were out of the aircraft in 18 seconds, that was 37 men. We
> were on the ground and had RV'd about 600–700 yards from where we
> had dropped in an hour and three-quarters, the whole Squadron together.
> This could have been shortened had it not been for the fact that we had
> an injury.

Here Major Thompson explains that this was the one thing they were
worried about, as evacuating a casualty by helicopter might compromise the operation's security. Trooper Mulcahy's parachute got stuck
in a tree 189 feet high, and while he was trying to extricate himself,
the branches gave way and he fell, breaking through lower trees and
eventually hitting the ground, badly damaging his back. The consequent helicopter rescue was a triumph of bold and skilful flying – 'the
finest entry into the jungle I have ever seen . . . this DZ would never
have been passed by the R.A.F. in a thousand years . . . the pilot,
Showell, if he had wanted to, could have said no, but he came in and
I saw the branches of the trees coming in on top of his rotors; he came

in and hovered beside this log ... then we put him in and Showell got him out, the most brilliant piece of flying we'd ever seen.' Such were the hazards of parachuting in Malaya and such the debt of gratitude which the S.A.S. acknowledged to the gallant R.A.F. pilots. In the event no security was compromised and the next ten days were spent patrolling either side of the Sungei Tinggi river. They found camps and signs of recent movement, but no actual terrorists. After a big re-supply lift, Thompson instructed Sergeant Sandilands to patrol the river by night using rubber dinghies:

> That troop then proceeded by night to move down the river in these dinghies, with instructions to keep their noses awake for the smell of fires, because we were quite sure that the CTs were just cooking fish and turtles on the side of the river ... sure enough they contacted a group of CTs who were living on the side of the river and unfortunately the chaps in the boat had shotguns and they fired off, but their range wasn't great enough ... we got a lot of equipment, cooking gear and a pack, and we saw one CT move off with a large sack on his back, which we presumed were probably turtles, a pretty casual effort, we felt, but he got away.

Later, however, Sergeant Sandilands was luckier. An aborigine boy arrived to say that he had seen a terrorist on the other side of the river, with a woman standing nearby. At first Sandilands did not believe him, thinking that the boy might have seen some of his own men. But he went to have a look:

> He and Corporal Finn went out to the river very quietly and got behind a log. Sandilands was carrying an FN and Finn was carrying a Patchet. Sure enough here the CT was still standing and Sergeant Sandilands fired twice and killed him outright. Corporal Finn fired his Patchet at the woman, but the range was too great and she got away. There was a follow-up. Other members of the troop had heard the firing and came straight back ... they followed the woman who left a glaring trail for some 3,000-4,000 yards through the swamp. They came to two camps, both of them had been occupied by four men and presumably the woman. And then we got a general picture, south of the river and near its mouth, where a group of 4 or 5 CTs was obviously operating. ... I felt that the time had come to put the main emphasis over by the river and west of it, where there was definitely movement, so I got hold of my fourth troop and had it helicoptered straight into Sungei Tinggi, and at the same time moved myself, my squadron HQ, up to the river by foot. ... By this time I felt we had got certainly one group pin-pointed into an area south of the river. I then decided that, as a result of 6 Troop's operations in the Sekinchang

area, I was getting a very clear picture of Babykiller's [another name for Ah Hoi, who in terrorizing villagers had been guilty of killing baby children] group. They were going over the river north of the police post, they were going into the paddies, staying there 2 or 3 days and coming back about 4,000 yards down river, very cool ... we were getting on now for about the ninth week of the operation. We reckoned we knew there were 4–5 CTs outside the jungle in the paddy fields – Ah Hoi's bunch. ...

Information came through via Special Branch to say that a female CT, Ah Niet, had been seen in the paddy. ... 24 hours after that I got another signal to say that she had been met officially in the paddy by Special Branch and she had said she was prepared to surrender, that they were very short of food because of pressure, they'd been moved around by Security Forces, in fact they'd been moved 18 times from separate camps in 3 months and they'd had two people killed [both had been killed by the S.A.S.]. She then explained the conditions under which she felt she could get the main group to surrender, Ah Hoi included.

These conditions were totally unrealistic. She was demanding huge sums of money for them all and the release from detention of Communist sympathizers. Special Branch made it clear that they would be lucky if they avoided prison, and had the opportunity either to return to China or live a normal life in Malaya. This particular meeting was unfruitful, but soon the situation changed:

One night at 7 o'clock I got a signal to say that Ah Niet had come out again, and she was prepared to bring the whole group out ... We moved out of the jungle through the dark with torches and started to move down to Sekinchang to find out what was going on. As we moved along the track, we suddenly came across a group of five in the paddy. It was the Sekinchang group surrendering. The most extraordinary bunch. First, a little creature wearing a woman's sort of blue silk jacket, and I said: 'For heaven's sake, who's that?', and they said: 'That's your Baby-killer'. I said I didn't believe it, it was a woman, so I told them to take the hat off, and there was this desperate man, Ah Hoi, who was 5ft nothing, dressed up as a woman, pathetic. Next came what appeared to be a man, but in fact was a woman, Ah Fung, suffering from venereal disease as most of them were, and then three more appeared ... Ah Niet said she knew where another group of 3 were.

In for a penny, in for a pound, and Ah Niet then agreed to guide the S.A.S. back to where this group of three would be waiting by the canal at the jungle edge. Ah Niet was horrified at the noise the soldiers made in crossing the canal, she herself making not a sound. Once inside the jungle, she made some clucking noises to attract the attention of her terrorist friends, but to no avail that night. Within forty-eight hours, however, they had all surrendered.

At that stage the operation seemed to be at an end ... about two days later two more gave up, which was in fact the end of the Sekinchang branch, and the Sungei Tinggi branch was then contacted by a battalion of the Malay Regiment, who had been guided by one of the surrendered terrorists ... this happened on the completion of the three months to a day, which was our standard time. In fact, it was, I would say, a complete and utter fluke, but it just happened that way.

Life in the jungle or in the swamps could be hard enough. But even when having a break from operations, the S.A.S. would give their people some training which was thought of as having particular application in war itself, as opposed to internal security campaigns. One particular aspect of this was to prepare people to resist interrogation, of the sort, for example, that the Chinese and North Koreans had subjected their prisoners to. Captain Raven has recorded the sort of training to which S.A.S. men might be treated by the Intelligence Corps teams:

Just to try the chaps out and it was quite amazing, off the record, how many of our big tough soldiers in fact weren't quite so tough under the skin. No physical violence whatsoever, it was purely mental. For example, you'd sit a chap down in a chair and you'd put a latrine bucket over his head, and a chap would sit there going bong, bong, bong with a spoon for about half an hour, and then he'd be taken outside and tied to a tree that had been smeared with jam, with ankle cuffs and wrist cuffs, so he had to keep away from the tree, because the ants were pouring up and down it, red ants, all sorts of lovely tortures they devised, these chaps. If you take a bicycle wheel with the spindle still in the centre, and put it on the ground and make you kneel on the rim, kneel inside the rim on the spokes, with your hands behind your back tied to a rope over the ceiling, and you had to keep this bicycle wheel absolutely dead flat. You can't do it, because you get cramp in the ankles and knees, and every time you moved, you got a jerk on the wrists and it was very painful. It didn't leave any mark or sign; you weren't actually beaten up. And they wouldn't give you any sleep for 36 hours or no food, you just didn't get a thing, and they'd put you in solitary confinement, and you'd be in this little cell all on your own with a board on the floor to sleep on, and every time you got on the board, somebody would open the door and throw a bucket of water over you. Or they'd put you in a pit and surround you with guard dogs and turn the hose on you from time to time just to keep you cooled down. It was great fun and it gave everybody a very good insight into the sort of chaps you had. You picked out then the really good and you picked out the doubtful ones.

Apart from these rather extravagant methods of testing people – and there was to be much criticism in later years of certain S.A.S. practices in their selection procedures – the great value of the Malayan campaign from the S.A.S. point of view was not simply that it had been the vehicle for their reconstitution. It had been the further demonstration that S.A.S. troops, operating in their special way in small numbers, could do things which other troops could not do. Moreover, it had sharpened the minds of those who believed in their future – such men as John Woodhouse, Dare Newell, Peter de la Billière and many others – that they had to get their administrative arrangements right, that their selection methods required constant watching and improvement, that however good a constant inflow of new men from other regiments might be, with new ideas and original approaches, some kind of permanent cadre was needed to form a hard core of skill, dedication and leadership which would keep the whole thing going. They had learned, too, special jungle techniques, which were to stand them in good stead for more campaigns to come; they had polished their training techniques and acquired new ones; understood how vital it was, if hearts and minds were to be won, to talk the languages of indigenous peoples, live with them and care for them. The S.A.S. were learning how to wage the savage wars of peace. Mistakes had been made. They had had no end of a lesson. It had done them no end of good. And almost immediately after leaving Malaya they did themselves another powerful piece of good in southern Arabia.

15

DJEBELS AND REBELS

From the point of view of the army as a whole the most important effect of the campaign was that it ensured the continued existence of the Special Air Service.

Frank Kitson

In his entertaining and revealing book *Bunch of Five* General Sir Frank Kitson has explained how it came about that the S.A.S. was involved in the operation to capture the Djebel Akhdar, the Green Mountain, in Oman in 1958. In the first place the British had certain treaty obligations to the Sultan of Muscat and Oman. In the second place the Sultan's interests were being challenged by Sulaiman ibn Himyar, chief of the Bani Riyam, and his nominee, the Imam, Ghalib ibn Ali, together with Ghalib's brother, the ambitious and powerful Talib. The row which had broken out in 1954 between the Sultan and the Ghalib-Talib alliance had been temporarily won by the Sultan, but in mid-1957 Talib, who had raised an army of expatriate Omanis in Saudi Arabia, returned to the Djebel Akhdar, made himself master of central Oman and declared himself independent of the Sultan. The strength of his position rested with the sheer dominance of the Djebel, not only in its apparent impregnability, but in its effective control of the communications between the coast and Nazwa in the interior. Also Talib enjoyed the support of two of the local tribes, the Bani Himya and Bani Riyam. The Sultan had neither the money with which to bribe his way back into authority nor the military wherewithal to coerce it. He therefore turned to the British.

Britain's precise obligation was far from clear as regards responsibility for suppressing internal dissension. Interference in Arab affairs did not always prosper, as the ill-conceived and ill-executed interference with Nasser in 1956 had shown. Moreover, the whole trend of our defence policy, as illustrated by the Sandys White Paper of 1957, was moving away from intervention in troublesome areas which demanded expenditure of ships, men and money, and turning towards the totally fallacious idea of reliance on nuclear deterrence alone. Nonetheless, being a business people and having regard to the expediency of combining self-interest with reassurance of friendly, oil-rich or otherwise strategically useful Arab nations like Kuwait, Bahrain and Qatar, Britain decided that the better part of discretion was valour and came to the Sultan's aid.

In 1957 a British infantry brigade from Kenya had restored the Sultan's authority at Nazwa, its surroundings and the important communications. Talib and his partners had withdrawn into the remote heights of the Djebel. Then in mid-1958 the trouble flared up again. From his mountain retreat Talib's patrols would set forth to attack isolated posts of the Sultan's Government and would mine the roads and tracks round the Djebel. Although the Sultan's army received some reinforcements from the Royal Marines and the Trucial Oman Scouts, it was becoming clear that in the end only an assault on the Djebel stronghold itself would ever scotch the snake. A number of plans made their appearance and were rejected. At last a good one came up. Frank Kitson has recorded that he had already put forward ideas gleaned from his previous experiences in Kenya where he had put together counter-gangs of surrendered Mau Mau to take on the terrorist gangs themselves. Why should not a similar way of doing things work in Oman? Selected officers would position themselves in the villages surrounding the Djebel, find out when some of Talib's men would be emerging, ambush and capture some of them, persuade them to change their allegiance, eventually get some teams on to the plateau of the Djebel itself, and then start sorting out Talib's irregulars. The difficulty that Kitson encountered was in getting hold of the right men to start the whole thing off. Then the Director of Military Operations, for whom Kitson worked, thought of the S.A.S. As the Malayan Emergency was nearly over and it had been decided to bring them home where they could be held ready to do comparable tasks elsewhere in the world, why not, so argued the D.M.O., use ready-made teams for this new purpose?

Of course, the country was very different from the jungles of Malaya. The Djebel Akhdar plateau was roughly twelve miles by eighteen miles in extent at an average height of 6,500 feet above sea level. It was surrounded by mountain peaks which rose even higher, up to some 10,000 feet. This meant that to get to the plateau it was necessary to go through narrow passes, mere tracks, dominated by high, inhospitable ground on either side, almost designed for ambush. Moreover there were very few tracks running through these mountain passes to the plateau. A few determined soldiers could laugh to scorn siege and assault by an entire army. It was reminiscent of the Great Game played between the British Army and the Pathan tribesmen on the North-West frontier of India. But the D.M.O.'s idea sounded sufficiently promising for a meeting to be arranged in Aden between the Commander British Forces there, Kitson himself and the Commanding Officer of 22 S.A.S., Lieutenant-Colonel Deane-Drummond, a man who possessed all the daring, dedication and determination inherent to the S.A.S. soldier, but who was perhaps deficient in the elegant and philosophical persuasiveness which David Stirling had so personified. The performance of Deane-Drummond and his men in capturing the Djebel Akhdar was decisive.

Deane-Drummond considered that, in spite of the very extensive reconnaissance that would be necessary to mount an operation, there was a good chance of killing Talib before the hot weather set in in April the following year, and that even if Talib's elimination were not achieved, it would be possible to 'condition' the rebels' frame of mind to such an extent that negotiations could be successfully concluded. He gave the task to D Squadron which had a total strength of seventy men. It was ready to move from Malaya by 15 November, 1958.

D Squadron, commanded by Major John Watts,* arrived in Oman on 18 November. Deane-Drummond was there too. In consultation with Colonel David Smiley, Chief of Staff to the Sultan's Armed Forces, plans for patrolling and blocking exits from the Djebel were made. It soon became clear to the S.A.S. that night operations were going to be more attractive than moving about by day. One veteran, Corporal Duke Swindells, was shot dead by a rebel sniper as he moved forward up a ridge of the mountain. Despite advice by the Sultan's own experienced officers, therefore, D Squadron began its programme of reconnoitring by night. Quite apart from the new freedom of movement they thereby gained, they also avoided the heat and consequent exhaustion of daytime operations. And soon they met with some success.

On the northern side of the Djebel two troops under Captain Rory Walker, guided by one of the locals, managed to reach the top of the mountain at a twin peak, later nicknamed Sabrina, and established themselves in sangars on the plateau, only 3,000 yards away from a rebel position. Before long they were attacked by groups of Talib's

---

* Who later commanded 22 S.A.S., the entire S.A.S. Group and the Sultan's Armed Forces.

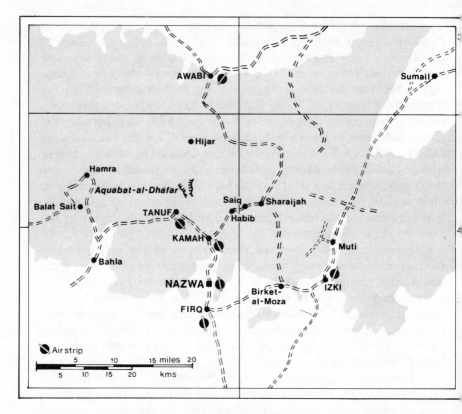

men, but by holding their fire until the enemy were a mere hundred yards away, an S.A.S. group commanded by Sergeant Hawkins was able to account for nine rebels and disperse the rest. Walker actually raided the peaks of Sabrina on another occasion. Although detected on the way to the summit and fired on, Walker was able to hurl a grenade over the top while engaged in climbing a rope. This not only killed a rebel who was firing at him, but enabled Walker and his group to reach the top and engage more of the rebel tribesmen, killing a further eight of them. Thus was a foothold on the northern side of the plateau made and maintained.

Meanwhile there was more S.A.S. activity on the Djebel's southern slopes. A reconnaissance patrol had discovered a rebel cave used by them to block any attempt to reach the plateau by that route. The cave was also a weapon and ammunition cache, just the sort of target likely to appeal to the S.A.S. Another future commander of both 22 S.A.S. and the whole Group, Peter de la Billière, was in charge of one troop which made a long and difficult night approach through country normally controlled by the rebels in order to be able to achieve surprise as to the direction from which their attack on the cave would come. With their guns and a rocket-launcher they got themselves to a position a few hundred yards from the mouth of the cave and at the same time within view of other caves in the upper slopes of the mountain from which enemy snipers could conveniently engage them. But surprise was achieved and when at dawn the rebels woke, they were greeted with a stream of rockets and machine-gun bullets. The calibre of Talib's men was evident from their being undismayed by this unexpected attack. There was no question of panic or surrender. They simply got themselves into fire positions and coolly engaged the attacking S.A.S. party as best they could. What is more, rifle fire was directed at de la Billière's men from the mountain slopes above. Yet the S.A.S. were able to get in some telling shots against retiring rebels, and had also laid on an air strike against rebel positions, one of which made a spectacularly successful direct hit on an enemy mortar and its crew. Nonetheless it was necessary for the S.A.S. to effect a fighting withdrawal to high ground held by their own people, with excellent covering fire being provided by another veteran, 'Tankie' Smith, wielding a Browning machine-gun. It was all very different from the jungle in which they had been operating such a short time earlier. At night it was cold, by day the wind hardly stopped. But at least there was some actual fighting to do. Daring and winning were once more on the menu.

All these preliminary actions, which took place in December, 1958, and involved other British troops from the Life Guards, Royal Corps of Signals and R.E.M.E. as well as the Trucial Oman Scouts and the Sultan's own forces, did little more than whet the appetite of both the S.A.S. and the rebel tribesmen. It was clear that more men would be needed if the plateau were actually to be cleared of Talib's men. After some discussion, during which Colonel Smiley expressed the view that the campaign could hardly be brought to a successful conclusion with present resources before the beginning of the hot weather in April, it was agreed that a second squadron of S.A.S. should be sent for from Malaya, and tactical command of the next operation was given to Deane-Drummond.

It was a classic battle of practising deception and seizing tactical opportunity. It was also a further demonstration of what superlative physical and mental hardness could do. The broad idea was that there would be feints on the northern and western sides of the Djebel, while the main assault would be made from the south-west. The newly arrived *A* Squadron under John Cooper (David Stirling's driver in the desert) started with an operation against the twin-peaked Sabrina in the middle of January, while a comparable advance was made from Tanuf, which was some eight miles further south. The word was also circulated in local circles, from which its passing on to the rebels could more or less be guaranteed, that the principal thrust would be coming from the area of Tanuf. Meanwhile *D* Squadron, part of which had been reinforcing the feinting activities, was assembling to the south of the Djebel, for after much consultation and study of air photographs, a kind of route along the top of a ridge, not even a track, but which led from the village of Kamah, held by the Sultan's soldiers, up into the Djebel, had been chosen by the S.A.S. commanders as the way for the main assault. A reconnaissance of this route carried out by one of Peter de la Billière's groups had discovered, about three-quarters of the way up what was a 4,000 foot climb, a small machine-gun post with a .5 inch Browning and its two-man crew, fortunately asleep.

It seemed at this time as if the deception was succeeding, for whereas large numbers of rebels were in the areas of Sabrina and Tanuf, the southern side, where the assault was about to go in, had far fewer. But there was still an important decision to be made, for it appeared to Deane-Drummond and Johnny Watts that if they pursued their way upwards with their full loads of rucksacks and ammunition, they might well be caught at sunrise short of the summit and overlooked by an ambushing enemy. They therefore chose to lighten their loads to minimum weapons and ammunition and make a dash for the top. It took on something of the nature of a race towards the end, but it worked. Among those who got there first were Deane-Drummond, Watts and de la Billière. A rapid consolidation of their hold on the summit was followed at first light by the pre-arranged air strike and supply drop by the Royal Air Force, which had the effect of convincing the enemy that an airborne assault was in progress. They melted away leaving large hauls of weapons, ammunition and documents. As Frank Kitson put it: 'The Djebel was captured and the rebellion came to an end. Unfortunately the rebel leaders made good their escape to Saudi Arabia.' There was nothing unusual in rebels escaping in that part of the world.

These are the bare bones of the operation. But its complexities and difficulties can only be understood by looking at it in more detail, and what follows is an extract from a report written by Major J.S. Spreule on the final assault:

D–Day 26 January, 1959. Both Sqns were in camp at Tanuf. Donkeys and handlers brought from the Aqabat under animal transport officer provided

36 Captain Peter de la Billière and Major Johnny Watts on top of the Djebel Akhdar, Oman, January, 1959.

37 Captain Walker, standing on right, opposite Suleiman's Cave after the assault on the Djebel Akhdar.

38 16 and 17 Troops, D Squadron, on the Aqbat el Dhuffar, Oman, 28 December, 1958.

39 .5 in Browning machine gun fired by Sergeant 'Tanky' Smith supporting the cave raid on the Djebel Akhdar, December, 1958.

40 A Royal Navy Wessex helicopter flying over typical jungle terrain in Borneo. (*Imperial War Museum*)

41 Sergeant Lillico on patrol in Borneo, 1966. He was awarded the MM after an action against Indonesian troops in which he was badly wounded. (*Soldier Magazine*)

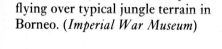

42 A 22 SAS patrol returns to a jungle outpost in Borneo. (*Imperial War Museum*)

43 The Tanuf Slab – Djebel Akhdar,

of the sort of country in which 22 SAS operated in 1958/9.

44 Major Peter de la Billière, OC A Squadron, after a patrol in the Radfan Mountains, Aden, May, 1964.

45 Royal Navy Wessex helicopters flying over typical Radfan terrain. In the background is the Djebel Huriyah. (*Imperial War Museum*)

46 Sergeant Geordie Tasker at Thumier, Aden, immediately after returning from the patrol on which Captain Robin Edwards was killed, April, 1964.

47 A Bren-gunner of 22 SAS in the Radfan Mountains, Aden.

48 A patrol signaller in Borneo.
One of the brave and
invaluable Fijian soldiers who
joined the SAS. (*Soldier
Magazine*)

49 Geordie Shipley in Borneo.

50 Major Peter de la Billière talking to Lieut-General Sir Charles Harington,
C-in-C Mideast, during operations in the Radfan. Lieut-Colonel John
Woodhouse is on the left, Major-General John Cubbon in the centre.

by the Trucial Oman Scouts were at Tanuf. All ranks were briefed by
Colonel Deane-Drummond in the morning. The donkeys left at 1000 hrs
to walk to the donkey assembly area at Kamah Camp. Both Sqns left
Tanuf in transport and arrived at Kamah after last light at 1930 hrs.
Troops debussed in the assembly area where there was half an hour's wait
for the moon to rise. The Sqns then re-embussed and were driven to the
start line. The start line was crossed as planned at 2030 hrs. Owing to a
strike by donkey handlers, the F echelon donkeys, which were to follow *A*
Sqn and precede the Commander's HQ party, failed to arrive at the
appointed time. These 25 donkeys, 10 for each Sqn and 5 for HQ, were
to carry the Sqns' Browning machine-guns and ammunition and HQ's
wirelesses. The donkeys eventually followed 15 minutes behind the Commander's party. At 2030 hrs the diversionary attack by 4 Troop was put
in. This could be heard by the assaulting troops. The climb was without
incident, but the going was harder than expected. A few unfit or overladen
soldiers were left behind to make their own way, while the Sqns pushed
on.

27 January. By 0500 hrs 27 Jan progress had been slower than expected.
A Sqn was in position on VINCENT, but *D* Sqn had one troop on PYRAMID
and three troops bunched round the point where it was thought a track
began to lead to BEERCAN. It was vital to reach the top – BEERCAN – by first
light and so *D* Sqn commander made two troops leave all their extra loads
behind and push on. They reached BEERCAN at approx 0630 hrs. By 0645
hrs the first of the Valletas began the re-supply drop. ... The troops were
too exhausted after 10 hrs almost continuous climbing to do more than
collect sufficient ammunition to hold off an expected counter-attack. At
0700 hrs they were joined by the Commander's party carrying equipment,
with an Air Liaison Officer and ground to air radio. The third troop was
left to deal with a rebel .5 machine-gun team which they did by 0630 hrs.
They then moved up the ridge arriving at 0800 hrs. The .5 machine-gun
was in a perfect position commanding all approaches. Had it been manned,
the outcome might have been very different. During the morning snipers
in caves to the east put up desultory fire at troops on the machine-gun
position and on troops moving to BEERCAN. These snipers were attacked by
Venoms and were not eventually silenced until about 1430 hrs after holding
up the leading troop of *A* Sqn, which reached BEERCAN by midday. A
grenade, exploded by a chance shot, wounded Troopers Carter, Hamer
and Bembridge. Carter and Bembridge later died of their wounds. By 1500
hrs the last troop of *D* Sqn on PYRAMID was relieved by the Life Guards
and rejoined its Sqn at 1630 hrs. At 2130 *D* Sqn moved to occupy a feature
overlooking the Kamah Wadi, leaving *A* Sqn to hold BEERCAN. The Com-

mander went with *D* Sqn and later returned to BEERCAN. *A* Sqn sent a troop reconnaissance patrol out at last light to the village of Habib. In the event it went to an unmarked village on the far side of Nantos because of an inaccuracy of the map. Going was difficult and the village was reported deserted.

28 January. *D* Sqn took an airdrop and later pushed forward to a feature overlooking Kamah Wadi. *A* Sqn collected previous airdrops and accepted further drops. Offensive air support against rebels throughout the day ... a 62-set was manpacked from PYRAMID and with this the Forward Observation Officer was able to range the guns. A request was made to begin psychological warfare. 15 Tribals arrived and spent the night on BEERCAN. On the night 28/29 Jan *D* Sqn with Sqn HQ and two troops occupied a feature which overlooked the village of Habib. The same night half *A* Sqn occupied a feature called Nantos 1,500 yards in front of BEERCAN.

29 January. *D* Sqn now had positions overlooking the Kamah Wadi and Habib. They took an airdrop at 1100 hrs. Half *A* Sqn was on Nantos, the other half on BEERCAN. Colonel Deane-Drummond with his HQ accompanied a patrol of *D* Sqn which together with 15 Tribals entered Habib at 1200 hrs. The village was deserted and had been damaged by bombing. *A* Sqn troops on Nantos detained 38 Arabs including women and children. They were sent under escort to BEERCAN for interrogation where a PW compound was set up.

30 January. Colonel Smiley and Said Tariq, Wali of Nazwa, landed at BEERCAN by helicopter and spoke to prisoners, who were later released. Half of *A* Sqn joined half of *D* Sqn, and together they occupied the village of Saiq. Later HQ was helicoptered to Saiq, which was deserted. A number of prisoners were taken and Suleiman's cave was located and searched. Vast quantities of documents and a substantial number of weapons were collected. A further supply drop took place at Saiq. Some prisoners were taken at Sharaijah, and a number of Talib's manacled prisoners released.

31 January. One troop of *D* Sqn was left at Saiq, while two Troops of *A* Sqn, one Troop of *D* Sqn, Sqn HQ and the Commander's Tactical HQ moved to Sharaijah. All resistance on the Djebel had ceased, except for a few minor pockets on the south slopes. These were dealt with by S.A.S. and Sultan's Armed Forces. S.A.S. troops started work on landing strip between Saiq and Sharaijah. A report was received that Talib and Suleiman were in the Wadi Salut area with their families. A party of *A* and *D* Sqn troops from Sharaijah searched south and a composite patrol from HQ searched north from Mi'aidin. The search was fruitless and was abandoned on 1 Feb.

There was little more to be done. Some other villages and caves were searched, the collection of arms, ammunition and documents continued, the airfield at Saiq was proved by a Twin Pioneer. Then, on a report that rebels had been seen in the villages of Biddah and Muti, further searches took place. The area was deserted. On 5 February the last of these searches was called off, S.A.S. troops were withdrawn from the Djebel and the HQ at Nazwa closed down. Some small rear parties were required to bring ammunition down from the Djebel by donkey, but, apart from this, by the following day the S.A.S. troops who had so successfully dealt with the Djebel Akhdar were enjoying a rest at the base camp. They may not have caught Talib. They had certainly seen him off. Many decorations for gallantry were awarded to the S.A.S for this brilliant operation.

One of those who was awarded the Military Cross for his part in the action was Tony Jeapes,* who like many other members of the S.A.S. returned to Oman again and again. Writing in 1980 about his experiences in the long Dhofar campaign of the 1970s, he recalled briefly his first acquaintance with the Green Mountain:

> The Djebel Akhdar rose straight out of the desert to a height of seven thousand feet and there were only a certain number of routes up it. These, of course, were guarded and it took a month of probing and skirmishing until an unguarded route was found. Then, after a feint squadron night attack in the north to draw the enemy's attention and reserves in that direction, the two squadrons of S.A.S. climbed the Djebel in one night from the south. It was a hard, long climb and only just accomplished. The leading troops dropped their bergen rucksacks and pushed on, carrying only their rifles and belt equipment to reach the crest just at first light. Had the squadrons been caught in the low ground still climbing up those bare slopes at dawn it might have been a very different story. As it was, there was very little opposition. My own troop accounted for four who tried to hold us up; one did a spectacular Hollywood-style death dive over a sheer cliff. Another troop killed the crew of a heavy machine-gun in a cave with hand grenades; but that was all. Once the squadrons had consolidated on top and had taken a parachute re-supply of water and ammunition, the rebels gave up and the three leaders fled for shelter to Saudi Arabia.

Before returning to Southern Arabia and dealing, not only with Oman, but also with what happened in Aden and the Radfan it is now neces-

---

* I had the good fortune when commanding 39 Brigade to have Tony Jeapes as my Brigade Major. With his guidance we did our best to turn Brigade Headquarters into a kind of S.A.S. squadron. The men loved it.

sary for the sake of chronology to go further east once more and take a look at what Sukarno's declaration of confrontation with Malaysia brought about in the jungles and rivers of Borneo. It was clear that there was going to be no shortage of jobs for the S.A.S.

16

CONFRONTATION

The year 1962 was a vitally important and eventful one for Sarawak. It saw rapid progress towards the realization of the Malaysia concept which would bring the country independence in an association of democratic states in South-East Asia and, unfortunately, the close of the year saw the outbreak of the tragic and futile rebellion in Brunei which caused serious disturbances and loss of life in the adjoining areas of Sarawak.

Sarawak Annual Report

The abortive Brunei rebellion of December, 1962, was followed by a declaration by President Sukarno of Indonesia of 'confrontation' – a military and political attempt to disrupt the planned formation of Malaysia. I had the good fortune to take over command of my Regiment at the beginning of 1963 just as the Borneo campaign was getting under way. From my headquarters in Kuching as Commander British Forces West Sarawak, I was required to ensure the security of the 1st, 2nd and 3rd Divisions, a huge area which had 750 miles of border with Kalimantan or Indonesian Borneo. The threat to West Sarawak was twofold: external, that is incursions from Kalimantan by Indonesian-led guerrillas, some of whom were the remnants of Azahari's Brunei rebels and others were Indonesian soldiers; and internal, from the so-called Clandestine Communist Organization, which numbered anything from ten to twenty thousand.

To do this I had one squadron of my Regiment, equipped with armoured cars, a company of infantry supplied by the Royal Marines, a few administrative elements, two Royal Navy minesweepers, two Auster aircraft *and* a squadron of the S.A.S. – a mere three hundred troops in all. The task for the S.A.S. was clear – surveillance and intelligence gathering, for, with so lengthy a frontier and so few troops, it was necessary to conserve my limited infantry and armoured cars to the role of securing certain key communication centres and patrolling widely, by road, by river [Sarawak is a country of rivers] using the long boats, and by penetrating the jungle on foot. In this way we hoped to reassure the local people and, together with the police intelligence system, learn enough about what was going on to deter those who might put either the external or internal threats into operation. It was also agreed early on that we should re-establish a force of Sarawak Rangers for patrol and intelligence activities.

However, the S.A.S. squadron commander, who had set up his headquarters in the renowned Tom Harrisson's house in Kuching, earnestly reminded me that his men were trained in intimidation. Was there anyone whom I would like intimidated? In fact there was one, but as this person was an official of the Sarawak administration whose attitude to the whole question of seizing and keeping the initiative was less robust than was in my view desirable, I restrained myself and assured the S.A.S. squadron commander that I would bear this particular capability in mind. His squadron deployed itself near the frontier and began its task of surveillance, intelligence gathering and the so-called 'Hearts and Minds' campaign, so necessary to win the loyalty of the Sarawak peoples and so dear to the Director of Operations in Borneo, the famous and brilliant jungle fighter, Major-General Walter Walker. The campaign was waged to bind the local people to our way of thinking with hoops made of kindness, medical supplies, radios, moving people and things about, and generally giving help in a thousand ways.

Having visited all my outposts, taken the invaluable advice of that great expert on Sarawak affairs and curator of the Kuching Museum, Tom Harrisson, made myself known to the various civil administrators and policemen of Sarawak's 1st, 2nd and 3rd Divisions, and attended regular conferences held by the Governor in Kuching and General Walker in Brunei, I put in an eloquent plea for some helicopters, was refused and then awaited the moment when their indispensability would be demonstrated. It was not long in coming. Early on the morning of 12 April, 1963, a Good Friday, as I was shaving in my room in the building we used as a mess, the Sarawak Steamship Company's villa, my Adjutant burst in and announced that a group of some thirty guerrillas had crossed the border at Tebedu, a village twenty-five miles from Serian in the 1st Division, had killed a few policemen and generally looted and terrorized the place. Had I, the Adjutant asked, any immediate instructions? After ensuring that the proper messages had been sent and the proper people alerted, I sensed that it was

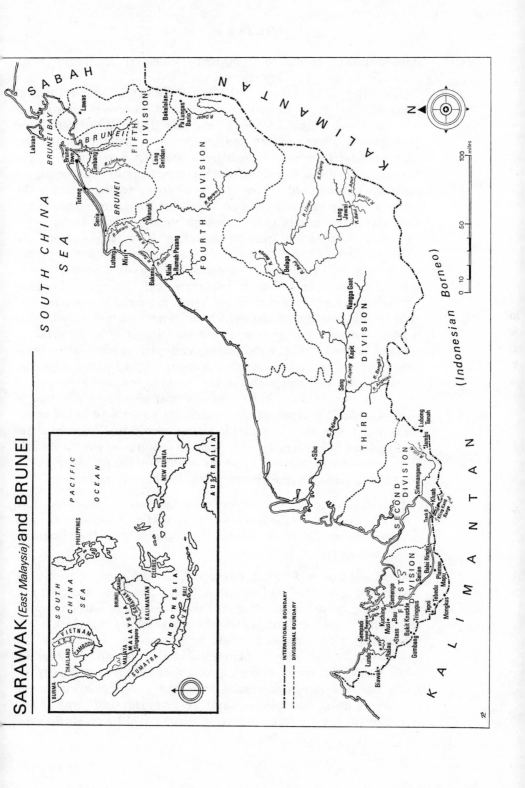

SARAWAK (*East Malaysia*) and BRUNEI

important to say something for posterity: 'Please arrange for my breakfast to be served in the Operations Room'.

The situation in Tebedu was restored by despatching a troop of Royal Marines there, yet never was the lack of helicopters more keenly felt, for it was a long drive over very poor tracks. What could have been done in a mere twenty minutes took more like four hours. But soon after the Tebedu raid, intelligence from S.A.S., police and other sources as to the likelihood of further incursions by Indonesian-led guerrillas concentrated my mind. It was confirmed by Sigint – the information we received through various radio transmissions which were picked up and processed through various special signal units. Moreover there were disquieting indications from the police and the civil administrators that 'some of the natives were restless', in other words that the Clandestine Communist Organization were about to make their presence and their grievances felt. Having by this time persuaded General Walker to let me have a few naval helicopters – the skill, courage and commitment of whose officers and men were beyond praise – we were able to step up our patrol activity in the sense of covering far more ground and making each platoon seem like a company. But the imminence and the measure of further enemy action seemed to be such that with the few hundred men we had to make secure so vast an area, it was unlikely that any reasonable sort of success could be guaranteed. Fortunately the police were in full agreement and I was able to persuade the Governor that substantial reinforcements were necessary if he were to continue to govern the first three divisions of Sarawak. For the only time in my life I sent a FLASH signal to General Headquarters, Far East. It read:

> In view of likely further incursions from Kalimantan and probability of C.C.O. insurgency, I have recommended to H.E. The Governor, who agrees with me, the instant despatch of a brigade of troops from Singapore to ensure the security of Sarawak.

Like an eagle in a dovecote this signal had the gratifying effect of fluttering a number of staff officers in GHQ Singapore, and next day a posse of generals and other senior fellows arrived in Kuching, courtesy of the Royal Air Force, to talk the matter over. Before long it was agreed that HMS *Bulwark* would bring a substantial part of 3rd Commando Brigade, Royal Marines, and the rest would follow by other means. So began a gradual escalation of military activity by either side, the Indonesians using more and more regular units, our own forces being strengthened until we eventually had some 15,000 troops in Borneo – infantry mainly, but supported by armoured cars, light aircraft, gunners, sappers, signals and all the logistic units, to say nothing of the huge and continuous support given by the Royal Navy and Royal Air Force. It was in many ways a most interesting and satisfactory war – plenty of excitement and interest, not too many casualties and a military success which led to a political result, greatly valued by all – the fall of Sukarno. Throughout the campaign the S.A.S. played their unique part.

Their initial tasks are best described by those who were on the spot at the time. I have already explained what I asked the squadron under my command to do, but here in a letter dated 1 February, 1963, is what John Woodhouse had to report to the Commander of 3 Division, stationed on Salisbury Plain, under whose administrative direction, but *not* operational control, 22 S.A.S. Regiment came:

> We have had orders to deploy a further six patrols close to the frontier. Two of these are south of Kuching; the other four will be in North Borneo. Their role is limited at present to recce, and collecting information from local tribes. The latter, of course, involves language ability and using our medical capabilities where necessary to win their confidence. In the event of small scale enemy infiltration from Indonesian Borneo, they will first report it and then either attack if enemy are weak, or wait to receive helicopter or parachute reinforcements and guide them to the enemy. Patrols have been ordered to recce DZs and LZs for reinforcements far enough away from their locations to avoid enemy discovering the drop or landing and near enough to be reached by the patrol within 2 or 3 hours ...
>
> In all cases so far patrols are near friendly Iban settlements. They have money to pay trackers and can live off the land by buying rice and catching fish ... The rebel situation, I assume, will be known to you in outline from the intelligence summaries. They are a feeble collection. The difficulties of infiltrating guerrillas from Kalimantan [Indonesian Borneo] to Brunei are mainly topographical. It takes 2–4 weeks to walk from the frontier to target areas. By river it would be quicker but insecure ... The civil population [Woodhouse was referring here to the people of Brunei, not of Sarawak or North Borneo] is still largely pro-rebel, but they are not the stuff of which revolutionary soldiers are made ... We shall get valuable training and experience in radio communications, administrative support of widely spread detachments, medicine, Malay language and of working with and getting the confidence of the native people.

Harry Thompson, writing from Brunei to John Woodhouse, explained a week later how he was getting on, and how like everyone else who came into contact with the great Tom Harrisson, whose knowledge of and concern for the Iban tribes was unrivalled, he had to pull his punches from time to time. Having told Harrisson that he would like to go and see some of the special surveillance groups that Harrisson had deployed near the border, Thompson was slightly taken aback when Tom blew another gasket. 'I thought at least,' observed Harry, 'that he'd have some respect for my age – I took off my hat deliberately!' [Harry Thompson, who was not only a marvellous S.A.S. soldier, but one of the nicest men going, was undeniably bald.] His letter went on:

> Ray England's 4 groups are all in position, and some interesting information on C.C.O. meetings in the area. They appear to be trying to organize the masses for an armed struggle in that area [Sarawak] ... I flew to Jesselton the other day and in conjunction with Colonel Sweeney, 1st Green Jackets, Commissioner of Police, and John Warne, arranged the locations [N. Borneo]. The deployment is now in process and is an involved one. Sandilands is in Tawau and moves to his location on 10 February. Two patrols fly to Sapalut tomorrow and are physically put in position and briefed by John Warne. He is an excellent chap. Parachuted in here during the war ... he visits on his flat feet over vast areas. He hit it off with all of us immediately ... briefed all our patrols [which] are moving into position on ponies, on bicycles, mainly on foot. The Governor, Goode, a pretty sharp nut, is adamant we keep well away from the border ... This whole area is fascinating ... We all move to the Haunted House tomorrow. Praise be!

During the Borneo campaign the value of S.A.S. troops was such that not only were they everywhere in demand, but other regiments of the British Army became anxious to get in on the act. In September, 1964, we find Mike Wingate-Gray writing to John Woodhouse about the way to meet future requirements – it being assumed at the time that certain Far East and Middle East commitments would persist. Of the nine squadrons proposed, three were regular S.A.S. Squadrons, two were from the Brigade of Gurkhas [whose performance in Borneo was, as everywhere else, second to none], three from the Parachute Brigade, and one was the Guards Independent Company, which survives now as *G* Squadron, 22 S.A.S.

At about this time too the S.A.S.'s role was changing. John Woodhouse had been pressing General Walker and others for agreement to take the war across the border, to discover where the Indonesian raiding parties were, disrupt their preparations, ambush their patrols and generally complete the domination of the border areas. He also wished to continue keeping friendly contacts with the Muruts and

Kelabits, to use the S.A.S.'s language and medical skills for continuing to win hearts and minds, and of course persist with surveillance and getting intelligence. This variety and abundance of roles were what necessitated participation by other parts of the Army. As Woodhouse wrote to Napier Crookenden in September: 'We are changing our role to recce and offensive operations in Kalimantan and expanding our guerrilla support operations [Woodhouse meant disrupting this support]. The Gurkha Parachute Company and their relief from the Parachute Regiment will probably continue the Border surveillance role.' In the same month Woodhouse's letter to Mike Wingate-Gray spoke enthusiastically about this new role: 'We are allowed 5 miles for *attributable* operations, ie. we can bash anything up to this range. *A* Sqn should have five patrols for cross-border ops by end of month ... Gurkhas killed at least twelve at Nantukor in a really good deliberate attack on their base'. As if all this were not enough, Woodhouse tells Wingate-Grey that he is sending an Arabic speaker, Jenks, plus ten men from *D* Squadron to reach Aden by 6 November. Borneo was still not the only place where the S.A.S. were doing their stuff.

But one of their most valuable contributions undoubtedly came about when these so-called 'cross-border operations' were eventually authorized by Whitehall. There had long been pressure by those on the ground, particularly General Walker, to do the obvious thing – not simply sit back and wait for the Indonesian patrols to cross into Sarawak or North Borneo [now Sabah] to make their raids and get their information, but to take the initiative, cross into Kalimantan, find out where the Indonesian camps were, what routes they were using to cross over the border and generally disrupt their capability. Indeed as early as 1963, when I had the good fortune to discuss the whole situation on the ground with John Woodhouse and Harry Thompson [soon after tragically killed in a helicopter crash with two other S.A.S. men*], even then we had asked ourselves the time-honoured question – how to dominate the border areas? The answer was clear enough, but there was a curious reluctance in Whitehall to acknowledge that, despite no declaration to that effect, British and Indonesian soldiers were at war with each other. By 1964, however, although with tight control being exercised from the Ministry of Defence, General Walker was authorized to mount operations across the border, all such actions being given the overall codename 'Claret'. It was appropriate enough, as a good deal of blood was spilled. The S.A.S. patrols were usually involved, not always successfully, as one particular action, admirably

* Including Major Ron Norman, the Regiment's 2 i/c

recorded in the Regimental Journal, *Mars and Minerva*, showed:

On a recent February morning [1965] a small SAS patrol was moving down from a ridge on a jungle track towards an old Indonesian Border Terrorist camp. This camp had been found the day before and appeared as though it had not been used for some six months. As the leading scout, Trooper Thompson, ducked under some bamboo across the track – there was a lot of it in the area – a movement attracted his attention. He looked up and saw an Indonesian soldier six yards away to his right, just as the latter fired a burst at him. Several other enemy opened fire simultaneously. Thompson was hit in the left thigh, the bone being shattered, and was knocked off the track to the left. He landed in a clump of bamboo two yards away from another Indonesian soldier lying concealed there. As the latter fumbled for his rifle, Thompson picked up his own, which he had dropped as he fell, and shot him.

The second man in the patrol, the commander, Sergeant Lillico, was also hit by the initial bursts and had collapsed on the track, unable to use his legs. He was still able to use his rifle, however, and this he did, returning the fire. The remainder of the patrol had meanwhile taken cover. Thompson, unable to walk, hopped back to where Sergeant Lillico was sitting and joined in the fire fight. As he had seen Thompson on his feet, Sergeant Lillico was under the misapprehension that he could walk and therefore sent him back up the track to bring the rest of the patrol forward and continued to fire at sounds of enemy movement.

As Thompson was unable to get to his feet he dragged himself along by his hands and, on arriving at the top of the ridge, fired several bursts in the direction of the IBT camp. Whether the enemy thought that this fire came from reinforcements moving into the area is not known, but about this time, some ten minutes after the initial contact, they apparently withdrew. During the remainder of the day Thompson continued to drag himself towards where he expected to find the rest of the patrol. He had applied a tourniquet to his thigh, which he released from time to time, taken morphia, and bandaged his wound as best he could with a shell dressing.

After sounds of enemy movement had died down, Sergeant Lillico pulled himself into the cover of a clump of bamboo, took morphia, bandaged his wound, and passed out until mid-afternoon. He awoke to hear the sound of a helicopter overhead. Realizing that it would never find him amongst the bamboo he decided, in the morning, to drag himself to the top of the ridge which was covered in low scrub. The balance of the patrol had decided that the best course of action was to move to the nearest infantry post, close by, and lead back a stronger party to search the area. This they did, starting back towards the scene of the contact late the same day.

The following morning Thompson continued on his way and by evening had covered 1,000 yards, about half the total distance he had to cover. However, soon after he had stopped for the night, a short while before last light, he heard the search party and was found about 1800 hours. An attempt was made to winch him out by helicopter but this failed due to the height of the trees. The next day, therefore, he was carried to a larger clearing nearby and was successfully evacuated at 0930, 48 hours after the contact.

Meanwhile, Sergeant Lillico had dragged himself to the ridge as he had planned – a distance of 400 yards – and on arriving there at 1500 hours, had fired some signal shots to attract the attention of the search party which he expected to be looking for him. These were immediately answered by three bursts of automatic fire some few hundred yards distant. Not by the search party, however, which at that time was too far away to have heard him firing. He therefore hid in the scrub as best he could and was able both to hear and see the enemy looking for him. One man climbed a tree about forty yards away and remained there for about half-an-hour in full view as he looked around and about.

While this was going on, he heard a helicopter close by but because of the enemy's nearness and obvious risk to the aircraft, he decided to make no use of the means at his disposal to attract it towards him. Not until the observer climbed down from his tree was he able to drag himself further away from the enemy and out into the scrub. The helicopter, continuing its search operation, returned in the early evening. This time he signalled to it and without delay it flew over, lowered the winch and lifted him out. In all, a rescue operation reflecting great credit on both RAF and Infantry, but most of all on Sergeant Lillico and Trooper Thompson for their courage and determination not to give in.

For this action Lillico was awarded the Military Medal and Thompson was mentioned in despatches. Once more the S.A.S. had shown that exceptional men could perform exceptional feats of gallantry and fortitude. The effect of their activities in Borneo had once again the benefit of focusing the eyes of those in Whitehall on the need for enough of them. With *A* and *D* Squadrons both having seen service in Borneo and HQ 22 S.A.S. in the so-called Haunted House in Brunei, it was decided to raise *B* Squadron in England. Other units were also given the chance to learn something of S.A.S. techniques, including the Guards Parachute Company, which later provided a nucleus for forming the S.A.S.'s *G* Squadron, which still exists, and also the 2nd Battalion, Parachute Regiment, which has recently added the Goose Green affair to its many battle honours. Nor were the Australians and

New Zealanders left out, both of whom sent S.A.S. squadrons to Borneo. *Mars and Minerva* contains another passage which gives just the colour and authenticity which should be conveyed:

> The parts of Borneo they have seen and got to know intimately are as varied as nature and man's complexity could make them: swampland, deep forest, high mountains, barren hills, fertile valleys; up to twenty races and ethnic groups; as many languages and almost as many religions. In the east of North Borneo the mangrove-swamp-lined waterways give access to the sea and the piracy-ridden coast of the East Coast Residency. These waterways form a labyrinthine maritime Hampton Court maze through which a brisk smuggling trade flourishes and the likelihood of Indonesian infiltration persists. Patrols here are mainly waterborne and it was here that an S.A.S. patrol report included sighting an Indonesian submarine.
>
> From the mid-reaches of the Serudong and Kalabakan Rivers to the River Pagalluggan 154 miles westwards in the Interior Residency there stretches an area entirely uninhabited, uncharted and until July this year untraversed. This is an area of dense rain forest, where rivers rise twenty feet in a night, broken ridges rising to beyond 4,000 feet, great waterfalls and in which game of all kinds is as prevalent as man is absent. In a 31-day journey an S.A.S. patrol traversed and reconnoitred this area with complete success. The report produced was of permanent value. Air supply and a diet of monkeys and venison sustained the patrol throughout its journey.
>
> Patrols have ranged widely in the Interior Residency of North Borneo, amongst the tough, individualistic Muruts. Here, to the accompaniment of frequent pulls at the *tapai* jar (containing rice wine) and finger-fulls of rancid fish, the tall tales of the Japanese occupation are still heard. Murut attacks on retreating Japanese columns were effective and many a shrivelled head still nods from the eaves of the long-house roof. Many of the Regiment will long remember 'Murutania' with affection, and already the doings of the long-haired *Orang Puteh*, the white men, are finding their way into the Murut folk-lore.
>
> The oil state of Brunei saw us frequently, but after the initial stages of the rebellion and the swift retribution that followed, our eyes were turned mainly outwards towards the new threat on the borders of Sarawak and beyond. The Haunted House, one of two headquarters – for the squadron commander operated from two HQs as far apart as London and Edinburgh linked only by air – will long be remembered. Hidden away behind the Sultan's Palace in Brunei, it had just the right atmosphere of sinister seclusion. No one saw many of the snakes* reputed to plague it, and the

* To the disappointment of John Edwardes.

ghost of the pale, fair-haired girl said to have been tortured by the Japanese never materialized.

To Sarawak, and from the Ops Room amidst fairies at the bottom of Tom Harrisson's garden to the Kelabit Highlands of Bario, Long Banga and Bakelallan, to Belaga and the upper reaches of the Rajang, to the Ulu Katibas and the S.A.S.-reported gang now active there,* to the Ulu Ai, to Sibu, Song, Simanggang and to the Land Dyak country of the First Division – these are a series of giant strides across the doodle of rivers that encompass Kuching, west along the sparkling coastline and past the Turtle Islands to Tanjong Datu, or south and east across thousands of square miles of jungle – barren, broken and spent by Iban cultivation in the lower reaches of the 2nd and 3rd Divisions, or luxuriant and magnificent as elsewhere.

Over the long muddy tongues of rivers, almost endless, tortuous and yet life-sustaining for the long-houses echeloned along their banks. To more than a score of patrol locations, past and present, where in each, four men, living as members of the long-house itself for months at a time, watch, listen, patrol and report. Where, day by day, the sick come for treatment, the women to bring presents of fruit and vegetables, the men to gossip and bring news, the children to watch silent-eyed and the leaders of the community to discuss their problems and to ask for and offer advice. The patrol slips as easily into the primitive rhythm of the day and season as the people themselves; soon the cycle of burning, planting, weeding and harvesting becomes a part of life itself and customs, rites and celebrations as familiar as the Cup Final or Bank Holidays at home.

Here or there we may find one of the ten or more training camps established for the Border Scouts we have raised and trained. Here a strong patrol of five or six men will train ten or twenty times that number of tribesmen in counter-terrorist warfare. In each camp there is a simple long-house for the Scouts; a similar but smaller one for their instructors. The daily programme is long and arduous, though the syllabus is basic and directly related to the skills required to be taught. The patrol embraces all responsibilities for its charges: training, administration, discipline and morale. The language difficulty is ever present, even fluent Malay does not reach everyone, pantomime is popular and some are skilful exponents of the art: helicopter training without helicopters is a test-piece. Throwing live grenades presents other problems, but no pantomime is necessary.

There from the horse's mouth is an account of the various activities which the S.A.S. pursued in Borneo and which make up the story of

* This sketch of life in Borneo was written while the campaign was still in progress and S.A.S. men still deployed there.

how a combination of good intelligence, strong patrol bases, aggressive patrolling and ambushing, artillery plus helicopters did the trick.

It was in this way that the S.A.S. made their indispensable contribution to the successful waging of a campaign which lasted not quite four years. The British Army, together with their colleagues from Malaysia, Singapore, New Zealand and Australia, with major participation by the brave and brilliant Gurkha battalions and the local Scouts raised and trained by the S.A.S., had succeeded in both winning the hearts and minds of those they were defending and in dismaying a courageous and skilful enemy by mastering the problems of getting reliable intelligence and using it with speed, perseverance and an absolute determination to prevail. The result was a Malaysia freed from a danger which had threatened to strangle it at birth. The S.A.S.'s unique ability to combine local omnipotence with general omnipresence had done much to bring this about, and it was fitting that in the closing victorious stages of the campaign an S.A.S. officer, General George Lea, who had commanded 22 Regiment in Malaya years before, was the Director of Operations in Borneo.

17

ADEN AND THE DHOFAR

But there is neither East nor West, Border, nor Breed, nor Birth,
When two strong men stand face to face, though they come from
the ends of the earth.

Rudyard Kipling

There had been a certain irony about the Malaysian campaign. From the British point of view the formation of Malaysia was designed to secure tenure of a strategic base, promote political and racial unity and reduce our defence effort. Precisely the reverse was achieved as a result of Indonesia's confrontation and Singapore's secession from the federation. In military terms it had been a kind of study in escalation, albeit in a minor key. At its peak the Indonesians had threatened Malaysia with some 35,000 guerrilla or regular fighters – 20,000 in Kalimantan, 10,000 in Sumatra, 5,000 in Rhios. The British, with their Commonwealth and other friends, had deployed some 15,000 soldiers in Borneo to counter the threat there, but had retained far more powerful means of waging war in the hands of the Royal Navy and Royal Air Force to deter real escalation and available for use should this fail. The concept had been one of defeating minor and deterring major aggression. The skilled and determined activities of British, Australian, New Zealand, Malaysian, Singaporean, and of course the indispensable Gurkha troops had won the border war. Good intelligence, strong patrol bases, aggressive patrolling and ambushing, artillery plus helicopters had done the trick. Casualties had been light. The Indonesians had lost about 600 killed, 800 wounded, 200 captured; the British far fewer, more like 100 killed and 200 wounded. The coalition of a politically supportable objective and adequate military resources had ensured that Sukarno's ambitions had suffered a check which led to his own downfall and reasonably cordial relations between Malaysia and its great southern neighbour.

The campaigns in southern Arabia, one of which began while operations in Borneo were reaching their zenith, were to be very different, although some of the recipes for winning them were not. The first campaign was in essence a hesitant, half-hearted, almost humiliating exit from colonial rule; the second a protracted and triumphant exercise in winning the hearts and minds of actual and potential rebels away from the false claims of those who led a Communist-armed insurrection against the Sultan of Oman. In each case the result had much to do with whether or not the legitimate Government was likely to survive. Frank Kitson has pointed out that the key to eliminating subversion, whether armed or unarmed, is for the government concerned to gain control of the population. Just as those who are promoting subversion are seeking to control the people, so those eager to defeat subversion must do so. It follows that the government, if it is to realize this aim of control, must be seen as being likely to win. This was so both during the Malayan Emergency and Confrontation. But it was not so in Aden. And, as Kitson writes: 'Few individuals can possibly support a government which is obviously going to lose, even if they sympathize with its policies and detest those of the insurgents.' It was therefore necessary that the government's campaign was seen to be based on an absolute determination totally to destroy the subversive movement, and that if there were an eventual intention to hand over power to some other authority, it had to be made plain that this would not be done before that authority was powerful enough to prevent any serious renewal of subversion. This point was ignored by the British in Aden, and by announcing its intention of withdrawing from the country when it became independent in 1968, Britain forfeited any possibility of fulfilling the two conditions necessary to ensure the loyalty and support of moderate representatives of the people. The people of Aden did not doubt, when this announcement was made, that sooner of later the insurgents would get control of the country. In his book, *Last Post in Aden*, Julian Paget pointed out that it was 'a disastrous move from the point of view of the Security Forces, for it meant that from then onwards they inevitably lost all hope of any local support'. The hearts and minds campaign had been lost before it had started.

Mind you, in this part of southern Arabia the cards were heavily stacked against the British from the early 1960s onwards. The left-wing Army coup in North Yemen of 1962 had successfully overthrown the Imam, even though he and his royalist supporters, reversing the normal course of events, conducted a guerrilla campaign against the newly established Republic of North Yemen. Indeed in this campaign the Imam and his men were assisted by a number of former S.A.S.

members, including the renowned John Cooper, who has already appeared several times in these pages. But it was clear that the new North Yemen would not only be able to preserve their own revolution, but had every intention of exporting it to the south, declaring their support for the southern Yemen revolutionaries in their fight against colonialism. Support not only took the form of words, but plenty of guns, ammunition, and even, ironically enough, British mines, supplied to the Egyptians.

When you first catch sight of the barren rocks of Aden, whether approached by sea or air, it is unlikely to prepossess you with great affection for Arabia, no matter how deep your fascination with other parts of that great tract of desert, rock and mountain. Nor will the inescapable stink of natural gas burning at the waste funnels, which strikes you as you step ashore, change your mind. But get away from Aden or Little Aden, drive up the Dhala road towards the frontier with north Yemen, visit a frontier fort, or take a look from an Auster aircraft at the grim, dry, rocky mountains of the Radfan, and the magic at once returns. When it became clear that Britain's attempt to produce a federal link between Aden colony and the tribesmen of the sheikh-doms of the interior was going to meet fierce opposition – it was in December, 1963, that the Emergency there was formally declared – it also became clear that there would be two sorts of uprising to deal with, one among the Radfan tribesmen of the Protectorate, another from urban guerrillas in Aden itself. The S.A.S. were to be involved in both.

In April, 1964, *A* Squadron arrived at Khormaksar airfield. It had been agreed that the S.A.S. would assist other troops, including those of the Federal Regular Army, the Royal Marines, the Parachute Regiment, artillery, engineers and armoured cars, in re-establishing themselves in the Radfan. It was clear from the beginning that there was very little intelligence available about the nature of the country, whether there was any water or what sort of enemy they would be meeting. They were soon to find out that they would be taking on an enemy as hostile as the scorching, arid mountains themselves, for the Qotaibi tribe of Radfan were men who would endure terrible wounds and crawl away to die rather than surrender or be succoured by an enemy. Fanatically proud, independent and brave, the tribesmen had the additional advantage of fighting in territory where a few men could argue the toss with complete battalions.

All this notwithstanding, *A* Squadron instantly established itself at Thumier, a base some sixty miles north of Aden, just off the Dhala road near Habilayn airstrip, on the edge of the Radfan and about thirty

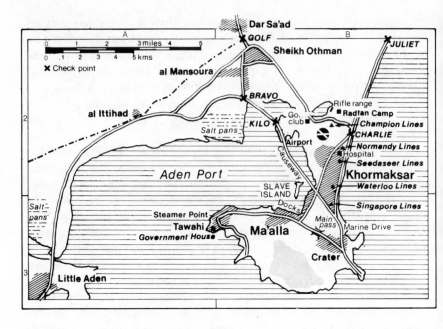

miles from the border with Yemen. They at once began proving patrols in preparation for the operation which was to 'bring sufficient pressure to bear on the Radfan tribes; to prevent the tribal revolt from spreading; and to stop attacks on the Dhala road'. Two mountain objectives were to be taken by the Royal Marines and the Parachute Regiment, and to assist the latter, an S.A.S. patrol would go out on the night of 29 April in order to establish and mark a dropping zone for the parachutists. The story of Captain Robin Edwards's ill-fated patrol has been told before, but it must have its place here too.

The aim of Edwards's nine-man patrol was to move up the Wadi Rabwa in armoured cars, then dismount and move on foot to their objective. In the event, although the intelligence boys had predicted light opposition, they came under fire almost at once while still mounted in the armoured cars. They therefore dismounted and made their way on foot, initially up the Wadi Rabwa, and then climbed the Djebel Ashqab, where Edwards decided to spend the night of 29 April in some old stone sangars where they could hide. All this was explained by radio to the base at Thumier, where another famous member of the S.A.S., Mike Wingate-Gray, was positioned. The patrol intended to lie up during the day and still reach its objective in time during the next night. In the morning it was seen that the patrol was only about

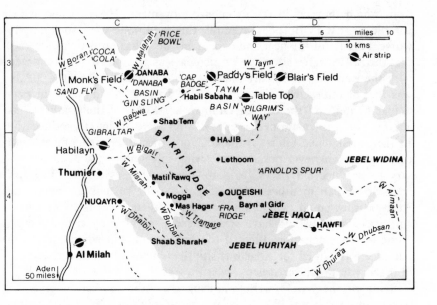

a thousand yards from a village, Shab Tem, from which both armed tribesmen patrolled and goat herdsmen directed their flocks. One of these herdsmen came so near that he caught sight of the S.A.S. men and gave the alarm. He was immediately shot and killed by Edwards's patrol, but they then found themselves pinned down by enemy snipers. Although Edwards was able to call for air support and Hunter aircraft fired their cannons at enemy positions, neither this nor artillery support could prevent the enemy pressure increasing and casualties among the S.A.S. patrol rising. Two men were wounded and another killed. Edwards decided that there was no longer any question of reaching the objective. They would have to break out at dusk and try to get back to Thumier. During the first few minutes of the breakout Edwards was hit and killed. The remainder of the patrol, pursued by bullets and tribesmen, managed to make their way back to the Wadi Rabwa and safety. One of them, Lance-Corporal Baker, was awarded the Military Medal for his part in the operation.

Although it was learning the hard way, the benefits of this patrol were that the whole military plan was altered to a much slower and more modestly conducted operation, which eventually occupied the battalions and other units of a complete brigade. Later the S.A.S. returned to the Radfan with the task of establishing observation posts from which they could report enemy movement. It was a task comparable to that in Borneo, although the conditions were so infinitely worse, because of the heat and exhausting dehydration which followed, that the S.A.S. referred to the Borneo days as gracious living compared with the Radfan. An equally unattractive role which fell to the S.A.S. was that of undercover work in the alleyways of urban Aden, in particular Crater and the Sheikh Othman area. One of their targets was a group of Yemen-trained assassins who were trying to reduce the British intelligence effort by picking off Special Branch officers and their agents whenever possible. In trying to counter this, it was necessary to produce a type of 'bait' to lure out the assassins. On other occasions Fijian members of the S.A.S., made to look as much like Arabs as they could, would simply position themselves in likely places and occasionally would have some success in engaging armed Arabs. None of these activities affected the final result, but some useful experience was gained for what was still to come in Ulster and elsewhere in the way of urban terrorism.

Some of the letters written during the Aden operation give the flavour of what it was like. Mike Wingate-Gray, then Second-in-Command, in a letter dated May, 1964, writes about what he and others had been doing. The letter was sent to John Woodhouse in Borneo, for at that time the Regiment had two campaigns on its hands:

> The last operation by *A* Squadron took place from 13–19 May. It was purely an intelligence-gathering one to find out about the enemy's use of supply routes at the east end of Wadi Taym, and if possible to get a prisoner from the dissidents. It was rather a negative operation and slightly dull, as after two days we had really achieved our first aim, and after this the axis of the battle had swung southwards into the main Radfan Hills, into which it was apparent the main body of the dissidents had escaped. As a result there were few enemy about in the Taym apart from some civilian camel trains. The Infantry could have done, and later did, much the same job as us, though we were some 4,000 yards ahead of them. The Squadron worked extremely well and succeeded in killing a couple of enemy by ambush, but unfortunately did not get a prisoner as there were few dissidents about. They stayed out the whole six days without resupply as they managed to find their own water locally ... I think there is no doubt but that the S.A.S. image is good ... the GOC told me that HQ Middle East have definitely requested the permanent use of a Squadron next year ... I think that it is the intelligence gathering role that they are especially interested in ...

This report is well complemented by what Peter de la Billière, who at that time was commanding *A* Squadron, had to say about the actual conditions of operating:

> The Squadron has done a magnificent job under the most gruelling conditions, even by our standards. I have never been on such tough patrols physically as the two we have completed out here. They knock Oman into a cocked hat. As a result of the intelligence they have produced, the next phase of operations has been planned, and we are more than ever in demand ... Our task is now to recce the best route for attacking the Hajir plateau which is the next rebel stronghold ... There is no doubt that this operation has shown several weaknesses in our training, and also has underlined our lack of knowledge in this type of fighting. A further interesting aspect is the manner in which the tough conditions out here have sorted out the weak and the strong individuals in the Squadron. The mental and combined physical strain here are never approached in Borneo, and an average man can bumble along quite happily out there. Here, however, a man has to be master of self-discipline and of his job, or he will start to waver.

Meanwhile John Woodhouse was reporting all the Regiment's activities in Aden and Borneo to the Colonel Commandant of the S.A.S., Major-General Sir Robert Laycock, former commander of Layforce, from which the S.A.S. was born. In replying, Bob Laycock wrote of Woodhouse's 'most interesting and inspiring letter', adding 'I am full of admiration for the splendid achievements of the Regiment'.

One of the last contributions made by the S.A.S. in the doomed battle for the Radfan was only about ten days before the British withdrawal. One of their observation posts spotted a group of three tribesmen moving along a wadi about fifteen miles south-west of Thumier. By this time the drill of having troops instantly ready for action with helicopters standing by was more or less a routine, and the S.A.S. report resulted in a Royal Marine troop moving rapidly into action and killing all three. It made no difference to the British withdrawal from Aden and the emergence of the Peoples' Democratic Republic of Yemen, which in no time at all became, instead of a British colony, a lackey of the Soviet Union and a base from which to launch a serious and prolonged attempt to subvert and overthrow the régime of the Sultan of Oman. This was the second of the two southern Arabian campaigns in which the S.A.S. took part. It was also one in which their methods, their perseverance, their adaptability and their daring once again won.

The war in Dhofar was not quite as long as that in Malaya, but it was long enough and, as Colonel Tony Jeapes points out in his excellent account of the campaign there, *Operation Oman*, it had in common with Malaya the distinction of being one of the very few wars which have been won against a Communist-inspired armed rebellion. In the introduction to his book Tony Jeapes explains that in numbers the affair was on a fairly small scale. There were about two thousand guerrillas opposed by a brigade of infantry, supported by air and naval power, which were part of the Sultan of Oman's Armed Forces. The S.A.S. role was in support of these forces and in particular was concerned with raising and training the *firqats*, or Dhofari irregulars, to fight for the Sultan. Colonel Jeapes rightly claims that here the S.A.S. were crucial to success and that 'without the S.A.S. the war would not have been won'. As in other campaigns, like those of Malaya and Borneo, 'the aim was not to obliterate the enemy, but to persuade them to join the Government side. It was first and last a war about people, a war in which both sides concentrated upon winning the support of the civilians of the Djebel Dhofar and which was won in the end by civil development, with military action merely a means to that end'. Tony Jeapes commanded his S.A.S. squadron in Dhofar in 1971 and 1972, and was there again from 1974 to 1976 in command of the Regiment itself. He has some fascinating stories to tell and a few of them will explain what it was like to be there. One of them concerns the gun on the Djebel Aram.

In May, 1971, it was decided by the then Major Jeapes and Lieutenant-Colonel Fergus Mackain-Bremner, commanding one of the S.A.F.* battalions, to mount an operation to deal with a gun, which the *adoo* – the Arabic word for enemy – had positioned on the Djebel Aram and were regularly shelling the village of Taqa with, thereby diminishing the morale of its people. It was agreed that a joint *firqat/ S.A.F.* operation, with two S.A.S. troops, should be enough to do the trick. The force was assembled at Mamurah, some twelve miles from Taqa, and when one of the S.A.F. officers caught sight of the *firqats*, he observed that they were a murderous-looking lot, adding that he was glad they were on his side. There was a long approach march across the plain before the joint party began their climb of the djebel. Shortly before dawn, after climbing to within three hundred yards of the summit, Tony Jeapes decided to pause with some members of the *firqat* until dawn clarified the situation. He need not have worried. Daylight clarified it all right:

> The world exploded. It was broad daylight and I realized that I must have dozed off. Bullets seemed to whipcrack from every direction punctuated by

* Sultan's Armed Forces.

long bursts of machinegun fire from very close at hand. A grenade exploded. A chip of wood clipped off the tree above my head. It had seemed quite a substantial tree before; now I began to wonder. The breath was knocked out of my body as three *firqat* men hurled themselves flat on top of me. One kept glancing up to the left of the high ground, muttering, 'This is not good. This is not good'.

He was right. It was not good. We were in clear view of the top of the djebel three hundred yards away and if the *adoo* were up there and they were attracted by this shooting we could be in difficulties. The high ground dominated us completely. The shooting began to slacken. One by one each of the *firqat* men behind the tree waited for a lull and then sprinted for the nearest sangar, Laconde's, until I was left alone. A small voice said, 'Remember your Sandhurst training. You should set an example. Get slowly to your feet and walk calmly across to the sangar', but another smaller voice said, 'Remember, no casualties. What do you think the effect will be in Whitehall if the Squadron Commander gets himself killed? The S.A.S. will be out of Oman tomorrow'. The voice of pragmatism shamefully won. I eased into my bergen straps, rose to my feet and ran pell-mell for the sangar, where at last I learned how the contact had happened.

It seemed that one member of the *firqat* had stumbled across a group of *adoo*, had flung a grenade at them and precipitated a fire fight. Fortunately an S.A.S. gun team had observed the exchange and succeeded in pinning down the *adoo* with G.P.M.G. fire. While Tony Jeapes was later talking to this group, he came across the member who had started it all off, a splendid *firqat* leader called Salim Said Dherdhir, whose near escape was clearly visible from two bullet grazes on his neck and shoulder. When Jeapes jokingly told him he must be more careful, Dherdhir replied that a man could only die once. It was plain that no matter how gallant was the conduct of S.A.S. men in the Dhofar, and there was repeated and overwhelming evidence of this, it was a different kind of bravery from that of the *firqat* leaders, which was a combination of devotion to Islam and a fatalistic philosophy. Eventually, after a good deal more fighting, the combined efforts of the S.A.F. under Mackain-Bremner, the *firqats* and the S.A.S. under Jeapes, succeeded in reaching the site of the big gun, which had been shooting at Taqa. The gun itself had gone, withdrawn by the *adoo* during some intense mortar and machine-gun fire. It had been cleverly sited and concealed, and there was still a supply of 75 mm ammunition. The subsequent withdrawal to Taqa was achieved with the aid of helicopters and artillery support, accompanied by a good deal of small arms shooting on either side.

All that the S.A.S. did at this time was part of the 'Five Fronts' campaign devised by the Commanding Officer of 22 S.A.S., Lieutenant-Colonel Johnny Watts. He had recommended that the S.A.S. should help in five ways: first, and indispensable to any counter-insurgency operation, an *intelligence cell*; second, to ensure that the people were properly informed about civil development, about future benefits and also to counter the propaganda of Radio Aden, an *information team*; third and fourth, bearing in mind that the Dhofari people put more value on their own health and that of their animals than anything else, a *medical officer supported by S.A.S. medics* and a *veterinary officer*; fifth, the raising of *Dhofari soldiers* to fight for the Sultan. This was the Five Fronts plan, but it must be remembered that the whole idea was for the S.A.S. to help the Omanis to help themselves.. At first the S.A.S. would carry out certain tasks, then train the Omanis to do them, so that at length the Omani Government would be able to embark on a programme of development which would gradually use resources for the well-being of the Dhofari people. In this way the spark of revolution would be finally extinguished.

If civil development were to take place on the djebel itself, however, it would be necessary to secure firm bases there, and Operation *Jaguar*, mounted in October, 1971, under Watts's command did much to achieve this. It was a large operation with about 100 S.A.S., 250 of the Sultan's Armed Forces, some Baluchi soldiers and five *firqats* totalling about 300 men. While a feint was made by one S.A.S. team under Captain Branson, who with two *firqats* climbed the djebel to the east of Eagle's Nest, the main force under Watts, with a squadron of S.A.S., the Baluchis and two other *firqats*, A'aasifat and Salahadin, climbed up to seize a former S.A.F. airstrip at Lympne, a few miles east of Jibjat:

> It was a terrible march. The route itself lay across the negd, winding its way through the boulder-strewn wadis and across the flinty little plateaux between – an area devoid of water and breeze. The night was hot and humid and before long, the combination of wrenching ankles and knee joints, the weight of their bergens and ammunition and the lack of water began to make itself felt even upon the S.A.S. The much less heavily equipped *firqats* began to throw away their rations to lighten their loads still further. The pace became slower and the final climb up the steep slope to Lympne seemed endless. At last no more than half the force stumbled on to the airstrip at 0435 hours and set about making it secure, but they were in no state to fight without a rest. Fortunately, the *adoo* were conspicuously absent and remained so for the rest of the day.

Thus began an operation which led, despite setbacks and disappointments, to a clear demonstration that the Government writ ran on the djebel as well as in the coastal towns. Jibjat was secured next, and then Watts began the second phase and took the war to the enemy. Two separate S.A.S. groups, each with *firqats*, advanced respectively down the western and eastern sides of the Wadi Darbat and, by seeking out and engaging the enemy in a series of fierce battles, had succeeded by 9 October in hunting the *adoo* off the plateau. A further base was established at White City, subsequently renamed The Place of Truth. It was at this moment that Watts planned to deliver a further blow by driving the *adoo* out of their wadi hiding places. The *firqats* had other ideas, and in spite of the dispensation granted to them by both the Ruler and the religious leader, they insisted on stopping the fight in order to observe Ramadan. Watts was obliged to abandon some of the important positions captured and re-establish his force at Jibjat. It was here that he threatened, after further *firqat* recalcitrance, to withdraw his S.A.S. teams altogether unless they agreed to do what he wanted. During the month that followed, further actions at Shahait and in the Wadi Darbat enabled Watts to make White City his operational base and to establish three positions above the Djebel Khaftawt. These positions became known as the Leopard Line, and it was clear from the sharp *adoo* reaction that this kind of linear blockade strategy was a sound recipe for controlling infiltration and inflicting defeat. Yet although Government forces were on the djebel, they needed to do more than simply be there if they were to win over the people. Above all water-wells and dwellings were required. Then, the Government might be said to have won the population's support.

But it was clear that much had been done. In some areas military security was now in the hands of the S.A.F., while S.A.S. teams were handing over medical responsibilities to Dhofaris. On the djebel at Jibjat and White City the *firqats* now had their families with goats and cattle. But, and this was a key point, there had to be a market for these herds. It was then that the Governor of Dhofar, Sheikh Baraik Bin Hamood, took a crucial decision. He had to show that the Government's promise to look after the people was no idle thing. It would be done. Therefore the goats would be flown out and the cattle would be driven to Salalah:

> Next day saw what must surely be unique in military history, a Texan-style cattle drive supported by jet fighter cover and 5.5-inch artillery. Amidst scenes like shots from a Boulting Brothers comedy mixed with a John Wayne Western, fire fights between pickets and *adoo* on the high

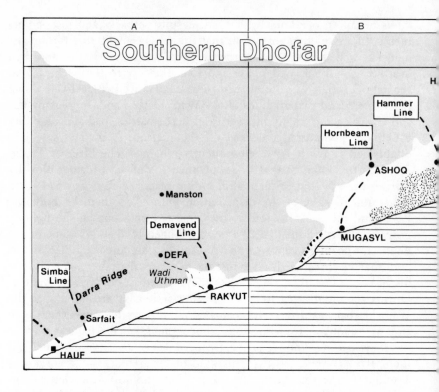

ground, whoops of delight from the *firqat* and expressions of amused disbelief by the S.A.F. and S.A.S., five hundred head of cattle were driven across the plateau and down the djebel to Taqa. Most of the animals were owned by *firqat* families, but many of them belonged to men serving in the *adoo*, and were 'confiscated' by the *firqat* during the drive.

It was a remarkable illustration of Government control and created a deep impression. By the end of 1971, the situation in Dhofar had been transformed from that at the beginning when, except for Salalah and part of the plain, the Government writ ran nowhere. Now there were firm bases on the djebel, the expanded S.A.F.'s presence was being felt, the *firqat* policy had resulted in some 700 Dhofaris being under arms fighting for the Government, the plain and the coastal towns were under Government control and the whole development policy for agriculture, medicine and education had been set up and further plans made. The Peoples' Front for the Liberation of the Occupied Arabian Gulf had lost much ground. And as Tony Jeapes recorded:

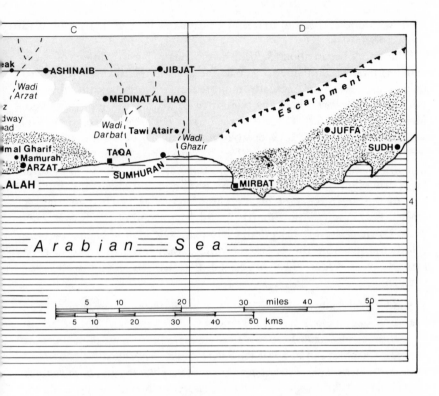

It had been a composite effort in which many people had played their part towards the same end, but if any one man could be given more credit than others it must surely be Lieutenant-Colonel Watts. The 'Five Fronts' plan had been his, it was his S.A.S. Regiment which had raised the *firqats* and secured the three towns, and it was he who had personally led the Government forces on to the djebel to seize the two firm bases at Jibjat and White City. It was an impressive record and more than enough to satisfy most men, but he was a man who set and demanded the highest standards ... more than anyone else it was the strategy he had devised and the groundwork he had completed that was to lead to the ultimate defeat of the enemy.

Before that day came, however, there was another day in the long Dhofar war which was crucial to the struggle for men's minds being waged between the Front and those loyal to Sultan Qaboos. This day was 19 July, 1972, and will long be remembered by the S.A.S. It was the day of the battle for Mirbat, when some 250 *adoo*, with artillery, machine-guns and mortars in support, attacked a small party of defenders – eight S.A.S. men, about thirty armed tribesmen, a few *firqat*

men, with one 25-pr, a mortar and a heavy machine-gun. In command
was Captain Mike Kealy.*

The attack began about 5.30 am with a heavy bombardment of shells
and mortars, accompanied by machine-gun fire. Unlike their normal
behaviour, the enemy actually mounted an infantry assault, directed
initially on the fort where the tribesmen gendarmerie were positioned.
Most of Kealy's S.A.S. team were in the BATT† house, some 400
yards away. A report came on the radio that one of the Fijian S.A.S.
men, Labalaba, who was in the fort, had been wounded and his fellow
Fijian, Savesaki, asked for permission to go and help him with medical
kit. Permission given, he ran to the fort, dodging shells and bullets,
and to the great relief of his watching comrades reached the sangar
where the 25-pr was positioned. At this point one of the S.A.S. men
with a machine-gun, Corporal Chapman, saw that the enemy were
calmly approaching the perimeter wire, going straight for the fort. At
first Kealy thought they might be friendly, so coolly were they
advancing:

> Suddenly all doubts were removed. At a signal, the men started to run into
> an extended line, raising their weapons to their shoulders. The crackle of
> small arms fire sounded paltry against the ear-splitting noise of the bursting
> shells. Chapman did not wait for orders. Short sharp bursts of fire ripped
> through the haze like a succession of tiny comets into the groups of running
> men, the ricochets bouncing and arching gracefully into the air until they
> burnt out. As if it was a signal to begin, the whole corner of the fort
> erupted with the sound of machine guns and rifles mixed with the explosion
> of shells. All the enemy's fire seemed to be directed at the fort and the
> S.A.S. men looked on with disbelief as it disappeared from sight. A cloud
> of brown smoke and dust, lit up in spasms by the bright flashes of shell
> bursts against the walls, hid the fort entirely. Above it all sounded the
> vicious cracking explosions of the big gun by the fort as it fired its 25-
> pound shells point blank at the wire forty yards in front of it.

Although the enemy's attack seemed to be concentrating on the fort,
they soon realized that much of the fire being directed against them
was coming from the BATT building, which then began to receive
its own share of machine-gun bullets. The enemy had reached the perimeter wire and attacked across it with extraordinary bravery. While the
S.A.S. men were still moving towards the fort, Kealy made a report
to his headquarters thirty miles away by radio, asking both for heli-

---

*Kealy died tragically from exposure and hypothermia as a result of disorientation
during a training exercise on the Brecon Beacons in February, 1979.

† British Army Training Team was the name given to S.A.S. groups in the Oman.

copters to evacuate wounded and air support. At this time of year during the monsoon the weather often prevented flying, as the rebels well knew in choosing low cloud and drizzle for their attack. Also, as Kealy could get no reply from the gun-pit at the fort on the short-range radio, he decided to go there himself with Tobin, a medically trained S.A.S. man, leaving Corporal Bradshaw in command at the BATT house. They had a highly hazardous dash for the gun-pit, one man running, the other shooting, while bullets hummed round them, but they got there. Then Tobin attended to the wounded Omani gunner, while Kealy found that both Fijians, Labalaba and Savesaki, were badly wounded. There followed a fierce fight, with the enemy through the wire and running up to the fort, Labalaba firing the 25-pr then falling at the gun, Kealy himself engaged at close quarters by several enemy, throwing grenades and aiming Kalashnikov machine-pistols at him. He shot one, shot at another, shouted to Savesaki to cover left, while he covered right, heard the 25-pr crash out again as Tobin fired it, only to fall a moment later, fatally wounded. Then Kealy radioed to Bradshaw to get his machine-guns and mortar to engage the enemy more closely, in fact as close to the fort as they could fire. More grenades, more bullets, and then the arrival of Strikemaster jets seemed to dissuade the enemy from any further immediate attack. Kealy and Savesaki tried to find out who was actually holding the fort, but could extract no sensible reply to Savesaki's shouted question in Arabic. The jets struck again, and then Bradshaw reported by radio that reinforcements were on the way.

By chance, and it was a very unlikely chance indeed, another S.A.S. squadron was actually in Dhofar, and although many of them were already deployed, twenty-three, including the squadron commander,* the sergeant-major and twenty-one troopers, all well armed for practice firing at a nearby range, were at Salalah airfield at 8 o'clock that same morning. By this time the seriousness of the attack was clear to all, and all twenty-three men were briefed and, having climbed into three helicopters, were quickly on their way to land south-east of Mirbat, where they split into three groups and made their way forward. The arrival of these reinforcements, together with the marvellous performance of the S.O.A.F.'s† Strikemasters and helicopters in difficult flying conditions, and, of course, the courage, skill and perseverance of Kealy's group of S.A.S., gendarmerie and *firqat* men – the combination of all these conditions saved the day and Mirbat. But the whole situation was very untidy and Kealy still had much to do to ensure that his

* Major Alistair Bowie.
† Sultan of Oman's Air Force.

own people, *firqat* and others, did not get caught in the fire of either enemy or friend. At length, the defences were reorganized, wounded evacuated, the enemy in retreat and the danger of the *firqat* being caught in the path of withdrawing *adoo* averted. Kealy's task was nearly over:

> Once more he trudged back to the BATT house where he found that Bowie had wasted no time in reorganizing the town's defences and establishing order again. Two Landrovers had just returned with the dead and wounded and thirty-eight enemy bodies lay in a row, their weapons and ammunition belts, all new Chinese and Russian equipment, piled in heaps nearby. A gaggle of *firqat* clustered about them trying to persuade some stony-faced S.A.S. men that they needed the weapons to claim reward money to feed their families. Within the house a medical officer and the S.A.S. medics applied dressings to the minor wounded, both friendly and enemy, while in a separate room the prisoners were being interviewed by Chapman. The three sat quietly smoking cigarettes and drinking tea and Kealy was struck both by their youth and by the dignity with which they accepted their lot. These were brave men.

Kealy's own bravery and leadership were acknowledged by the award of the Distinguished Service Order. There were many other names which appeared in the despatches dealing with the battle, for if ever there was a day in Dhofar when once again it was shown that who dares wins, it was on 19 July, 1972, at the battle of Mirbat.

Mirbat had been a serious set-back for the Front, but there was still much to be done. Colonel [now Brigadier] Tony Jeapes has described in his book how the campaign continued in 1974 and on to 1976. The various positions on the djebel had to be maintained and extended, the *firqats* had to be kept going, wadi searches made, government control established, development programmes supported. The particular value of the wadi searches was that it demonstrated once and for all that the *adoo* could not rely on safe refuge anywhere. It was for this reason, as Tony Jeapes has observed, that the searches were initially so fiercely resisted. 'But there were always more S.A.F., more BATT, and more *firqat*, whilst the *adoo*, their losses exacerbated by the continually rising SEP* rates, could not be replaced ... By the middle of 1975 the *adoo* in the Central and Eastern Areas had split into small bands on the run.'

There are many other names synonymous with the winning of the

---

* Surrendered Enemy Personnel, who did more than surrender – they changed sides.

ADEN AND THE DHOFAR

Oman war – John Graham, Tim Creasey,* Ken Perkins, Jack Fletcher,
John Akehurst. It was Akehurst who insisted that the *firqats* should
always accompany S.A.F. units, for, as he pointed out, the *firqats*
'are what this war is all about. They are the future of Dhofar'. He was
right. The S.A.S. had always had the same view and their B A T Ts
had raised, sustained and inspired the *firqats*. Of course, they had done
much more than this. In the battles already recorded, and in the
further engagements at Shershitti, point 985 and Defa, they proved
again and again what David Stirling had so often insisted on – that
the regiment is the Man and the man is the Regiment. No one can
read accounts of what these men did and what the S.A.S. Regiment as
a whole did without feelings of awe and pride. Gradually the Western
Area was pacified, or at least as pacified as it ever would be. Although
the Sultan of Oman announced in December, 1975, that the war was
over, it was not until three or four months later that armed action by
the regular army of the Peoples' Democratic Republic of Yemen and
the Peoples' Front for the Liberation of Oman ceased. The path to
peace, to civil development, to schools, Government Centres, to
bore-holes for water was open. It had been opened by the military
defeat of Communist rebels. To this defeat the S.A.S. with their
ubiquitous B A T T activity had made an indispensable contribution.
By the autumn of 1976 the last squadron had been withdrawn after a
campaign which for them had lasted six years.

Yet even in 1976, as Tony Jeapes has written, 'the *firqat* were stoned
by village women in a scene more like one from Northern Ireland than
Dhofar'. In Northern Ireland the British Army was to be engaged
much longer than in Dhofar, or in Malaya, or anywhere else for that
matter. Indeed it is impossible to think of a time when the British
Army was not engaged there. The S.A.S.'s participation is of relatively
recent date. But its importance was never more great.

* General Sir Timothy Creasey returned to Oman in 1981 as the Sultan's Chief of
Defence Staff.

18

THE UNTELLABLE STORY

A truth that's told with bad intent
Beats all the lies you can invent.
Blake

The S.A.S.'s part in Northern Ireland, however, is not going to be included here. Indeed it will shortly be necessary to begin to bring the story to a close, not because it has all been told, but because it cannot be told by me. When I agreed to undertake this work, I agreed also to conform to the wishes of the S.A.S. as to what should be left out. It is clear that no service either to them or to the nation can be done by attempting to recount their recent activities in a number of countries, including our own. That there have been such activities, no one doubts. But as far as Northern Ireland is concerned, it is permissible to say only something of a very general nature and perhaps to clear up one misunderstanding which may still linger in the public mind.

Most campaigns in which the S.A.S. have taken part resulted either in outright victory for them or an honourable draw. In the urban jungle and bandit country of Ulster this has not been so. There are several reasons for it. In the first place there were no means by which a victory over the hearts and minds of the Republicans could ever be won; secondly, the absence of a clear, consistent and realizable political objective has for nearly fifteen years rendered the task of the soldier at best a Micawber-like holding operation; thirdly, the mere existence and proximity of Eire has provided a virtually unassailable sanctuary and store-house; fourthly, if it is true that a necessary condition for defeating insurgency against legal government is to win control of the population, then it is plain, has indeed always been plain, that this condition cannot be attained, that there is no such thing as winning total control of Ulster's population, and therefore no such thing as defeating the I.R.A. Yet, as for all the other soldiers involved, the S.A.S.'s position is to continue to do what is required, avoiding if possible, becoming subject to the contract's unlimited liability clause, death in the course of duty.

As in all other counter-insurgency operations in which the British Army has indulged, the name of the game in Northern Ireland has been proper acquisition of intelligence, and it is no secret that in accordance with their traditional role the S.A.S., whether in rural or urban surroundings, have played their part, as have many other intelligence-gathering agencies. And it is perhaps here that the misunderstanding referred to above should be cleared up. Robert Nairac, whose courage and spirit and tragic death gave rise to so much comment and speculation in the press, was not a member of the S.A.S. What they have been up to in Northern Ireland and elsewhere has been the subject of much irresponsible conjecture in newspapers and books. Far more responsible was the R.U.S.I.'s publication, *Ten Years of Terrorism*, which contains two passages of interest in this area, both written by Tony Geraghty. One concerned the Mogadishu incident of 1977:

> The Mogadishu hijack later the same year was a more complex *mélange* of terrorist techniques and counterrevolutionary warfare. It is significant for two reasons. First, through the use of British diplomacy and S.A.S. specialists, it opened a new phase of European cooperation against terrorism. Until Mogadishu only the Israelis – notably at Entebbe – had dared to use the 'long-arm' approach in attacking terrorists outside home territory.
>
> Second, the Mogadishu operation was important as a reminder of the potential perils of the hard-line approach. It was the merest luck that both terrorist and security forces' grenades did not blow up the aircraft, 86 hostages and the assault group as well as the four hijackers. ...

Nonetheless:

> As Group 9's commandos smashed the emergency doors in, they hurled 'concussion grenades' supplied by two British S.A.S. men on the scene into the cabin. The noise and flash effect of these stunned the terrorists for eight vital seconds, just long enough for the operations to get under way.

The second passage is about the I.R.A. gunmen involved in the Balcombe Street siege in London in 1975:

> After four days the gunmen were beginning to realize that they too were hostages and that the police meant it when they said they were prepared for a long siege ... After six days the gang finally negotiated for food and

cigarettes. Next day they were planning to make a break for freedom, using the Matthews car, taking John Matthews with them when the news – deliberately leaked by the authorities – reached them that S.A.S. marksmen were being brought into the operation.

After that, as Matthews reported, the gunmen seemed to lose interest, and as the I.R.A. men chose not to indulge in a shooting match with the S.A.S. and others, they surrendered.

I have quoted these two passages simply to remind the reader that such things have happened and will go on happening. But to discuss such secret and sensitive matters would be to do the S.A.S. and others a disservice. It is enough to know that the S.A.S. and other comparable groups of what we might call the Anti-Terrorism International are active and that they cooperate in trying to defeat the international terror network. Journalists may speculate about what they do to their hearts' and editors' content. Authorized historians will wish to be more circumspect..

Yet it *is* possible to say something of the changing – and enduring – nature of the S.A.S.'s purpose and methods. Origins are notably capricious, and we find sometimes that a military force raised for one purpose is before long being employed for precisely its opposite. The whole idea that David Stirling had and then put into practice was roughly the same as that embraced by terrorists now: to make havoc, to disrupt, distract, destroy, and, by so doing, enable the principal military, or political, objective to be achieved. Small bands of bold, skilled men would throw spanners in the works, slow down the enemy machinery, cause adversaries to withdraw strength from the maelstrom to counter a thrust and anxiously wonder where the next blow would fall. And so, during the Second World War, when properly used, the S.A.S. courted stealth, speed, secrecy and surprise, operating well away from the main battle areas, blowing up aircraft and supplies, ambushing unsuspecting convoys, harassing enemy far in rear of the battle, discovering the situation, directing air power on to profitable targets. Sabotage, intimidation, demolition, the striking of uncertainty and terror into their enemies' hearts – these were the watchwords. As we shall see, they were to do it all over again in 1982. Above all they prided themselves on bold, imaginative ideas, excellence in a dozen skills, endurance, daring and identification with the Regiment. But in fact they behaved in the same sort of way as those whom in the last decade or so we have come to call 'terrorists'.

Then, during the years following the last war, when Britain was either defending its own territories against rebels and insurgents or helping other countries to do the same, the pattern changed to one of *countering* terrorism, of beating the guerrillas at their own game, of training and supporting the security forces of Asian, Arabian and other nations until these people could defeat insurgency by themselves. To start with, these activities were largely conducted in the confines of jungle or the spaces of desert. Then came another change – urban guerrilla warfare, kidnappings, killings, the taking of hostages, larceny on a grand scale, hijacking aircraft or taking over buildings, and always enjoying instant and maximum publicity. Some of these terrorist acts meant that counteraction was necessarily restricted to a very small area – an embassy, an aircraft, a train – although the very freedom of manoeuvre enjoyed by security forces in response to such terrorist action was in sharp contrast to the cabinned and cribbed environment of those guerrillas who were supposed to hold the initiative. In such cases when national or international groups of men and women dealing in violence declared war on the public or on a particular part of the community, the police were instantly involved. In Britain it was the police backed up by the S.A.S. Elsewhere in the world, such is their reputation and record, requests for S.A.S. advice and assistance were frequently made and met. If violence has to be countered by violence, there are no greater experts than the S.A.S. Trouble is their business.

In 1965, for example, an S.A.S. Training Mission assisted the Kenya Government to organize and train a Special Force Unit for their Police Force. This unit has provided the President's Bodyguard and has also been available for counter-revolutionary operations. There has in recent times been the need for such a force. In many other countries the S.A.S. have carried out similar tasks of giving both advice and help with training.

The range and versatility of the S.A.S. was admirably illustrated in a paper written by Mike Wingate-Gray in June, 1966, when he was commanding the Regiment. His paper was primarily concerned with the Regiment's capabilities overseas and drew largely on the experience it had gained in the previous years during operations in the Far East and Middle East, together with a great deal of training and research into new equipment and new techniques. He explained that whether thinking of counter-guerrilla operations, limited war or total war, there was always a crucial role for the S.A.S. because of their particular skills. Indeed, leaving aside total-war, we have had recent examples of this in the Dhofar, where couter-guerrilla operations were entirely successful, and in the Falkland Islands, where limited war was won outright with a major contribution to victory being made by the S.A.S.

Wingate-Gray went on to list the various skills in which his men were trained. Apart from the fact that every man is a driver, swimmer and parachutist, each of them possesses the basic skills of combat survival, resistance to interrogation, close-quarter combat, knowledge of foreign weapons, jungle warfare, and either radio, medical, or sabotage and demolition. Indeed as far as possible these last three skills are acquired by everyone. On top of all that come languages, for apart from a wide knowledge of Malay, the Regiment possesses many speakers of Arabic, Thai, German and Swahili. Quite apart from all these individual accomplishments, each squadron of the Regiment is able to deploy its troops in special environments demanding special capabilities, such as desert, snow and mountains, amphibious operations or free fall parachuting. As if this were not enough, training also deals with such things as bodyguards, V I P escorts, police Special Branch work, and industrial sabotage. What is more, the Regiment's ability to carry out a variety of separate operations world-wide, with the advantages of independence from the home base and of secure, dedicated communications, reinforces their unique capabilities.

In summing up what it was that his Regiment was able to do, Wingate-Gray pointed out that they could operate for long periods in small parties in enemy-occupied or -dominated territory; they could deal with extremes of terrain and climate at very short notice; they had secure and reliable communications over long distances; they could enter areas of conflict in many ways, parachuting, boating, mountaineering, ski-ing; their medical skills served their own needs and could win support from local peoples; they could talk to Asian, Arabic and other peoples in their own languages; they could raise, train and command indigenous irregular forces; they were trained to take part in clandestine, highly classified operations, if necessary with intelligence agencies; they were trained in sabotage; they could move anywhere to do practically anything within 24 hours and in strict secrecy. It is perhaps now clear why at the beginning of this book, there appears a couplet from Charles Churchill's *Epistle to William Hogarth*:

> By different methods different men excel;
> But where is he who can do all things well?

Of course, at this time Wingate-Gray's thinking was influenced by what the Regiment had been doing overseas. He had seen how competently his men had carried out frontier surveillance and clandestine offensive operations in Borneo; he had arranged for the raising and leading of indigenous forces there; he had observed how expertly they had carried out counter-guerrilla activities in mountainous and desert country, or long-range desert operations; he knew their effectiveness in amphibious reconnaissance or attacks; and he had thoroughly understood the incalculable value of winning the 'Hearts and Minds' of those with whom the S.A.S. worked and fought, by virtue of their linguistic and medical skills and their mere presence and support. Indeed, it was this ease with which the S.A.S. soldier was able to adapt to the conditions and ways of life of those whom he was supporting that won him golden opinions from all sorts of people. He talked their language, he ate their food, he wore their clothes if necessary, he lived and worked among them, he respected their ways. No wonder he enjoyed their confidence. Once again the British soldier had shown himself to be the very best ambassador that Britain could deploy among the peoples of the Third World.

All this Mike Wingate-Gray and others understood. But they also realized that the pattern was changing. It was not really until the 1970s that what one writer has called the secret war of international terrorism got well under way, but even in the late 1960s, quite apart from Northern Ireland, it had begun, as Claire Sterling has graphically described:

'I killed two,' the girl said, glancing up at her bulky companion with a small smile of content.

'Quite right; I killed one myself,' he replied. . . .

They were chatting in the Vienna headquarters of OPEC, where they had come in a mixed team to kidnap eleven Arab oil ministers for a firmer Arab commitment to annihilate Israel. The girl was short, slight, smart in a furred gray wool jacket and matching knitted cap pulled down like an absorbed child's to her eyebrows; her Makarov automatic pistol was still warm. She had fired it into the stomach of an Iraqi security guard, and before that into the nape of the neck of an elderly Austrian plainclothesman. 'Are you a policeman?' she had asked, and when he said yes, she shot him dead from four feet away, shoveling his body into an elevator, and pressing the Down button.

She was Gabriele Kröcher-Tiedemann of West Germany; he was Carlos the Jackal – Ilich Ramirez Sanchez of Venezuela. It was a shape of things to come. Yet before this incident in 1968, the S.A.S. had been turning its thoughts to the possible need to back up either M.I.5* or M.I.6† with its military skills and experience. In a paper written soon after that of Wingate-Gray, Colonel John Waddy, at that time known

---

* M.I.5 is responsible for security within the United Kingdom.

† M.I.6, the Secret Service, or Secret Intelligence Service, is responsible for security matters external to the U.K.

as Colonel S.A.S., spoke of 'tasks of a more delicate nature which have properly required the S.A.S. skills'. He went on to point out that if the Army were to help in countering certain subversive activities, they would need more information and intelligence. Conventional methods of dealing with outbreaks of subversion or armed guerrilla action would not do. The 'military' would have to be on hand ahead of such an outbreak to try and prevent it, or if this were not possible, to help put out the fire. This called for close cooperation, even joint action, between the secret services and the military. 'The Army organization,' Waddy concluded, 'to do this task is obviously the S.A.S.' The S.A.S. would therefore have to be capable of carrying out not only reconnaissance and offensive operations in enemy territory, but also special tasks in support of M.I.6 or Special Branch.

Both types of task could be said to be clandestine, but whereas the first, if this is not paradoxical, might be further classified as overtly clandestine, as they were in David Stirling's day with S.A.S. men operating deep in enemy territory, using military equipment and dressed in uniform, the special tasks in support of M.I.5 or M.I.6 would be *covertly* clandestine, of intensely high security, and perhaps involving the wearing of civilian clothes or other disguises. Examples of each of these types of action, carried out in the last few years, appear in the two following chapters. The crucial points which John Waddy was making were these. Although the S.A.S. had done much in the past, they still had not developed their full potential. Changing political and military circumstances, particularly those of the cold war and the beginnings of international terrorism, would enable them to reach this full potential, but it would mean adding to their previous activities in hostile territory the more special tasks demanded by M.I.5 and M.I.6. The need for exceptionally high military standards would persist, but more emphasis on liaison with the Secret Intelligence Services would be needed.

It is important to understand that while all this self-examination was taking place, the S.A.S. still had to be ready to undertake *any* of the three broad roles – in counter-guerilla operations, limited war or full-scale war between NATO and the Warsaw Pact – for which they were responsible. This demanded great imagination and flexibility of mind. Luckily, those who were conducting these studies had these qualities, as did some more senior members of the S.A.S. named below. It was fitting that one of those who most readily adapted to the ideas of assisting the police and secret services by providing them with highly specialized military skills during his time of commanding 22 S.A.S. Regiment, Peter de la Billière, also found that when he was later in charge of the whole S.A.S. Group he had on his plate the two operations which are described in the next chapters – one, a military back-up to the police at home, which *only* the S.A.S. could have done with such speed, skill and success; the other, a classic and traditional use of the Regiment in deep reconnaissance, offensive action behind enemy lines, sabotage, deception and at the end a use of psychological warfare which was a model of its kind. But it still has to be remembered that these changes of heart and methods were not made lightly or without some nostalgic doubts by some of the older hands, whose imagination could not match changing conditions.

It was no easy leap from the distant adventures which had a flavour of Ouida, of the Great Game, of T.E. Lawrence, or of William Hodson, whom Jan Morris described as:

> a soldier through and through, but unlike most of his colleagues, he was bred to the humanities. He was the son of a canon of Lichfield, was at Rugby under Arnold, took a degree at Cambridge and was a man of wide reading. He loved Shakespeare, and this was natural, for he was Hotspur brought to life. He enjoyed war for war's sake, fought it with superb panache, and was one of the greatest British leaders of irregular troops. . . .
> He was the sort of man who is commonly called fearless, a quality that so often masks some inner atrophy, and in his unquenchable hunger for physical conflict one senses an uncertainty of spirit. We are told that in battle, heedlessly slashing with his sabre or galloping pell-mell towards the enemy lines, his face was habitually wreathed in smiles: in a sword-fight he laughed out loud, and sometimes encouraged his opponent like a fencing-master – 'Come along now, make me sweat for it! You call yourself a swordsman? Try again, try again!'

Yes, it was a far leap from this sort of image, which had stood out during some of the S.A.S.'s adventures in the Radfan, Borneo and Dhofar, to a much grimmer game, almost comparable to the mean streets down which Philip Marlowe had to go, or the less romantic aspects of Commander Bond's work. Yet the leap was made, and much of the groundwork in facilitating this move by 22 S.A.S. away from the days of imperial adventure was carried out by successive Commanding Officers – John Woodhouse, Mike Wingate-Gray, John Slim, Peter de la Billière and others, together with the then Commander of the S.A.S. Group, Colonel John Waddy, and one of the S.A.S.'s longest-serving and most experienced officers, Dare Newell.

The major task which confronted these men was finding and fixing in the minds of Whitehall arbiters a proper and enduring role for the Regiment. It was a question which had long exercised S.A.S. Commanders during that lengthy 'Farewell the Trumpets' period of shoring up certain colonial and post-colonial régimes, a period which lasted some twenty years from the latter 1940s to the latter 1960s. Many were the discussions which they had among themselves during which they sought to define what the S.A.S. of the future should usefully do, while still remaining true to the principles laid down by David Stirling – that the S.A.S. should always be used strategically as a special force, and not simply employed as very high class infantry. There was even some disagreement within the higher echelons of the S.A.S. itself about this fundamental point, but it was fortunate for the Regiment both that the views of those who really understood what the S.A.S. was for prevailed and that at that very time a number of tasks, caused by what might loosely be called international terrorism together with Third World insurgency, became apparent. Thus just at the time when former campaigns in places like Malaya, Aden, the Radfan and Borneo were over [and even though operations in the Dhofar were to persist for some years still] it was becoming clear to those responsible for certain intelligence and security matters in this country that there was a need for a kind of armed branch of M.I.5 and M.I.6, a military back-up to such organizations, which could be called in as necessary both at home and overseas.

It was also fortunate for the Regiment that such men of the S.A.S. as those named above never hesitated to state their views in unequivocal terms and also understood the true value of salesmanship. That they were so successful in finding a new and world-wide role for the S.A.S. and thereby re-establishing the unique advantages which such a military option gives to this country owed much to what they themselves have referred to as a full-scale marketing and sales operation, both at home and abroad, for it was always clear that, apart from the Home Office, the Foreign and Commonwealth Office's approval and support were indispensable. In addition Colonel Waddy and his colleagues created the S.A.S.'s own command and communication structures as an independent group. The result of all this was S.A.S. activity and employment in a score of countries overseas. But once more discretion obliges me to draw a veil over the precise nature and whereabouts of the operations which were undertaken.

It was nonetheless an evolutionary period of great significance, indeed it was a turning point, for from that time forward the need for this special capability and its manipulation at the highest level has never again been questioned. Wherever terrorism or illegal armed violence or whatever we care to call it may occur, there is also the opportunity for those in authority to call upon the services of the

S.A.S. If Her Majesty's Government chooses to respond to such a call, it is able to put at the disposal of those in trouble the most professional, deadly and dedicated group of men trained in the business of countering terrorism that is available anywhere in the world.

Nor is this all. We are also able to call upon them ourselves, and it might now be fitting to demonstrate their extraordinary versatility in describing two operations which are well known to the public, and in doing so present some aspects of each not so well known. The two form a great contrast, one typifying the problems of urban guerrilla warfare, the other a strange interlude which gave back to the S.A.S. their almost classical roles of deep infiltration and destructive raiding. The two operations were separated by two years and many thousands of miles. The first was an admirable example of the S.A.S. being employed as an armed and expert back-up to the police and took place at the Iranian Embassy in Princes Gate in the spring of 1980. It showed the S.A.S. at their deadly and professional best in their newer tasks of eliminating urban guerrillas. The second made it necessary for them to go to South Georgia and the Falkland Islands on what must have seemed, except for one tragic circumstance, almost like a busman's holiday. It took them right back to the days of David Stirling. It is their part in these two affairs which forms a fitting epilogue to this story.

19

NEGOTIATION IN PRINCES GATE

Nought's had, all's spent,
Where our desire is got without content:
'Tis safer to be that which we destroy
Than by destruction dwell in doubtful joy.
Macbeth

The story of the Princes Gate siege is well known. Indeed the two instant books about it produced by *The Sunday Times* and *The Observer* were admirable both in detail and expedition. Whether such high marks may be awarded to them for accuracy or commentary will be a matter of opinion. While, therefore, there is no need here to repeat *all* the circumstances which led to the S.A.S.'s use in 'negotiating' the terrorists, it will be fitting to set down some matters of fact, and based on them offer some shades of opinion. This may perhaps be done best by asking three questions: first, what are the principles governing the S.A.S.'s use in such situations and what were they up to before the event? Secondly, why was their negotiation not one hundred per cent successful, in that one hostage was killed and others injured *after* they began their assault? Thirdly – and this question was posed by John Le Carré in his introduction to *The Observer*'s book – was it necessary for the S.A.S. to go in at all?

The principles governing the use of the S.A.S. in a terrorist/hostage situation are the same principles which govern the use of force by any citizen of the United Kingdom who comes to the aid of a Constable when a breach of the peace is taking place. A person under English law is only permitted to use reasonable force to achieve his aim. He remains answerable as an individual to the court for his actions. No extra powers are granted to S.A.S. soldiers under the law. The aim of the S.A.S. therefore, when invited by a Chief Constable to act in a terrorist/hostage situation, is to rescue the hostages using only as much force as may be necessary. Clearly the level of resistance by the terrorists will dictate what force is judged to be reasonable and the activities, the weapons and the threats made by the terrorists are all fully considered before the S.A.S. is deployed. During the Iranian Embassy siege, each incident, which resulted in the death of a terrorist was subject to forensic testing by the police, including the test firing of all weapons and a detailed examination of witnesses at the inquest.

The sequence of events of the Iranian Embassy siege followed classic lines of any terrorist/hostage situation:

a. The first phase was the publicity-seeking phase in which the terrorists sought to attract world attention to their cause. They were lucky enough to have four or five journalists within the building when they seized it. There were also over two hundred journalists present at the scene of the incident who were given regular releases of information by the police. Two of the journalists were also released bearing messages and, in addition, the BBC broadcast a message by the terrorists in return for further releases of hostages. The publicity phase lasted from Wednesday 30 April (when the incident began) until Sunday 4 May.

b. The second phase was the period when the terrorists abandoned their original demands (which were only a form of public relations exercise) and started talking about the resolution of the incident and their own return to the Middle East.

c. Finally came the dénouement in the late afternoon of Monday 5 May.

First notification of the incident, which had occurred at about 1115 on 30 April, came about lunchtime when an ex-S.A.S. non-commissioned officer, called Dusty Gray, who had by then left the Regiment and joined the Scotland Yard dog-handling squad, telephoned the Officers' Mess in Hereford and said that the S.A.S. would almost certainly be required at the scene of the incident from where he was speaking. Formal official authority to move from Hereford finally arrived from the Ministry of Defence after they had, in fact, arrived in London (without authority) 6 hours later.

The S.A.S. soldiers were all located in a building close to the Embassy and spent their time during the five days avoiding the Press (who never suspected their presence), in planning, training and rehearsing. Hyde Park, incidentally, had an abnormally high proportion of unusually fit looking men running around that Bank Holiday! A small scale model of the Iranian Embassy was built and, later on, a full scale model was built in a nearby barracks. Because the terrorists had said they would not surrender until their aims were met but would rather kill themselves and all the hostages if they could not achieve their objectives, the S.A.S. soldiers prepared for a violent dénouement from the onset. Most of the ideas for the plans of attack came from the soldiers themselves, although outside assistance from government scientific departments and other agencies was available.

So much for the first question. In order to deal with the second one, we must remind ourselves of the situation facing the S.A.S. just before their assault, a situation in which the terrorists – even though at that point it could be said that they still had the option of killing every one of their hostages – had psychologically already surrendered the initiative to the security forces outside. Shortly after 7 p.m. on 5 May, 1980, the terrorist leader, Salim (or Oan), was talking to the police on the telephone, which was positioned on the Embassy's first floor. With Salim were P.C. Lock and Simeon Harris, a BBC sound recordist. On the floor above in two separate rooms were the hostages – the men in the Telex room, guarded by a gunman; the women in a back office, also guarded by a gunman. Two more gunmen were in the corridor of the second floor, while the last and sixth terrorist was in the hallway on the ground floor near the front door. As we shall see, one of the Iranian hostages had already been killed by the gunmen and, some hours after the killing, his body had been pushed out into the street.

The task facing the S.A.S. was to enter the Embassy, ensure the safe release of twenty hostages and somehow guarantee that six terrorist gunmen would not prevent this happening. The gunmen were on three different floors, the hostages mostly on one floor. The S.A.S. knew some of this, but not all of it. Indeed in one vital detail what they thought they knew turned out to be wrong. Yet they had to have a plan flexible enough to deal successfully with whatever circumstances confronted them on actually breaking in. They knew therefore that to succeed they would have to stun the gunmen into temporary inactivity by themselves acting with such speed and daring, creating such shock and surprise, countering terror with an even greater degree of paralysing counter-terror that they would give themselves the time to 'negotiate' the terrorists. There was also the problem of how to tell which were the gunmen. Changing clothes with hostages was an old trick. In short, somehow or other the S.A.S. assaulting the Embassy had to minimize the danger of precipitating the very thing they were there to prevent – the hostages' instant death by shooting. These were some of their problems.

Although the second question posed above was, why was the attack not totally successful, it must be said at once that the very high degree of success was both astonishing and an absolute vindication of all the S.A.S. had for so long been doing.

On Monday 5 May, Salim knew – and this was apparent to all – that he would have to start using force that day in order to try and get his plan to fly out to the Middle East accepted by the British Government. No one had been killed up to this point but he now would have to start killing if he was to make any further progress. At midday, he said, in response to a request by the negotiators for further delays, that he would now kill a hostage. He then fired two shots with a three-second interval between each shot. It seemed that one shot had been fired into someone and, as he or she fell to the floor, a second shot or *coup de grâce* had been administered. Later in the afternoon, Salim again said he would shoot a hostage. Up to then no body had been put out of the Embassy but, following two more rapid shots, a body was in fact put out and, when examined by a doctor, was proved to have been killed some hours before.

The actual assault into the Embassy was relatively simple and no more than a platoon attack carried out in a vertical plane, although some delay was caused when the main assault was mounted into a room where there were no hostages or terrorists and which was barred to further access to the building. As a result the terrorists succeeded in killing one hostage and injuring others before the S.A.S. could get to them but, because they knew the inside of the building so well, other groups were able to locate the hostages and terrorists and save further bloodshed to the hostages. The main assault had to be mounted from the rear of the building because of the presence of the Press to the front and, although the police had tried to prevent media coverage of the rear of the building following an S.A.S. request, ITN managed to infiltrate one camera team to the rear. However, the effect of this team's coverage was neutralized when the news editor, in a monitor van controlling the electronic news gathering, unwittingly switched coverage to the front thinking that the occurrences to the rear were unimportant!

By 0500 hours the next morning all S.A.S. troops were back in Hereford, including one injured soldier who had received severe burns while trapped outside the burning building. He was hijacked out of St Stephen's Hospital in the Fulham Road, still with his drip inserted in his arm and in his National Health pyjamas and borne away in a helicopter to Hereford where he was put in the care of his wife – who, in fact, was a nurse.

In spite of the severe fire which followed the freeing of the hostages, considerable forensic evidence was obtained from the scene and it was conclusively shown that all the terrorists had weapons on them at the time they were killed. This put the lie to the wild allegations that were made about the S.A.S. following the incident.

And so we come to the third question – was it necessary for the S.A.S. to be used at all? It had been the police's hope that gradually the gunmen's resistance would be worn down, that they would recognize the hopelessness of their position, would release their hostages unharmed and themselves surrender. Such expectations were sharply disappointed when the body of Larasam was unceremoniously shoved on to the pavement outside the Embassy. At this point use of force to end the siege became inevitable. It was simply a question of when and by whom. The *when* was determined by the hearing of two more shots a few hours later. The *whom* was never in doubt, for once the remedy of force had been decided on, it was clearly necessary to apply force in the most efficient, expeditious and economical way open to the authorities. This in turn meant the S.A.S. They were there, they were ready, had been ready for four or five days, they were trained for just such a situation. If success were to be as certain as it ever could be in such conditions, it was essential to use the right tool, and the S.A.S. clearly was, and is, the right tool. The proof of the pudding was in the 'negotiation' itself.

There is the further point – once bitten, twice shy! As a mere exercise *pour encourager les autres*, it may have had the same sort of effect as the incident Voltaire referred to had on Admiral Byng's contemporaries. There almost certainly had to be a first time for H.M.G. to play its anti-terrorist ace in London, for the S.A.S. to dare and win there, to show any other terrorist groups who might be thinking of something similar that all they can expect is a similar fate – to be negotiated by the S.A.S. If Lord Jellicoe is right in his contention that London might become the future battleground of Arab extremism, then perhaps the almost excessive coverage given by the media to the S.A.S.'s resolution of the siege of Princes Gate will yield some benefit. Yet it is perhaps ironical that the fourteen minutes of this particular action should have received more publicity and acclaim than any other incident or campaign which the S.A.S. have brought to a successful conclusion. Its very violence and the coining of a new significance to the word 'negotiation' have perhaps concealed that negotiations of another sort, the psychological power of communication, can reveal the S.A.S., not just as tough killers, but as gentle persuaders too. In the Falkland Islands the Regiment had an opportunity to excel in both these categories of daring.

20

GENTLEMEN IN KHAKI
ORDERED SOUTH

The S.A.S. and S.B.S. will be secretly landed on the islands to
begin special operations.

Buenos Aires intelligence report 17 April, 1982

On 5 April, 1982, two carriers of the Royal Navy, *Hermes* and *Invincible*, together with the assault ship *Fearless*, sailed from Portsmouth.
Operations to retake the Falkland Islands were literally under way. On
the same day the S.A.S. began their own part in the affair. In fact they
played several parts – infiltration for surveillance and reporting information; destruction of enemy aircraft; diversionary attacks and seizing
important ground in advance of the main forces. With the exception
of these latter tactical operations, it was a return to the good old days,
a re-enactment of traditional S.A.S. roles.

D Squadron and half of G Squadron, 22 S.A.S. Regiment, were
used in these operations. D Squadron began its work at once, joining
the Task Force on 6th April, only four days after the Argentinian
invasion, its first duty being to assist in Operation Paraquat, the re-
taking of South Georgia. To start with it was as hazardous as anything
they had ever done. The Task Group commander for Paraquat wanted
information about enemy positions at the two main settlements, Leith
and Grytviken, in order to make his plan. He therefore instructed the
Royal Marine S.B.S. men to land and get intelligence about Grytviken,
while D Squadron S.A.S. was allotted Leith. In the plain, unemotional
report by Headquarters S.A.S. on how they got on appear these words:
'Initial attempts to insert S.A.S. observation posts from the landward
side towards Leith resulted in two helicopters crashing when the patrol
had to be extracted because of extremely adverse weather conditions.
A no less dramatic insertion by boat finally got the patrols ashore.'

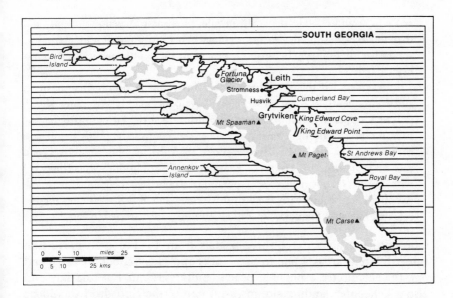

Some of the drama is provided by a member of D Squadron, Corporal Davey, who wrote an account of his adventures after returning to this country in June, having been wounded during later action on the Falkland Islands themselves.

He has described how he and his comrades were initially briefed on 4th April, then flew to Ascension Island, embarked in the Royal Fleet Auxiliary *Fort Austin*, and in company with HMS *Antrim* and HMS *Plymouth* sailed on 9th April for South Georgia:

> We met up with *Endeavour* a week or so later. 19 Troop [this is the troop of which Corporal Davey is a member] and S.B.S. were cross-decked into *Endeavour*, and here we were able to get our first intelligence on South Georgia from the crew of the ship. This information included plans of Stromness, Husvik, Leith, Grytviken and the British Antarctic Station (B.A.S.) at King Edward Point, also meteorological, topographical, coast-line and climatic conditions, together with a large amount of first-hand information literally only two weeks old. Map coverage of South Georgia was very inadequate but the Squadron managed to put together photo-copied maps, with a grid overlaid, after having to agree with the Royal Marines which grid was to be used.
>
> Actual intelligence on the Argentine Forces and Scrap Merchants* was scant – suffice to say it was thought most probable that the whaling station

---

* The first Argentines to land on South Georgia were scrap merchants on legitimate business. They aroused suspicion when they raised the Argentine flag.

at Leith would contain the scrap people, plus some Argentine troops, and that the B.A.S. would also be occupied. Any planning at this stage was somewhat preliminary because no orders to carry out operations had yet been given.

It was decided that 19 Troop would insert on to South Georgia first, and consequently we started to receive arctic kit, mainly skis, snow shoes, polks and a mass of climbing gear. We also raided the kit on board *Endeavour* for bivi-bags, lightweight sleeping bags, mittens etc. 19 Troop was then moved on to HMS *Antrim* about 18 April. At this time 18 Troop was in *Plymouth*, 16 Troop in *Endeavour*, 17 Troop and Squadron HQ with us in *Antrim*, where an Operations Room had been set up in the Admiral's day cabin with the Royal Marines and S.B.S. Planning for the retaking of South Georgia, Operation Paraquat, then started in earnest.

The outline plan was for three patrols from 19 Troop to move into three different areas – one to Stromness and Husvik, one to Leith and one to reconnoitre a possible beach landing area in Fortuna Bay and also a helicopter landing site in case more of the Squadron should be required to move in. The idea was that as soon as enemy positions were known, either 19 Troop would handle the situation by itself, or bring in more of the Squadron if they were needed for an assault. Like many plans, these did not survive contact with the enemy, the principal enemy in this particular engagement being the weather.

About midday on 21 April, after two unsuccessful attempts hampered by bad weather, the troop was landed by one Mark 3 Wessex from *Antrim* and two Mark 5 Wessex from *Tidespring*. They were dropped on the Fortuna glacier and almost at once the weather closed in with rapidly deteriorating conditions. The winds were up to 50 mph with spindrift which blocked the ammunition feed trays of the machine guns and then froze. Despite this, the machine guns' working parts, largely because they had been properly greased, continued workable, while the muzzles were taped. The troop had intended to move over the Fortuna and Nuemayer glaciers in order to carry out their tasks, but they found it so difficult to move forward because of crevasses, deep snow and all the kit carried, that they managed only about 500 metres in four to five hours. They were therefore obliged, when the wind became very strong and they were subjected to almost continuous whiteouts, to call a halt. However, some protection from the wind was found in a crevasse. The so-called arctic tents proved to be quite inadequate. Poles broke and one was torn away by the wind. As Corporal Davey remembers: 'Each tent had five men in it; we managed to get into sleeping bags, but only by sitting against the tent sides were we able to keep the tent from collapsing. Every hour one man had to go out and dig the snow out from around the tent to stop us being buried. The rest of the troop slept out in the open as best they could, either under polks or in bivi-bags with all their clothing on. To say the least it was an uncomfortable night!'

Next morning they signalled HMS *Antrim* asking to be extracted before they suffered serious casualties from frostbite or hypothermia. After many attempts three helicopters managed to pick them up, but then things went very wrong indeed. Again the story is best told by Davey:

> The helicopters lifted off, the Mark 3 Wessex with navigational equipment leading and the two Mark 5s following. I was in the first Mark 5. The flight plan was to follow the glaciers down to a land fall and then out to the ships. The Mark 3 put in a shallow right-hand turn, height probably about 200–300 feet, the first Mark 5 started the turn but was hit by a sudden whiteout in which the pilot lost all his horizons and we crashed into the ice. The pilot managed to pull the nose up before impact so that the tail rotor hit first and the helicopter rolled over on its left-hand side. The main door being uppermost everyone got out quickly, the only injury being Corporal Bunker who had hurt his back.
>
> The remaining Mark 5 and Mark 3 then landed and we transferred to them ... the two helicopters lifted off again and exactly the same thing happened, whiteout followed by crash. This time the Mark 5 rested on its right-hand side. The Mark 3, unable to return because of extra payload, then flew back to *Antrim*. I and the other passengers were taken to the wardroom where an emergency medical room had been set up. After re-fuelling, the Mark 3, with the same crew still aboard, returned to the area of the second crash, but was unable to land because of weather. It returned to the ship, having contacted the troops on the glacier who had no serious injuries. They had in fact managed to erect a survival tent carried by the helicopter and had also retrieved equipment from the first crash.
>
> The Mark 3 then returned again to the second crash, and this time picked everyone up and returned to *Antrim*. It had seventeen passengers, very much overloaded, and the pilot had to fly the helicopter straight onto the flight deck as he was unable to hover and approach normally. It was now 22 April.

Insertion by air having failed, the S.A.S. now tried it by sea. On the following day 17 Troop, or rather part of it, for two of the Gemini landing craft had engine failure, did succeed in getting ashore at Stromness Bay. Some S.B.S. men were also inserted near the northern whaling stations. Soon after this the British succeeded in taking back South Georgia. In summary what happened was this. Grytviken was captured by Squadron HQ and one troop of D Squadron on 25 April as part of a rapidly mounted operation by the S.A.S. and Royal Marines, when the Task Group commander decided to exploit the damaging of an Argentinian submarine, *Santa Fe*, on the same day. During operations on South Georgia the S.A.S. found, as the rest of the Task Force were later to find during the main battles on the Falkland Islands themselves, that naval gunfire support 'was used to good effect in persuading the enemy that our intentions were serious'. The S.A.S. report on this part of the affair ends with a simple statement that Argentinian resistance on South Georgia collapsed finally when their troops at Leith surrendered to the S.A.S. on 26 April. Our friend, Corporal Davey, is able to fill in the picture here and there. After the news came of the successful attack on the *Santa Fe*, men of D Squadron were given orders for the re-taking of Grytviken and the B.A.S:

We boarded all available helicopters. The first helicopter lift consisted of Captain Hamilton's patrol of which I was a member. Would you believe it was the same Wessex Mark 3 from *Antrim*? All S.A.S. troops were helicoptered ashore, landing on an area of flat ground known as the Hesterleten, two kilometres south-east of the B.A.S. The troop formed up in all-round defence to await the arrival of some thirty men from M Company, 42 Commando, and the commander of the operation, Major Sheridan, Royal Marines. Prior to our insertion a Forward Observation Officer and party had inserted to control the naval gun support. Having shaken out for an advance to contact, we engaged likely enemy positions, and by this time naval gunfire was supporting our advance.

In the area where the Brown Mountain ridge line joined the coast we saw what appeared to be men in brown balaclavas among the tussock grass. They were engaged by GPMG fire from approximately 800 metres and by naval gunfire. Captain Hamilton and I also engaged a possible enemy position on the top of Brown Mountain with Milan. Advancing across open ground towards the ridge line we discovered that the balaclava'd enemy were in fact seven or eight elephant seals, which were now somewhat the worse for wear! The enemy position on Brown Mountain had been a piece of angle iron on which we had scored a direct hit.

By this time they were able to see the B.A.S. and could hear some small-arms and machine-gun fire near King Edward Cove. Although the Argentinian flag was still flying outside the station, it was surrounded by white sheets on almost every building. They observed the *Santa Fe* tied up by the jetty, but at first there was no sign of the enemy. Then, about a quarter of an hour later, Argentinian troops marched out of Discovery House and formed up by their flag. The S.A.S. moved from the ridge line, now occupied by Royal Marines, went past the Argentinian Puma, shot down during their invasion of South Georgia, and, having moved through the deserted whaling station at Grytviken, reached the station. There the Argentinian garrison surrendered to Major Delves, while Sergeant-Major Gallagher lowered the Argentinian flag and hoisted the Union Jack. It was by these actions that the S.A.S. contributed to the initial British successes in re-establishing their sovereignty over their possessions in the South Atlantic. Their major contributions were still to come.

On 1 May the first intelligence-gathering patrols of G Squadron were inserted by Sea King helicopters onto East Falkland. Most of them stayed in their positions which they established close to the enemy, in extremely uncomfortable weather, for nearly a month, that is until after the main landings were made on 21 May. The S.A.S. of G Squadron provided just the information needed for the Amphibious Group and Land Force commanders to make their plans for the assault. They also provided information as to the whereabouts of enemy aircraft and stores which both Harrier strikes and naval guns were then able to give their attention to.

D Squadron rejoined the main Task Force soon after their South Georgia activities and were then allocated tasks of direct action. One of these tasks was against an enemy airstrip at Pebble Island, off the north-east side of West Falkland. It was done on the night of 14/15 May. First an observation post was established by canoe and then the Squadron was flown in by helicopters about five miles from the airstrip. They then walked to the target area. It was a repetition of the very earliest S.A.S. raids which had been conducted by David Stirling and his men in the Western Desert during the Second World War forty years before. At Pebble Island some eleven aircraft were destroyed together with about a ton of ammunition and explosives. The ubiquitous Corporal Davey tells us what happened:

14 May 82 - 45-minute flight by three Sea Kings onto L S secured by 17 Troop. Captain Burls then briefed the Squadron and Troop officers on the ground. Distance from L S to base - six kilometres. The moon was bright and very little cover was afforded by the ground. Each man carried two 81mm mortar bombs, which were dropped at the base-plate. 16 and 19 Troops were led to their respective targets by scouts from 17 Troop.

Base-plate to forward RV four kilometres. Captain Burls led 19 Troop onto the airstrip via the forward RV manned by Captain West and Sergeant-Major Gallagher. Once on the edge of the airstrip we began to engage visible aircraft with small arms and 66mm rockets. By this time naval gunfire and illumination were being produced by HMS *Glamorgan* and our mortars also fired some illuminating rounds. We were aware of some incoming enemy small arms fire, but it was totally ineffective.

I was a member of Staff-Sergeant Currass's patrol and was the extreme right-hand man. I was hit in the lower left leg by shrapnel at about 0700 hours. Staff-Sergeant Currass helped me put a shell dressing on the wound. The Troop moved onto the airstrip and started systematically to destroy the aircraft with standard charges and 66mm. Captain Hamilton covered Trooper Armstong who went forward to destroy the last aircraft. The Troop then shook out and started to fall back off the airstrip. We were at this stage silhouetted against the burning aircraft. A land mine was command detonated in the middle of the Troop, Corporal Bunker being blown some ten feet backwards.

I was beginning to feel faint from loss of blood and consequently was told to head back towards the forward RV with two others. Just off the airstrip we heard Spanish voices, at least four or five, shouting some fifty metres towards the settlement. I opened fire with M203 and put down some sixty rounds in the direction of the voices. Two very pained screams were the only reply. The Troop came down behind us and we moved back through the forward RV at about 0745 hours. During the move back I was helped over various obstacles and so was Corporal Bunker. The helicopter pick-up was on time at 0930, and the flight back to *Hermes* lasted about one hour twenty minutes. Corporal Bunker and I went directly to the sick bay where we were looked after admirably.

Such was one member of the S.A.S.'s account of the Pebble Island raid. He and his Squadron had certainly been active since the very onset of the operation to re-take the Falkland Islands. But his adventures and misfortunes were not over yet. The report by HQ S.A.S. Group contains one sentence which conceals much sadness – 'eighteen S.A.S. soldiers were killed in a helicopter crash while changing ships prior to the main landing'. Corporal Davey tells us that on 19 May most of D Squadron had already been cross-decked from *Hermes* to *Intrepid* during the day. The last lift was a mixture of people including himself and others of 19 Troop. They lifted off about two hours after last light with twenty-seven passengers and three crew in a Sea King. *Intrepid* was only half a mile away and what should have been a few minutes' flight was delayed because another helicopter was being

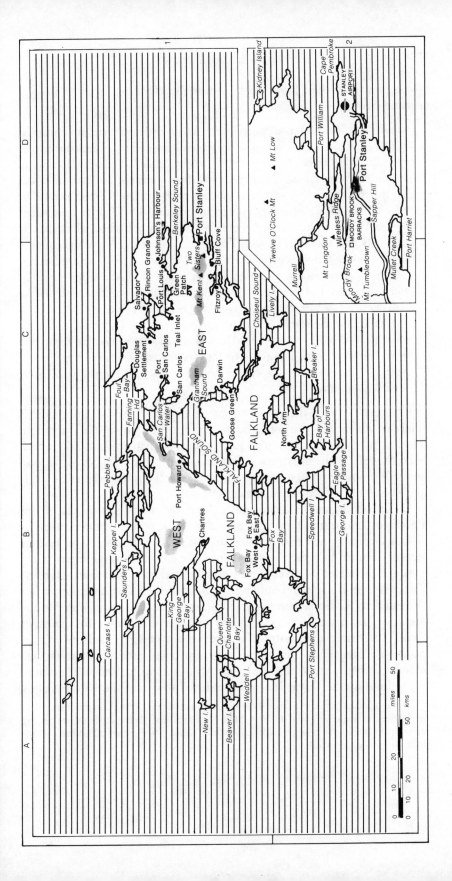

folded away on their flight deck. It was therefore necessary to make a second circuit:

> Suddenly and without warning there was an extremely violent impact at the front of the helicopter, near to where I was seated. Immediately the cab filled with water. All I remember was being thrown about under water and in complete darkness. I don't know how I got out but assume it was via the front passenger exit. The journey to the surface seemed to take for ever. Once on the surface, coughing and vomiting AVTUR and sea water, I looked back towards the helicopter but saw only one wheel which was by now only just above the surface. I became aware of a group of men around a small life-raft and swam towards it ... We spent a most uncomfortable half hour or so awaiting rescue. The majority of us had a life-jacket of some sort and had managed partially to inflate them, but without the one-man aircrew raft we would have really been in trouble.
>
> By the time the rescue helicopter came we were all very close to unconsciousness ... a dinghy from HMS *Brilliant* also arrived on the scene. We were hauled aboard. I must have lost consciousness at this stage as the next thing I remember was waking up in the sick bay wrapped in blankets several hours later.

Such were some of the recollections of Corporal Davey, who had his share of adventures during D Squadron's gallant part in the operation. He lost many of his comrades in that terrible helicopter crash, which was caused by an albatross flying into the engine intake. It is bad enough to lose men in a genuine action. It is far worse when fate deals out such a blow by sheer mischance.*

D Squadron was in action throughout the whole ten weeks of the Falklands campaign. They had played a major part in the recapture of South Georgia; they had carried out the brilliantly successful raid at Pebble Island; they then went on to cover the main amphibious landings at San Carlos by diversionary attacks at Darwin and Goose Green; three days after the main landings D Squadron, acting on information provided by G Squadron, inserted a reconnaissance patrol at Mount Kent, a vital piece of ground in the subsequent advance by the main force, and three days after that the whole of D Squadron was in position there. They ambushed enemy patrols, carried out raids, ascertained enemy strengths, and after Mount Kent had been taken over from them by the Royal Marines, returned to one of the Royal Navy's

* 'It is indeed a tragedy to lose 18 men in a pure accident,' wrote Commander S.A.S. in a letter to the author dated 26 May. 'The Regiment has taken it well and are getting on with the fighting at present ... I shall only be happy when we are all ashore and our lives are in our own hands.'

assault ships. Their final activities included operations on West Falkland and harassing and diversionary attacks against the Argentinian garrison of Port Stanley to facilitate its capture by the main attacking force. It was no surprise that the D Squadron Union Flag was raised on Government House on 15 June 1982.

The achievements of D Squadron are best summarized by the citation written for its Commander, Major Delves, who was awarded the Distinguished Service Order. Here is an extract:

In South Georgia his soldiers had to operate in extremes of climate which bordered on the limits of survivability. In spite of the difficulties, Major Delves was able to insert the necessary surveillance patrols into his area of responsibility overlooking Stromness Bay. This was achieved in spite of one of his patrols becoming involved in two helicopter crashes, and another one losing half its strength when it was scattered into the night by 100mph katabatic winds.

On 21 April after the engagement of the Argentinian submarine, the *Santa Fe*, Major Delves led his men into Cumberland Bay East and captured Grytviken, employing two of his SAS troops. By his quick decisive action and personal display of courage, he was able to accomplish the fall of Grytviken without a single loss of life. The next day he ordered his remaining troop to go ashore in Stromness Bay and accept the surrender of the remaining Argentinian forces in South Georgia.

On the early morning of 15 May Major Delves led his men in delivering a devastating blow to the enemy air capability on Pebble Island in the Falkland Islands. The operation has since been described as a classic of its time. In a daring and well executed series of moves in which he was able to determine the layout of the enemy positions, he infiltrated the enemy defences and by skilful use of his own men and Naval gunfire, he destroyed 11 aircraft on the ground and over a ton of explosive.

On 21 May only hours after his Squadron had received a most cruel blow when it lost a significant proportion of its numbers in a helicopter crash, Major Delves led his men out once again in order to carry out a deceptive raid on to the Argentine position at Darwin. So successful was he in his aim of drawing off enemy reserves from the real landing position that the enemy were heard to inform their higher HQ that they were under attack from at least a battalion of men.

Following the successful establishment of the beachhead in San Carlos Water, Major Delves took his Squadron 40 miles behind enemy lines and established a position overlooking the main enemy stronghold in Port Stanley where at least 7,000 troops were known to be based. By a series of swift operations, skilful concealment and lightning attacks against patrols sent out to find him, he was able to secure a sufficiently firm hold on the area, after 10 days, for the conventional forces to be brought in. This imaginative operation behind the enemy lines provided UK forces with psychological and military domination over the enemy from which it has not recovered.

In all the operations described above, Major Delves led his men from the front. Coolly directing operations when under intensive fire from the enemy, he maintained a control and gave an inspiration to his men which I have never seen in the field before.

Citations, as we know, are written with a particular purpose and tend to deal in superlatives. It is also necessary always to bear in mind that an award to a Commander is an award to his command. But in this account of what Major Delves and his Squadron did is contained all that is best in the S.A.S.'s tradition – their daring, perseverance, versatility, discipline, refusal to be dismayed by setbacks, and the way in which huge military dividends can be extracted from the proper strategic use of small, skilled forces. In this citation alone is enough for us to understand why we won.

Nor was G Squadron's part in the affair less significant nor less crammed with incident and success in discovering where the enemy were and were not, thus ensuring the facility with which the main assault landings were made. On 1 May the first intelligence-gathering patrols from G Squadron were inserted by Sea King helicopter on to East Falkland. Most of these patrols stayed in position, close to the enemy and in adverse weather conditions for up to thirty days, that is until and after the main force landings on 21 May. They provided intelligence on which the Amphibious Group and Land Force Commanders' plans were based and also gave the necessary information about enemy aircraft and stores for naval gunfire and Harriers to deal with.

The more or less continuous information they provided ensured that by 14 May, a week before the main landings, the main enemy positions to the west of Port Stanley, Port Howard and Fox Bay had all been identified. They also produced negative information that certain areas like Jersey Harbour and Bluff Cove were not occupied by the enemy. The reports they produced were both varied and detailed, including such matters as aircraft moving about from base to base, shipping, enemy defensive positions, logistic movements, enemy routine patrols, minefields, concentrations of administrative troops and stores, and what was happening at places like Darwin and Goose Green. Moreover, the two S.A.S. Squadron Commanders were able to brief other troops, like the 2nd Battalion, Parachute Regiment, before these latter forces were committed, by discussing the situation together on board one of the assault ships. Like D Squadron's raid on Pebble Island, this intelligence gathering activity of G Squadron was in the classic mould. Another citation for an officer commanding a four-man patrol which provided vital information about enemy dispositions in the Port Stanley area gives us the feel of what it was like:

> Inserted by helicopter on to East Falkland from HMS *Hermes* at a range of 120 miles, he positioned his patrol in close proximity to enemy positions, cut off from any form of rescue should he have been compromised. This position he maintained for a period of 26 days. During this time he produced a clear picture of enemy activity in the Stanley area, intelligence available from no other means, which has proved vital in the planning of the final assault.

> Throughout the period, the accuracy of his reporting has been exemplary. On one occasion he reported an enemy helicopter concentration against which an airstrike was directed resulting in the destruction of 4 troop-carrying helicopters essential to the enemy in maintaining flexibility and rapid deployment across the islands. This was complicated by the enemy changing the location of his helicopter holding area each day.

> In spite of his exposed position, vulnerable to air and ground search and the tactical DF of his communications, his intelligence reports were detailed and regularly updated. The conditions in which he and his men existed were appalling, with little cover from view, requiring observation from shallow holes scraped in the ground and covered by chicken wire camouflaged nets. His patrol existed throughout the period with little cover from the elements and weather conditions that varied from freezing rain to gale force winds with few clear days. In this respect the endurance and fortitude of all his patrol was magnificent.

> By his personal example he set the highest standards which his patrol both admired and responded to in the most positive way. His actions, carried out in a totally hostile environment, were in the highest traditions of his Regiment and the Army.

A more general survey of G Squadron's activities explained that from the time of their initial deployment in the Falkland Islands on 1 May the men had been in close contact with the enemy for over six weeks. They had been exclusively committed to carrying out long-term surveillance operations against Argentine forces throughout the islands to determine their positions, strengths and activities. Most of the detailed intelligence that became available during the first part of May was therefore gained by this Squadron. In the view of the Task Force Commander it would not have been possible to plan the amphibious

landing or subsequent operations without this intelligence. Not only
this, but nor could the offensive naval gunfire and air attacks have
been properly executed, and these attacks were essential to softening
up the enemy prior to landing the main force. It was all a typical
demonstration of clandestine operations, living behind enemy lines for
a month or so without respite, always close to the enemy, in a hazardous operational environment and extremely unpleasant weather. Yet
the patrols always maintained communications and never failed to pass
the required intelligence. It is important to understand that the detailed nature of their reporting meant that the men had to penetrate
enemy positions so that they could actually see the exact defensive
positions, weapons and aircraft which the enemy had. This in turn
ment that the patrols were constantly without shelter, eating only cold
food. Small wonder that many of them became debilitated. Yet none
had to be withdrawn from the field. Moreover G Squadron, like D,
suffered tragic loss in the helicopter accident already described. Their
leadership, resilience, discipline and training were such that it did not
affect their resolution or perseverance. Indeed no other men were lost
at all, whereas the toll taken of enemy men and machines continued to
be high. There can be no doubt that G Squadron's contribution to the
success of the whole Falklands operation, like D Squadron's, was
indispensable. And now one more reference to D Squadron will be
fitting. It is the story of Captain Hamilton, of whom it might well
have been said, 'The valiant never taste of death but once':

Between 19 April and 10 June, when he was killed in action, Captain
Hamilton and his S.A.S. Troop were responsible for some of the most
successful S.A.S. operations carried out in the entire campaign in the
South Atlantic. Having survived two helicopter crashes in appalling
weather conditions on the Fortuna Glacier in South Georgia, two days
later Captain Hamilton led the advance elements of the forces which captured the main Argentinian positions in Grytviken. This action led directly
to the total surrender of all Argentinian forces in South Georgia. Ten days
later Captain Hamilton led his Troop on the successful and brilliantly
executed raid on Pebble Island when 11 enemy aircraft were destroyed on
the ground. Acting quickly and decisively and with great courage and
coolness, he personally supervised the destruction of 7 aircraft.
   Even though his Troop had lost half its strength in a helicopter crash
the previous day, Captain Hamilton then led the remainder of his men on
a highly successful diversionary raid on Darwin in order to cover the main
amphibious landings on East Falkland. That he was able to do this after
such losses is an immense testimony to his resilience and leadership. Next

Captain Hamilton deployed with his Squadron to a position 40 miles behind the enemy lines overlooking the main Argentinian defensive positions in Port Stanley. Once again, his leadership and courage proved to be instrumental over the next seven days of continuous operations in seizing this vital ground from which the attack on Port Stanley was ultimately launched. On 27 May he identified an enemy probe into the Squadron position and in the ensuing battle captured a prisoner of war. The next night, he and his Troop successfully held off another enemy attack and by doing so enabled 42 Commando to fly in as planned to reinforce the position. On the following day he ambushed another enemy patrol, wounding three and capturing all five members of the patrol.

On 5 June he was deployed in command of a four-man observation patrol into a hazardous position once again behind enemy lines on West Falkland to carry out observation of enemy activities in Port Howard. He managed to establish himself in a position only 2500 metres from the enemy, from where he sent detailed and accurate reports. Shortly after dawn on 10 June he realized that he and his radio operator had been surrounded in a forward position. Although heavily outnumbered and with no reinforcements available, he gave the order to engage the enemy, telling his signaller that they should both attempt to fight their way out of the encirclement. Since the withdrawal route was completely exposed to enemy observation and fire, he initiated the fire fight in order to allow his signaller to move first. After the resulting exchange of fire he was wounded in the back, and it became clear to his signaller that Captain Hamilton was only able to move with difficulty. Nevertheless he told his signaller that he would continue to hold off the enemy while the signaller made good his escape, and then he proceeded to give further covering fire. Shortly after that he was killed.

In the action which lasted some 30 minutes, Captain Hamilton displayed outstanding determination and an extraordinary will to continue the fight in spite of being confronted by hopeless odds and being wounded. He furthermore showed a supreme courage and sense of duty by his conscious decision to sacrifice himself on behalf of his signaller. His final brave and unselfish act will be an inspiration to all who follow in the S.A.S.

He was awarded a posthumous Military Cross, but the officer recommending it added: 'I consider that his actions fall little short of the ultimate award of the Victoria Cross'.

Apart from sheer fighting, however, there was one more crucial contribution that the S.A.S. made to victory in the Falkland Islands. It was in the sphere of psychological warfare operations – 'psyops'.

It has long been understood by post-war S.A.S. that war is about people's attitudes as much as it is about killing people, and the war in the Falkland Islands proved to be no exception.

The war showed that the wide and varied training of the S.A.S. for their different roles and their flexible communications system undoubtedly enabled them to operate successfully both in South Georgia and in the Falkland Islands. For example, the covert observation techniques developed for the rural areas of Northern Ireland were entirely appropriate to the Falkland Islands situation and terrain. The S.A.S. training for the Northern Flank commitment required them to have special cold weather clothing and equipment which again produced benefits in the Falkland Islands.

The S.A.S. had not worked with the Royal Navy on large-scale amphibious operations since the last war and major adjustments had to be made by the S.A.S. to conform to the Royal Naval way of doing business.

Brigadier Julian Thompson, who commanded the ground forces during the planning stages of the war and during the initial phases of the land battle, was clearly going to be the person who would make the most meaningful decisions regarding the land battle. It was Brigadier Thompson who would establish the constraints and requirements which would govern the running of the entire war, including the deployments of the ships and aircraft belonging to the other Services. Furthermore, much of his intelligence was going to emanate from the S.A.S. who would thus have a decisive influence on his planning. The Regiment had worked with him when he was commanding 40 Commando in Bessbrook Mill in South Armagh.

The C.O. flew down to see Julian Thompson on Saturday 3 April and had a one-hour meeting with him, Commander Amphibious Warfare (COMAW) and General Moore, (at that time MGRM). Brigadier Thompson readily agreed that from 9 April onwards the S.A.S. would be integrated into his planning group. No S.A.S. action or plan went without his approval and he was fully appraised of everything in the way of intelligence that was gained. He also ordered the S.B.S. Headquarters to move to HMS *Fearless*, for the S.B.S. Headquarters had gone forward to Ascension Island and was intending to travel down with the Naval Task Force with Admiral Woodward. As a result, throughout the war, the S.B.S. were integrated into the headquarters on HMS *Fearless*.

Fairly early on it became clear that deception and psychological operations could be conducted by the S.A.S. The bombardment of Port Stanley, from an S.A.S. position on top of Mount Kent, on the first of June, and the sending of newspaper despatches also from

51 An NCO of 22 SAS with a *firqat* patrol during operations in Dhofar.

52 An SAS 'medic' starts his daily surgery in Dhofar.

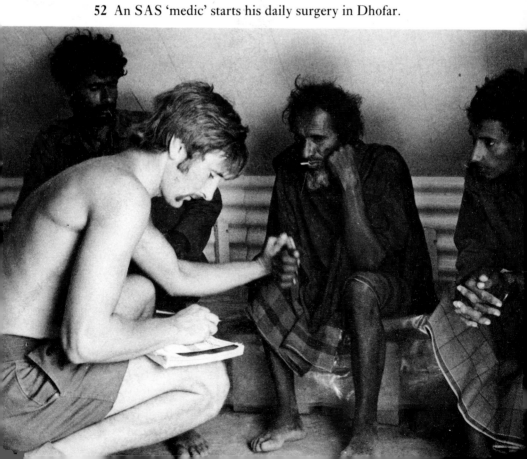

53 The Sultan of Muscat and Oman greets a *firqat* man at Qairoon Hairitti in Dhofar.

54 An SAS patrol in typical scrub country in Dhofar.

5 Corporal Labalaba, the great Fijian, killed at Mirbat, 19 July, 1972.

56 Danny Elliott, Oman.

57 A view of Mirbat from the air.

58 An SAS selection course in progress on the Brecon Beacons.

59 An extra-large T.A. selection course of 21 SAS (Artists) forms up at the Duke of York's HQ in London; only 11 passed.

60 Preparing to assault the Iranian Embassy, Princes Gate, London, May, 1980.

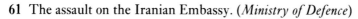

61 The assault on the Iranian Embassy. (*Ministry of Defence*)

62 The Falkland Islands, April, 1982. The damaged airstrip and Argentine aircraft at Pebble Island. (*Ministry of Defence*)

63 A Royal Navy Sea King Mark 4 helicopter taking off during the Falkland Islands war. (*Ministry of Defence*)

64 A crashed helicopter in the Falklands, South Georgia. (*Crown Copyright, Fleet Photographic Unit, Portsmouth*)

65 Signing the instrument of surrender, South Georgia. (*Crown Copyright, Fleet Photographic Unit, Portsmouth*)

Mount Kent at a time when the Argentinian radio was saying that British Troops were still bogged down in Darwin, Goose Green and San Carlos, were examples of psychological operations which sought to undermine the credibility of the Argentine high command amongst their soldiers. More important was the opening of a line to Argentine Joint Services Headquarters in Port Stanley. The idea for this came from the reports S.A.S. patrols had sent indicating that the Argentine Army were, in general, in a very demoralized state. This, coupled with the knowledge that their temperament was somewhat Italian, made them susceptible to this form of attack. It was thought that once the Argentine Army felt that it had satisfied its own sense of honour by putting up sufficient resistance (however token), to British attack, then it would accept a surrender as long as it was on 'honourable' terms. This view of their thinking was confirmed by the surrender of the garrison at Darwin and Goose Green. A plan, outlining various stratagems, was put to General Moore when he arrived in the Falkland Islands. He subsequently got clearance for this plan from UK.

The S.A.S. had a most useful asset in this psychological warfare campaign in the person of a Royal Marine Captain called Rod Bell, who was a Costa Rican-born Englishman who had spent most of his life in Latin America. He had had to learn English in order to join the Royal Marines. Furthermore, he had a genuine sympathy and understanding for the Argentine predicament in the Falkland Islands and this proved invaluable.

The main part of the psyops plan lay in getting the Argentines to open a line with the British and this was achieved on the 6 June after an initial failure to open a telephone line to Port Stanley from Estancia House which was the most forward position. This attempt had failed because the line had been destroyed by British artillery shelling. Assisting us at this stage was an Argentine Air Force Commodore – one Pedrozo Wilson – who agreed to act as an intermediary or go-between on our behalf (or on behalf of a cease fire as they euphemistically called it). He became surprisingly friendly and somewhat emotionally involved in achieving success; ie: in getting the Argentines to surrender! In the event, his voice on the air to the Argentine Headquarters was deemed by the Argentine Chief of Staff – and this was stated to the S.A.S. after the war had ended – to be a mistake, as he felt that the Commodore had not been acting honourably. (There then had to be a second psyops campaign on the Argentine Command to prevent Pedrozo from getting into trouble on his return to Argentina!). On 14 June at 1300 hours, the Argentine Chief of Staff, a naval captain called Melbourne Hussey, asked to speak to the C.O. The logic of our argument over a period of 8 days – that further bloodshed was useless, that it would only deepen the rift between the Argentine and the UK and would inevitably result in the Argentine Army being branded as the butchers of Port Stanley, the logic of all this was finally accepted by the Argentine Headquarters in the face of their hopeless military position. The C.O. arranged to fly to Port Stanley and RV with Captain Hussey at 1900 hours that evening. This he did, passing through a concealed S.A.S. position some three miles to the north of Port Stanley where a white flag was fixed to the helicopter for identification purposes because, although the ceasefire had largely been exercised across the battlefield by then, there was no trusting its effectiveness! The helicopter landed at the wrong RV, some quarter of a mile to the west of the Government House football field, and the S.A.S. party had to move across country, climbing over the Argentine obstacles and through their defensive positions round Government House which caused the Argentine soldiers manning them some surprise. They finally emerged, looking rather like scarecrows, on to the football pitch where the delegation was waiting, in immaculate, pressed uniforms and clean shoes. Melbourne Hussey said, in good English, that he had seen the helicopter land in the wrong place, to which the C.O. replied, 'Well, of course you know Port Stanley far better than we do'. He led the party to the main Secretariat where General Menendez was waiting with his staff. They went upstairs and started a two-hour long period of negotiations, which was broken off from time to time for each side to report back to their principals in order to get agreement to different points that were in contention. General Menendez was compelled to go off to his own Commcen in order to discuss points with General Galtieri in the Argentine. This put the team at some considerable psychological advantage. The main points of contention were whether the surrender by General Menendez should involve all forces in the Falkland Islands – including a fifty-mile *cordon sanitaire* round the islands – or whether, as the General wanted it, merely include his forces in East Falkland. Although the British were not in a position, because of the limited ammunition and troops available, to sustain a battle in Port Stanley, General Menendez was persuaded that, as Commander-in-Chief, he should surrender all his troops. He had opened the discussions by saying that he had been much impressed by the words the British had spoken to the Argentine Headquarters over the preceding few days because it had demonstrated to him that the British understood the true position of the Argentine Army and also recognized the valorous nature of his Army which had put up a good fight in difficult circumstances. In fact is was clear that the General was merely looking for a face-saving way out of his predicament and a peg on which to hang a surrender. After two hours of negotiation, he agreed to all the points made and General Moore was asked to come forward to sign the official instrument of surrender. After this formality, General Menendez retired to his billet and General Moore departed for his walk-about in Port Stanley, the time being after midnight. The S.A.S. party further discussed the situation with two Argentine Headquarter Company clerks who, relieved it was all over, produced a bottle of Southern Comfort from under their desk. After that, the S.A.S. party went off to Government House and hoisted the regimental S.A.S. Union Jack up the Government House flag pole where it remained for two days until the Royal Marines came and pulled it down in order to get television coverage of their own soldiers 'raising the Union Jack over Port Stanley'!

Only a small number of S.A.S. men took part in the Falkland Islands war. Between them they were awarded one DSO, three MCs, two MMs, fourteen Mentions in Despatches, four MBEs, two BEMs and three Commander-in-Chief's commendations. They had carried out their proper strategic tasks of intelligence gathering, raiding, diversionary attacks, and had even got themselves involved in tactical battles. Moreover the Commanding Officer's conduct of psyops had been decisive. As so often before the contribution to victory which they made demonstrated how much could be done with so few. They had dared, they had excelled, they had won! Had the Argentinians understood from the outset that it would be men like these they would be required to face in a battle for the Falkland Islands, it may be doubted whether they would ever have undertaken so unpromising an enterprise.

21

DARING TO EXCEL

The greatest pride of my husband, Airey Neave ... was to spend a day at the headquarters of the Special Air Service. His admiration for their regiment was unbounded.

Baroness Airey of Abingdon

.

What is it about the S.A.S. which makes us admire them so? Their daring, of course, for all of us admire courage; their reaching after and invariable attainment of excellence, for many of us would also wish to aspire to it; their versatility, for at heart most of us like a jack of all trades, whether he be master or no; their readiness, their dedication, their range, their success – yes, all of these too. But there is something extra, something less tangible and for want of a better word it is perhaps their sheer exclusiveness. They shun publicity for the best of reasons – security. For the most part they are nameless, shadowy, fleeting, tucked away in Hereford or London or the Dhofar or some other unheralded foreign field, until a journalist uncovers a story and blazes it across the headlines. It is perhaps this interchange of customary secretiveness and capricious publicity which add up to that quality so coveted and courted by the world of entertainment, yet so unwanted and eschewed by the S.A.S. – the quality of glamour.

There is something bewitching and awe-inspiring about their speed, their professionalism, their elusiveness, their single-minded dedication, their almost insolent certainty about being on top of the job, which endears them to us, which excites our imagination and fixes our wonder. There is, after all, despite the clinical efficiency with which they set about certain aspects of their business, something of the romantic image embodied by William Hodson* about them. Their panache, their physical toughness, their stealth and ingenuity, their unpredictability,

* See p. 217.

their extraordinary coalition of perseverance and dash, their matchless record of raising and leading irregular troops from far-off countries, their fearlessness - all these surely make up the very sort of being that David Stirling was thinking of when he equated the Man and the Regiment.

It is therefore David Stirling who should have the last word, for by insisting on a few principles which the last forty years have not changed, he has ensured that as long as the ordered application of violence by those in legitimate authority still has a place in the world in countering the evil forces of disruption and disintegration - and as General Sir John Hackett has made clear in his masterly little book, *The Profession of Arms*, this looks like being a long time yet - then the British Army will continue to need and take pride in the unique qualities and capabilities of the S.A.S. Regiment.

David Stirling described the philosophy on which the S.A.S. Regiment was founded like this:

> To understand the S.A.S. role it is important first to grasp the essential difference between the function of Airborne Forces and Commandos on the one hand and that of the wartime Special Operations Executive on the other. Airborne Forces and Commandos provided advance elements in achieving tactical objectives and undertook tactically scaled raids, while the S.O.E. was a *para*-military formation operating mainly out of uniform.
>
> In contrast, the S.A.S. has always been a strictly military unit, has always operated in uniform (except occasionally when seeking special information) and has functioned exclusively in the *strategic* field of operations. Such operations consisted mainly of: firstly, raids in depth behind the enemy lines, attacking HQ nerve centres, landing grounds, supply lines and so on; and, secondly, the mounting of sustained strategic offensive activity from secret bases within hostile territory and, if the opportunity existed, recruiting, training, arming and co-ordinating local guerrilla elements.
>
> The S.A.S. had to be capable of arriving in the target area by air and, therefore, by parachute; by sea, often by submarine and folboat; or by land, by foot or jeep-borne penetration through or around the enemy lines. To ensure surprise the S.A.S. usually arrived in the target area at night and this required a high degree of proficiency in all the arrival methods adopted for any particular operation.
>
> Strategic operations demand, for the achievement of success, a total exploitation of surprise and of guile - accordingly, a bedrock principle of the Regiment was its organization into modules or sub-units of 4 men. Each of the 4 men was trained to a high level of proficiency in the whole

range of the S.A.S. capability and, additionally, each man was trained to have at least one special expertise according to his particular aptitude. In carrying out an operation – often in the pitch-dark – each S.A.S. man in each module was exercising his own individual perception and judgment at full strength. The S.A.S. 4-man module could be viable as an operational entity on its own, or be combined with as many other modules as an operation might require.

In the early days of the S.A.S. Middle East HQ sometimes tended to regard us as a baby Commando capable of 'teasing' the enemy deep behind the lines during the quieter periods but available, in the circumstances of a major defensive or offensive confrontation, to undertake essentially tactical tasks immediately behind or on the flank of an aroused enemy. It took some further successful raids to persuade HQ to acknowledge that our role should remain an exclusively strategic one.

In today's S.A.S. the importance of good security is thoroughly instilled into every man. Certain delicate operational roles require the Secret Service to invest in the S.A.S. Command highly classified intelligence necessary for the effective planning of these operations and, just as importantly, for special training. For such intelligence to be entrusted to the S.A.S., its security disciplines have to be beyond reproach.

As the S.A.S. was operating at a distance of up to 1,000 miles from Army HQ, an exceptionally efficient wireless communication was essential. Frequently we would require interpretation of air photographs of target areas, taken while an S.A.S. unit was already deep in the desert on its way to attack them. An effective communication system became even more important to the S.A.S. in Europe. [Their own dedicated and special communications are still an essential feature of S.A.S. operations].

Recruitment was a problem, as we had to depend on volunteer recruitment from existing Army units. Not unnaturally, Commanding Officers were reluctant to see their most enterprising individuals transfer to the S.A.S., but eventually Middle East HQ gave us firm backing and we were usually able to recruit a few volunteers from each of the formations which had undergone general military and desert training. We always aimed to give each new recruit a very testing preliminary course before he was finally accepted for the S.A.S. Today the S.A.S. is even more ruthless in its recruitment procedures.

Once selected, our training programme for a man was an exhaustive one and was designed to give him thorough self-confidence and, just as importantly, equal confidence in his fellow soldiers' capacity to outclass and outwit the enemy by use of S.A.S. operational techniques.

We kept a careful track record of each man and capitalized whenever possible on the special aptitude he might display in various skills such as advanced sabotage technique, mechanics, enemy weaponry, night-time navigation and medical knowledge, etc. This register of each man's special skills was vital to make sure that each of our modules of 4 men was a well-balanced entity. Historical precedents, demonstrating how vital this concept could be to the winning of wars, were ignored and we, therefore, had to start again nearly from scratch. Luckily, the British, for one, now acknowledge the validity of the strategic raid, hence the continuing existence of the S.A.S. Regiment. The S.A.S. today fully recognizes its obligation to exploit new ideas and new development in equipment and, generally, to keep a wide open mind to innovation and invention.

From the start the S.A.S. Regiment has had some firmly held tenets from which we must never depart. They are:

1. the unrelenting pursuit of excellence;
2. maintaining the highest standards of discipline in all aspects of the daily life of the S.A.S. soldier, from the occasional precision drilling on the parade ground even to his personal turnout on leave. We always reckoned that a high standard of self-discipline in each soldier was the only effective foundation for Regimental discipline. Commitment to the S.A.S. pursuit of excellence becomes a sham if any *single one* of the disciplinary standards is allowed to slip;
3. the S.A.S. brooks no sense of class and, particularly, not among the wives. This might sound a bit portentous but it epitomizes the S.A.S. philosophy. The traditional idea of a crack regiment was one officered by the aristocracy and, indeed, these regiments deservedly won great renown for their dependability and their gallantry in wartime and for their parade-ground panache in peacetime. In the S.A.S. we share with the Brigade of Guards a deep respect for quality, but we have an entirely different outlook. We believe, as did the ancient Greeks who originated the word 'aristocracy', that every man with the right attitude and talents, regardless of birth and riches, has a capacity in his own lifetime of reaching that status in its true sense; in fact in our S.A.S. context an individual soldier might prefer to go on serving as an N.C.O. rather than have to leave the Regiment in order to obtain an officer's commission. All ranks in the S.A.S. are of 'one company' in which a sense of class is both alien and ludicrous. A visit to the Sergeants' Mess at S.A.S. HQ in Hereford vividly conveys what I mean;
4. humility and humour: both these virtues are indispensable in the everyday life of officers and men – particularly so in the case of the S.A.S. which is often regarded as an élite Regiment. Without frequent recourse to humour and humility, our special status could cause

resentment in other units of the British Army and an unbecoming conceit and big-headedness in our own soldiers.

It was thus that David Stirling summed up the idea of daring to excel and explained the rules of putting it into practice. They are rules which worked yesterday, work now and will work tomorrow. There is no doubt about the S.A.S. being élite and it is open for any man in the British Army to join – if he is good enough. There is no more to be said.

APPENDIX 1

ORIGIN OF SPECIAL FORCES

In 1938 a War Office research section, G.S.(R) examined how guerrillas might be used in future wars, and generally studied irregular warfare. The following year produced a further study of how to co-ordinate guerrilla operations with the main battle. It was thought that in the right circumstances such operations could greatly assist the main forces. G.S.(R) then became Military Intelligence Research. Fresh ideas for sabotage, deception and escape organizations were developed. In the spring of 1940 the War Office was persuaded to put some of these ideas into practice, and independent companies were formed to act as guerrillas. Three such companies were sent to Norway, but were misused as infantry, instead of being employed to harass enemy communications. Despite this, ten further companies were formed from the Territorial Army with some Regular content.

In June, 1940, Churchill urged the War Office to do something to hit back and 'set Europe ablaze'. Lt-Colonel Dudley Clarke suggested raising Commando raiding forces, and convinced the C.I.G.S., Sir John Dill, that it should be done. A special War Office branch was thereupon formed to co-ordinate operations, and late in June the first raids on France were carried out. They had little success, but the idea took hold and it was agreed to form a Commando Force of 5,000. It was in this way that the origins of the S.A.S. emerged. Men of 2 Commando started to train as parachutists, and later became 11th S.A.S.* In February, 1941, they raided the Tragino aqueduct in southern Italy, obliging the Italians to divert substantial forces to guard against such operations.

Proper exploitation of these ideas and the troops available was not at first possible because of general shortages of shipping, smaller craft and aeroplanes. Nonetheless a Special Service Brigade had been formed and plans for

---

*Later 1st Parachute Battalion.

attacking Dakar, the Canaries and Pantelleria were discussed. There was disagreement about the relative value of such raids compared with properly organized and supported operations, but the general concept of small raids both for sabotage and for gaining intelligence was taking hold.

These were not the only ideas for raiding Europe. In July, 1940, a number of peacetime canoeists had demonstrated their potential in reconnaissance and sabotage. It was proposed to form a section of 30 canoeists per Commando, and in this way the first Special Boat Section was born. Lieutenant Roger Courtney, who had been a big-game hunter before the war, trained a section of fifteen men, which was attached to 8 Commando. In early 1941 he took his section to the Middle East as part of Layforce, which consisted of three Commandos and was despatched to the Middle East with the purpose of capturing Rhodes. The aim was to clear the eastern Mediterranean of enemy forces, in conjunction with Wavell's successful campaigns in East Africa and the Western Desert. On arrival in the Middle East, however, the situation had changed so much that Layforce was split up and employed differently. Yet it was part of Layforce which gave birth to the S.A.S. [see Chapter 2].

APPENDIX 2

S.A.S. OPERATIONS
IN NORTH AFRICA 1941/3

Appendices 2, 3 and 4 have been compiled from official records, where they exist, and from various other sources. Some errors and omissions are inevitable in the circumstances.

Date / Means	Mission	Taking part	Results
1941 16 November By parachute drop from 5 Bombay aircraft onto 5 DZs at night	To destroy aircraft on 5 landing grounds in Tmimi/Gazala area on night before 8th Army offensive 18 Nov	64 members of original 'L' Detachment. 7 officers: — Stirling, Mayne, Lewis, Fraser, McGonigal, Thomas, Bonnington. 32 NCOs: — Yates, Riley, Cheyne, Stone, Lazenby, Almonds, Tait, Duvivier, Badger, Monachem, Kershaw, White, McGinn, Gryne, Orton, Storey, Leitch, Hildreth, Walker, Evans, Smith, Rose, Arnold, Cattell, Kendall, Bennett, Brough, Kaufman, Lilley, MacDonald, Cooper, Seekings. 25 Privates: — Keith, Cockbill, Warburton, Phillips, Davies, McKay, Westwater, White, Harvie, Trenfield, Morris, Hill, Sadler, Carrington, Baker, Bolland, Keenan, Bridger, Chesworth, Leadbetter, Rhodes, Austin, Hawkins, Blakeney, Robertson.	Due to very high winds and cloud not one aircraft dropped accurately. Sticks were widely dispersed on landing. One aircraft landed on German airfield. One group believed to have penetrated one target but all were killed. Stirling and Mayne reached coast road, then, with other survivors, marched south to RV with LRDG patrol. 4 officers and 18 NCO's/Ptes returned. The first and last parachute operation in the desert, which convinced Stirling that approach must be made by vehicle, then courtesy of LRDG.

Date	Target	Personnel	Results
6 December By air to Gialo oasis and then by LRDG patrol	To destroy aircraft on:— Agheila airfield Sirte (Tamet) airfield	Lewis, Fraser, Almonds, Kershaw, Rose, Lilley, Bennett, Storey, Baker, Rhodes, Warburton. Stirling, Mayne, Brough, MacDonald, Burns, White, Seekings, Cattell, Cooper, Chesworth, Hawkins.	Dropped off 20 miles from target and walked in. No aircraft on airfield. Destroyed trucks on road. Stirling and Brough on recce to Sirte but no aircraft. Mayne with main party attacked Tamet and destroyed 24 aircraft.
18 December As above	To destroy aircraft on Agebadia airfield	Fraser, Tait, Duvivier, Phillips, Burns.	Walked onto airfield and destroyed 37 aircraft. On return were attacked by RAF aircraft and LRDG lost 2 killed.
23 December As above	To destroy aircraft on Sirte airfield	Stirling, Brough, Cooper, Cattell, Seekings.	Airfield was defended and party could not penetrate. Some trucks destroyed.
24 December As above	To destroy aircraft on Tamet airfield	Mayne, MacDonald, White, Bennett, Hawkins, Chesworth.	Drove to within 3 miles of airfield and destroyed 27 aircraft. Party dispersed by enemy fire but rejoined. Celebrated Christmas Day on return journey with LRDG.
24 December As above	To destroy aircraft on Nofilia airfield	Lewis, Almond, Lilley, Storey, White, Warburton.	Walked in from 16 miles. Aircraft dispersed and enemy alert. 1 aircraft destroyed. On return with LRDG strafed by enemy aircraft. Lewis killed. White PW. 4 trucks destroyed. LRDG walked 250 miles to Gialo.

Date Means	Mission	Taking part	Results
24 December As above	To destroy aircraft on Marble Arch airfield	Fraser, Tait, Duvivier, Phillips, Burns.	Nothing on airfield. Waited 7 days at RV but remaining LRDG truck from Nofilia attack could not find it. Walked 200 miles in 8 days and finally hijacked German staff car.
1942 23 January As above	To destroy shipping and dumps in Bouerat Harbour	Stirling, Riley, Badger, Bennett, Kershaw, Seekings, Cooper, Cattell, Rose, Austin, Brough, Rhodes, Baker. Capt Duncan, Cpl Barr SBS, F/O Rawnsley, RAF	LRDG wireless truck lost. SBS canoe damaged. Destroyed 18 petrol bowsers and 4 food dumps.
8 March	To attack aircraft on; Benina airfield	Stirling, Seekings, Cooper.	Found only derelict aircraft. Blew 2 torpedo dumps.
By LRDG patrol from Siwa Oasis (due to 8th Army retreat Gialo was abandoned).	Berca airfield	Mayne, Rose, Bennett, Burns.	Walked in from 30 miles and destroyed 15 aircraft and 15 torpedos. Burns captured.
	Barce airfield	Fraser, Badger, Kershaw, Phillips, Chesworth, MacDonald.	1 aircraft and workshop trucks destroyed.
	Slonta airfield	Dodd, Riley, Duvivier, Brough, Cattell, Warburton, Storey.	Unable to penetrate airfield defences.

254

Date / Method	Objective	Personnel	Results
24 March By LRDG patrol	To destroy aircraft on Benina airfield	Stirling, Cooper, Seekings, Bennett, Elliott, Sinclair, Alston.	First made recce of Benghazi and on return stopped off at Benina. 5 aircraft in hangars destroyed but most aircraft on field were decoys.
April As above	To destroy shipping in Benghazi harbour	Stirling, Mayne, Lilley, Storey, Seekings.	Blew dumps and shot up trucks. SAS vehicle destroyed by accident.
21 May As above	To destroy shipping in Benghazi harbour	Stirling, Cooper, Seekings, Rose, Bennett, Alston, Capts Churchill, Maclean, Lts Sutherland, Allot (SBS), Maj Bob Melot.	Drove into Benghazi by car and stayed for 2 days. No damage done but useful recce.
13/14 June From Siwa by LRDG patrol. By Navy submarine to Crete.	To destroy aircraft on 8 airfields in Libya and Crete in order to assist passage of convoy from Egypt to Malta	*Derna* (3): Lt Jordan and 17 French SAS. Capt Buck and S.I.G. *Benghazi* (2): Stirling, Mayne, Cooper, Seekings, Storey, Lilley, Warburton. Lt Zirnheld and 7 French SAS. *Heraklion:* Capt Bergé and 3 French SAS. Capt Jellicoe. *Kastelli:* Lt Duncan ⎫ *Timbaki:* Lt Sutherland ⎬ SBS *Maleme:* Lts Kealy/Allot ⎭	Raid betrayed by German collaborator and all captured, less Jordan and Buck. 20 aircraft destroyed. 21 aircraft destroyed. All party except Jellicoe captured. 8 aircraft destroyed. Although these raids distracted German air effort against Malta convoy, nevertheless 15 out of 17 ships were sunk.

Date / Means	Mission	Taking part	Results
7/8 July Guided by LRDG to desert RVs and then by SAS armed jeeps	To destroy aircraft on 5 airfields close behind German line at Alamein	*Fuka*: British/French SAS. *Bagush*: Stirling, Mayne and party. *Sidi Barrani*: Schott, Warr and party. *El Daba*: Jellicoe, Lt Zirnheld and French SAS.	Some parties could not attack due to enemy defences on airfields. Stirling and Mayne's party destroyed 37 aircraft. Other parties destroyed 14 aircraft.
12/13 July By SAS jeeps	To raid enemy airfields behind Alamein line	*Fuka* (3): Parties led by Mayne, Fraser, Jordan. *El Daba* (2): Parties led by Jellicoe and Martin.	Mayne's and Jordan's parties destroyed 22 aircraft but other parties met opposition on airfields.
26/27 July By SAS jeeps	To destroy aircraft on Sidi Haneish airfield (near Fuka)	A force of some 50 British and French SAS in 18 armed jeeps under Stirling, with Mayne, Jellicoe, Scratchley, Jordan, Martin, Zirnheld and others.	A concentrated attack was made by whole party in 2 columns of armed jeeps on crowded airfield at night. About 40 aircraft were destroyed. Several SAS casualties including Lt Zirnheld.
1 September By SAS jeeps	To attack enemy transport on coast road	4 parties under Lts Jordan, Bailey, Russell, Mather.	Due to changed plans, there was not time to carry out the mission to any conclusion.

Date/Method	Objective	Forces/Commander	Results
13 September SAS by jeeps and 3 ton trucks to Benghazi	Large-scale raid (planned by GHQ Cairo) to attack Tobruk and Benghazi harbours	*Benghazi*: Stirling and some 200 SAS. *Tobruk*: Army Commandos.	Enemy in Benghazi were alerted and it was impossible to press attack. SAS lost 50 men and 50 vehicles from air attack during withdrawal.
	Gialo oasis to be taken and Barce airfield to be attacked	*Gialo*: Sudan Defence Force. *Barce*: LRDG.	The LRDG at Barce achieved some success.
October/November By SAS jeep via Kufra and Siwa Oasis	To disrupt German supply lines behind Alamein position.	Maj Mayne and A Squadron SAS.	Many small raids carried out against dumps, transport, airfields and railway with some success.
29 November–5 January By SAS transport from Egypt to desert RVs in Tripolitania	To disrupt supply lines along 400 miles of coast road Agedabia-Tripoli	*Agheila–Bouerat*: Mayne with A Squadron. *Bouerat-Tripoli*: Street and B Squadron (initially led by Stirling).	Due to more rapid 8th Army advance A Squadron had time to carry out only few attacks. B Squadron from 13 December made series of sharp raids causing damage, thus forcing enemy to divert large forces against them. Most of B Squadron were eventually killed or captured, less a few old hands. However, enemy transport was forced to use roads by day thus presenting good targets for attack by RAF.
1943 January/February By jeep patrols, mainly via Ghadames	To assist 8th Army's attack on Tripoli and the Mareth line by	*Tripoli area*: Lt Poat and party. *Mareth Line Recce*: Capt Alston and party.	SAS patrol first to enter Tripoli. Useful information on Mareth Line given to 8th Army.

Date Means	Mission	Taking part	Results
	harrassing enemy supply lines West of Tripoli and in Tunisia	*Gabes/Sfax:* Capt Jordan and French SAS. *Central Tunisia:* Stirling and party.	Some harassing raids carried out but eventually all French killed or captured. Stirling on way to raid near Sousse was captured by German anti-SAS unit, but remnants of his group were first to link with 1st Army near Gafsa.

During March/April 1943 patrols of 2 SAS, recently formed from 62 Commando and commanded by Lt-Col William Stirling, David's brother, attempted to carry out similar operations and to infiltrate around enemy lines near Pichon and Gafsa, but they found, like 1 SAS and the French, that it was very difficult by comparison with the desert, due to the hill terrain, the unfriendly population and a more compact enemy defensive line.

APPENDIX 3

S.A.S. OPERATIONS IN CENTRAL MEDITERRANEAN AND ITALY 1943/44

Operation Date	Unit	Method of entry	Mission
SNAPDRAGON 28 May	Detachment 2 SAS	By submarine	Reconnaissance of Pantelleria Island.
MARIGOLD 30 May	,,	,,	Reconnaissance of enemy airfields East coast of Sardinia.
HAWTHORN 7 July	,,	,,	,,
NARCISSUS 10 July	,,	By landing craft	To destroy Italian defence positions SE coast of Sicily in advance of Op Husky.
CHESTNUT 10 July	Various groups 2 SAS	By parachute	To cause disruption in enemy rear areas at time of invasion of Sicily (Op Husky) by dropping SAS patrols to take offensive action.
In support HUSKY 10 July	SRS complete (late 1 SAS)	By landing craft	To destroy Italian coastal batteries at Cape Murro di Porco, near Syracuse. After successful operation SRS re-embarked and landed again to capture Augusta harbour.
SPEEDWELL 7 September	Two groups of 2 SAS	By parachute	To interdict railway communications in Spezia–Genoa area, N.E. Italy, in order to slow up German reinforcements into South Italy.

Date/Operation	Unit	Method	Task
9 September	Composite Squadron from 2 SAS	By RN/US Navy Cruisers	To operate with Airborne Div as jeep reconnaissance force to infiltrate retreating German forces from Taranto–Bari–Foggia, S.E. Italy. Sqn. later joined with SRS, 2 SAS and Commandos at Termoli.
12 September	SRS complete	By landing craft	To dislodge German defences at Bagnara, S.W. Italy.
JONQUIL October	Detachment 2 SAS	Landing craft	To carry out harrassing operations against German transport in Ancona area, East coast Italy.
September/October	2 SAS	By parachute and landing craft.	A number of small operations were carried out to organize the successful evasion and evacuation of Allied ex-prisoners of war from Italian PW camps.
BEGONIA 2 October	Detachment 2 SAS	By parachute	To harass German road/rail transport Ancona–Pescara, East coast Italy.
3 October	SRS	By major assault landing	To land with Special Service Brigade (Army and Marine Commandos) near Termoli in order to dislodge German left flank. Fought major action as infantry. Sqn 2 SAS joined SRS.
CANDYTUFT 27 October	Detachment 2 SAS	By landing craft	To cut railway in Pescara area, East coast Italy.

Operation Date	Unit	Method of entry	Mission
SAXIFRAGE 27 October	Detachment 2 SAS	By landing craft	To harass German road/rail communications Ancona– Pescara, East coast Italy.
SLEEPY LAD 18 December	"	"	"
1944 MAPLE THISTLEDOWN 7 January	"	By parachute	To interdict German rail communications North of Rome in support of Allied landings at Anzio.
MAPLE DRIFTWOOD 7 January	Detachment 2 SAS	"	To interdict German rail communications Ancona–Rimini, East coast Italy.
POMEGRANATE 12 January	"	"	To raid German airfield San Egidio, Central Italy.
BAOBAB 27 January	"	By landing craft	To destroy railway bridge Pesaro, East coast Italy.

APPENDIX 4

S.A.S. OPERATIONS IN EUROPE
1944/5

Operation Date Area	Unit Strength Commander	Mission Method of entry	Results
1. TITANIC 6 June–6 July S. of Carentan, Normandy	1 SAS 6 troops Lt Fowles	To create diversions in order to assist U.S. Airborne landings by dropping dummy parachutists and pyrotechnics By parachute	Most equipment lost on drop. Operation did not cause enemy to react.
2. BULBASKET 6 June–7 July Haute Vienne/Indre Central France	1 SAS/Phantom 55 troops (dropped 6–18 June)	To cut railways:— Limoges–Orleans –Poitiers Nevers –Vierzon By parachute	Enemy road, rail and signal communications harassed continuously, causing them to deploy large numbers including SS troops. SAS base attacked with 37 casualties of which 33 were captured and executed.
3. HOUNDSWORTH 6 June–6 September Saone et Loire E. France	A Sqn 1 SAS Some 2 SAS 153 troops 14 Jeeps Major Fraser (Lt Col Mayne from 7 Aug.)	To cut railways:— Lyons–Châlons Dijon–Paris Le Creusot–Nevers By parachute	Area was too big and targets too distant. Bad weather hampered flying. 22 railcuts: 6 trains derailed: 70 vehicles destroyed: 220 enemy casualties: 3,000 Maquis armed and active.
4. SAMWEST (incl WASH) 6 June–23 July S.W. Guin Camp N. Brittany	4 French Para Bn 116 troops (dropped 6–9 June) Capt Le Blond (Sqn Ldr Smith)	To hinder movement of enemy forces from W. Brittany to Normandy To organize Resistance By parachute	Successful arming of Maquis but base heavily attacked (12 June) with losses. Groups dispersed and joined DINGSON and GROG bases.

Operation	Force	Task	Result
5. DINGSON/GROG 6 June–17 June N.E. Vannes Pontivy Central Brittany	4 French Para Bn 158 troops 4 Jeeps (dropped 6–17 June) Cdt Bourgoin Capt Desplante	As above and to arm FFI battalions By parachute	On 17 June base was heavily attacked by strong German force with heavy casualties. SAS dispersed to new base. Very successful arming of Maquis.
6. COONEY 7 June–15 June Brittany	4 French Para Bn 54 troops dropped in 18 parties of 3 men	To cut all rail communications throughout Brittany By parachute	Partly successful – most parties joined DINGSON groups.
7. GAIN 14 June–15 August Foret de Fontainebleau S.W. of Paris	1 SAS 61 troops Maj Fenwick	To harass enemy lines of communication in Orleans Gap To cut East-West railways South of Paris By parachute	Very successful operation resulting in considerable harassment and casualties to enemy moving towards Normandy. Maj Fenwick and 3 SAS killed. 14 captured, most of whom were executed.
8. LOST 23 June–18 July Brittany	SAS/4 French Para 7 troops Maj Carey Elwes	To discover situation on DINGSON and contact Cdt Bourgoin By parachute	Contact made 30 June with French group from DINGSON The large-scale operations by 4 French Para Bn were very successful resulting in over 2,000 enemy casualties and in the arming and organising of 25,000 Maquis. The Germans were forced to deploy large forces against them and later their movement out of Brittany was delayed.
9. HAFT 8 July–11 August Mayenne/Le Mans N.W. France	1 SAS 7 troops	To report on enemy movement and dispositions To report potential targets for air attack By parachute	Very useful intelligence was provided. Good contact with Maquis.

Operation Date Area	Unit Strength Commander	Mission Method of Entry	Results
10. DICKENS 16 July–7 October Vendee, W. France	3 French Para Bn 64 troops Capt Fournier	To attack railways: Saintes–Saumur–Nantes To report and harass enemy movement in area. To organize Resistance By Parachute	90 successful railcuts – all traffic ceased after 26 July. Enemy on main roads harassed and forced to use side roads. 500 Germans killed: 200 vehicles destroyed. Operation would have achieved more if carried out earlier.
11. DEFOE 19 July–23 August Normandy	2 SAS 22 troops	To infiltrate parties through U.S. lines to observe and report enemy	
12. RUPERT 23 July–10 September Meuse, E. France	2 SAS 58 troops Maj Symes (killed in air crash 22 July) Main body dropped 4 Aug (Maj Rooney on 24 August)	To attack railways: Verdun–Reims Metz–Meaux Chaumont–Sens To contact Resistance By parachute	Operation did not achieve spectacular results as area was too close to main battle zone. It had been planned to take place soon after D Day but was delayed by RAF and SF objections.
13. GAFF 25 July–13 August Rambouillet S.W. Paris	2 SAS 6 troops Capt Lee	To kill or kidnap Field-Marshal Rommel and senior members of his staff By parachute	Rommel was strafed by fighter aircraft and wounded 28 July. SAS harassed enemy road traffic with success, causing casualties.

Operation	Force	Objective	Results
14. HARDY (incl ROBEY) 27 July–18 September Haute Marne Plateau de Langres E. France	2 SAS 55 troops/6 Jeeps (dropped 27 July–1 September) Capt Hibbert	To cause maximum disruption to enemy withdrawing East through France By parachute	Enemy harassed and delayed and casualties caused. Major Farran's squadron joined 24 August (OP WALLACE) and they operated together.
15. CHAUCER 27 July–15 August N.W. of Le Mans, N.W. France	Belgian Independent Parachute Company 20 troops (in 2 parties) 28 July/9 Aug) Lt Ghys Capt Hazel	To cause maximum confusion to enemy retreating Eastward N. of R. Loire and West of Paris By parachute	Operation should have been carried out 2 weeks earlier, as only end of enemy retreat encountered. Operations on foot too slow.
16. SHAKESPEARE 31 July–15 August N.W. of Le Mans	Belgian Para Coy 22 troops (31 July–8 Aug) Lt Debefre Lt Limbosen	As above	Similar results. Also assisted Major Neave (MI9) in rescue of 150 Allied airmen.
17. DUNHILL 3–24 August Maine, N.W. France	2 SAS 54 troops (in 5 parties) Captains Bell, Baillie and Lazon. Lt Dimond	To establish recce party S.E. of Vitre to report enemy movement Rennes–Laval To receive reinforcement if opportunity to harass enemy retreat occurs By parachute	Due to unexpected U.S. advance operation was mounted too late. 4 parties overrun by U.S. troops within 24 hours. 200 airmen rescued. Some harassing by Party 5.
18. BUNYAN 3–15 August Chartres, W. of Paris	Belgian Para Coy 21 troops Lt Kirschen	To cause maximum confusion to enemy retreat East and North of R. Loire and West of Paris By parachute	German transport harassed and casualties caused. Information sent on targets for bombing.

Operation Date Area	Unit Strength Commander	Mission Method of Entry	Results
19. MOSES 3 August–5 October Poitiers, W. France	3 French Para Bn 46 troops: 4 jeeps (3–10 Aug) Capt Simon	To disrupt enemy communications Montauban–Limoges	Very successful operation causing considerable casualties and damage. Useful intelligence passed including one target which was attacked by fighter aircraft destroying over 400 vehicles.
20. DERRY 5–18 August Finisterre, Brittany	3 French Para Bn 88 troops Cdt Conan	To prevent enemy movement towards Brest To prevent demolition by enemy of viaducts at Morlaix and Plougastel By parachute	Successful operation causing considerable damage and casualties on Germans. Assisted U.S. Army advance into area.
21. SAMSON 10 August–27 September Limoges Haute Vienne	3 French Para Bn 22 troops Capt Le Blond	To harass enemy road movement To stiffen and assist French Resistance groups By parachute	Numerous minor harassing actions carried out causing some 100 casualties and damage to vehicles.
22. HAGGARD 10 August–23 September Loire et Cher Central France	1 SAS 54 troops Maj Lepine	To report and harass enemy movement on road and railway in area	Successful operation causing heavy casualties which assisted German collapse South of R. Loire. Would have paid bigger dividend if mounted a month earlier.

Operation	Unit	Task	Results
23. MARSHALL 11–24 August Correze L.E. Limoges	3 French Para Bn 31 troops Capt Wauthier	To disrupt enemy movement To organize and stiffen Resistance forces By parachute	Numerous successful ambushes on German transport caried out with FFI, including attack on 300 SS troops surrounded in a school.
24. SNELGROVE 13–24 August Creuse E. of Limoges	3 French Para Bn 28 troops Lt Hubler	As above	Enemy harassed in a number of actions.
25. BARKER 13 August–9 September Saone et Loire Central Massif	3 French Para Bn 27 troops Lt Rouan	As above	Continuous attacks on German troops and transport causing considerable damage and casualties, estimated at 3,000 including 500 prisoners.
26. HARROD 13 August–24 September Saone et Loire Central Massif	3 French Para Bn 85 (reinforced by party with 8 jeeps infiltrated OP Newton) Comdt Conan	As above	Numerous roads, bridges and rail lines cut: enemy harassed. SAS lost 6 killed and 11 wounded.
27. JOCKWORTH 15 August–9 September Rhone/Loire	3 French Para Bn 57 troops Capt Hourst	As above	Numerous attacks on German transport and troops causing damage and casualties. *Note:* These 5 operations by 3 French Para Bn enabled a large part of France to be liberated by FFI.

Operation Date Area	Unit Strength Commander	Mission Method of Entry	Results
28. KIPLING 14 August–25 September W. of Auxerre Central France	1 SAS (C Sqn) 107 troops: 46 Jeeps Capt Harrison (advance party) Maj Marsh (OC Sqn) (Lt Col Mayne joined operation)	Original mission: To drop advance party to prepare LZ for C Sqn to land by glider with jeeps to support large Allied airborne operations in Orleans area, which was cancelled. Mission then to extend OP HOUNDSWORTH area and harass enemy By parachute/infiltration	Advance party fought major action against SS troops, causing heavy casualties. C Sqn infiltrated via Orleans and relieved A Sqn; continued to harass retreating enemy, causing heavy casualties including 3,000 prisoners. Bad weather restricted supply drops.
29. NOAH 16 August–13 September French Ardennes	Belgian Indep Para Coy 41 troops/4 Jeeps (in 2 parties) Capt Blondeel	To obtain information of enemy situation in Ardennes To control further reinforcement, if required By parachute	A highly successful operation which obtained valuable information and achieved liaison with Resistance. Offensive action caused German casualties during their retreat Eastwards.
30. TRUEFORM 17–26 August R. Seine N.W. of Paris	1 and 2 SAS Belgian Para Coy 102 troops (in 25 parties on 12 DZs) Lt-Col Franks (co-ordinating operation)	To harass enemy in area during his retreat from Normandy, with accent on petrol tankers and dumps By parachute	A short-notice operation which did not achieve much as most parties had not enough time on ground to take action before being overrun by Allied advance. Some vehicles, dumps destroyed.

Operation	Force	Object	Result
31. NEWTON 19 August–11 September Champagne/Burgundy Central France	3 French Para Bn 1 SAS 57 troops/19 Jeeps Lt de Roquebrune	To reinforce existing bases in order to extend activity against enemy retreat	A generally successful operation causing enemy casualties. Some groups operated with FFI and with advancing U.S. troops.
32. WALLACE 19 August–19 September Plateau de Langres Burgundy Franche-Comté	2 SAS 60 troops 23 Jeeps Maj Farran (Lt-Col Mayne joined operation)	To strengthen SAS bases and thus increase offensive action To deceive enemy as to U.S. line of advance By infiltration	Party drove 350 miles to join HARDY and then (2 Sept) moved East for further offensive operation, causing heavy casualties. Many valuable bombing targets reported without reaction. A successful operation proving that a specially trained force can achieve results out of proportion to its numbers.
33. WOLSEY 26 August–3 September Compiègne/Soissons N.E. France	SAS/Phantom 5 troops Lt McDevitt	To report enemy dispositions and movement in area By parachute	Useful information passed including enemy convoy which was then attacked by 44 Mosquito aircraft, causing heavy damage.
34. ABEL 27 August–22 September Franche Comté/ Lorraine E. France	3 French Para Bn 82 troops Capt Sicand	To establish a base in Doubs area in order to: Block the frontiers Prepare to block the Belfort Gap	Successful offensive actions carried out but in conjunction with FFI and with advancing French and U.S. troops.

Operation Date Area	Unit Strength Commander	Mission Method of Entry	Results
35. BENSON 28 August–1 September N.W. of Compiègne N.E. France	Belgian Para Coy 6 troops Lt Kirschen	To report on enemy dispositions and movement in area	Some of party injured on landing so concentrated on Paris–Amiens road: excellent information sent back.
36. SPENSER 29 August–14 September E. of Bourges Central France	4 French Para Bn (now 2 RCP) 317 troops 54 Jeeps Comdt Bourgoin	To act as mobile harassing force to cause maximum loss to enemy withdrawal from S.W. France across the R. Loire By infiltration	German retreat across R. Loire seriously disrupted, causing heavy casualties, including 120 vehicles destroyed and 2,500 prisoners. Operation contributed to the surrender of 20,000 Germans to U.S. forces to the North.
37. BRUTUS 2–18 September E. of R. Meuse Ardennes	Belgian Para Coy 19 troops Maj The Hon Hugh Fraser GHQ Liaison Regt	To liaise with and assist Belgian Secret Army To obtain information and to contact Capt Blondeel (OP NOAH).	Operations co-ordinated with Secret Army: arms and supplies dropped. Intelligence sent back, but was more tactical than strategic due to short term nature of mission.
38. BERGBANG 2–12 September West Belgium	Belgian Para Coy 40 troops (in 2 parties) Capt Courtoy	To cut enemy communications East of R. Meuse	Not a successful operation due to blind drop too far from area, together with bad weather. Main party drop dispersed, with one stick dropped in Germany.

Operation	Unit	Task	Results
39. LOYTON 13 August–21 September Vosges E. France	2 SAS 91 troops: 6 Jeeps Lt-Col Franks Capt Druce } Recce Maj Power } Parties	To co-operate with Resistance To attack enemy installations and communications To report movement on roads/ railways By parachute.	1st recce party lost radio and met unco-operative Maquis. 2nd recce party dropped 25 miles to North. Main party had to keep on move due to German action including special anti-SAS unit, but casualties caused and two German divisions tied down. 2 SAS killed and 31 captured and executed. If operation had been carried out in July as planned better results would have been achieved.
40. CALIBAN 6–11 September S.E. of Bourg Leopold N.E. Belgium	Belgian Para Coy 26 troops Lt Limbosch	To cut enemy communications West of R. Meuse when ordered by SHAEF By parachute	Due to dispersed drop only limited guerrilla activity was possible, causing some casualties and parties were soon overtaken by advancing British troops. Lt Limbosch killed 8 Sept.
41. PISTOL 16 September–3 October Alsace/Lorraine E. France	2 SAS 51 troops (in 4 parties) Capts Scott, Holland Lts Darwall, Birnie	To attack enemy road/rail communications between R. Rhine and R. Moselle, South of line Nancy–Strasbourg By parachute	One party due to fog did not drop and others were dropped inaccurately. 4 trains derailed and some vehicles destroyed.
42. Un-named (N. of LOYTON) 9–18 September Vosges, W. of Nancy E. France	2 SAS/Franch Para 10 troops Lt Rousseau	To cut: railway Nancy–Saarburg road Luneville–Saarburg	Party dispersed on drop and soon overrun by U.S. troops. Lt Rousseau and 1 soldier captured and shot.

Operation Date Area	Unit Strength Commander	Mission Method of Entry	Results
43. REGAN (later FABIAN) 16 September–14 March ('45) Arnhem, Holland	Belgian Para Coy 4 troops Lt Kirschen	To obtain information of enemy in N.W. Holland To look for V2 sites By parachute	Operation coincided with Airborne operation Market Garden and after its failure at Arnhem, the party was heavily involved in organizing the evasion of many Airborne Div men over the R. Rhine in co-operation with Dutch Resistance. Useful intelligence was also sent back.
44. PORTIA/GOBBO 27 September–17 March N. Holland	Belgian Para Coy 6 troops Lt Debefre	To report enemy movement in N. Holland By parachute	Despite loss of radio and several close encounters with enemy this small group provided excellent information of enemy.
45. FRANKLIN 24 December–25 January St Hubert/Houffalize Belgian Ardennes	2 RCP (late 4 French Para) 186 troops: 31 Jeeps Capt Puech-Samson	To protect left flank of 8 Corps during operations to counter German breakthrough in the Ardennes Ground support role	This was more of a reconnaissance task than a SAS operation, but the situation was critical. Useful recce was carried out but as front stabilized there was less opportunity for infiltration.
46. REGENT 27 December–15 January St Hubert/Burl Belgian Ardennes	Belgian Para Coy Whole Company 22 Jeeps Capt Blondeel	To operate in recce role with British armour to counter German breakthrough in the Ardennes Ground support role	Continuous jeep patrols against enemy with British units or independently. Some men were used as assault troopers in this thickly wooded terrain.

Operation	Unit	Task	Result
47. GALIA 27 December–15 February ('45) S. of Reggio/Modena N. Italy	3 Sqn 2 SAS (detached to Italy) 33 troops Capt Walker-Brown	To co-operate with Italian partisans in order to harass enemy communications, to support offensive by 5th U.S. Army By parachute	A highly successful operation under difficult conditions of weather and terrain. Enemy were well harassed and 150 casualties caused with 25 vehicles destroyed. Partisans did not contribute much.
48. COLD COMFORT 17 February–Brenner Pass N. Italy	3 Sqn 2 SAS 12 troops Capt Littlejohn	To blow railway cutting in order to block Brenner Pass By parachute	Party scattered on drop and some later were betrayed by hostile peasants and captured. Capt Littlejohn and Cpl Crowley executed.
49. TOMBOLA 4 March–24 April S. of Modena/Reggio N. Italy	3 Sqn 2 SAS 40 troops Maj Farran	To organize Italian and other partisans To form a base in order to harass enemy communications To attack enemy retreat in the event of U.S. Army offensive	Another highly successful operation, causing considerable German casualties - 1,000, including 400 prisoners. A Corps HQ was attacked causing 60 casualties. Withdrawal of 4 German divisions continually harassed.
50. ARCHWAY 25 March–10 May N.W. Germany	Composite force of 2 strong squadrons from 1 and 2 SAS 300 troops: 60 Jeeps Lt-Col Franks Maj Poat 1 SAS Maj Power 2 SAS	Initial task to conduct short range recce for the Airborne divisions E. of R. Rhine at Wesel: after to achieve deeper penetration ahead of the Allied advance across Germany	SAS acting as recce troops fought numerous actions in conjunction with armour and infantry against German rearguards, reaching Kiel on 3 May. SAS skills with their fire-power and mobility contributed much to the rapid advance of British 21st Army Group to the Baltic.

Operation Date Area	Unit Strength Commander	Mission Method of Entry	Results
51. LARKSWOOD 3 April–8 May N.E. Holland N.W. Germany	Belgian SAS Regt (formerly Para Coy) 327 troops Maj Blondeel	To conduct reconnaissance and to protect left flank of 4 Canadian Armourd Div during their advance into N.W. Germany	Numerous recce and infantry actions were fought in support of Canadians and Polish armoured units, which contributed much to their rapid advance North to cut off German forces in Holland.
52. KEYSTONE 3 April–6 May S. of Ijsselmeer Holland	2 SAS 32 Jeeps: 10 Jeeps (in three parties) Maj Druce Capts Stuart, Holland	To disrupt enemy in conjunction with Canadian Army advance North from Arnhem To capture bridges over Apeldoornsche Canal (if possible) By parachute	Radio communications for both parties failed and thus no jeeps were dropped but groups harassed the enemy. The land party was unable to penetrate and were used as forward recce by the Canadians.
53. HOWARD 6 April–6 May Meppen/Oldenburg N.W. Germany	1 SAS 240 troops (all in jeeps) Lt-Col Mayne	To act as spearhead reconnaissance for 4th Canadian Armoured Div in their advance N.E. towards Wilhelmshaven	Due to dykes, movement off roads was difficult. Enemy opposition was strong, preventing penetration of their lines. Numerous patrol and infantry actions were fought, adding much to the speed of the Canadian advance.

54. AMHERST 8 April–16 April Assen/Hoogeveen N.E. Holland	2 & 3 French RCP (reinforced by ex- Maquis) 700 troops 18 Jeeps Brig Calvert (at Tac HQ SAS Brigade) Maj Puech-Samson Lt-Col Bollardière	To cause alarm and confusion in enemy rear area and thus prevent them taking up fixed positions To prevent demolition of 18 bridges and to preserve for use 3 airfields By parachute (46 aircraft on 46 DZs)	Cloud caused many aircraft to drop inaccurately. Jeeps were not dropped. Numerous ambushes and attacks were carried out, causing many German casualties and much confusion thus enabling Canadians to move rapidly North to seal off all enemy in Holland. French SAS lost 29 killed and 35 wounded.
55. APOSTLE 12 May–25 August Kristiansand Bergen Norway	HQ SAS Brigade 1 & 2 SAS Regts 845 troops 150 Jeeps (with additional Airborne units) Brig Calvert	To carry out occupational duties following German surrender in Norway To assist in arrest of war criminals	Airlift into Stavanger not complete until 23 May due to bad weather. Over 30,000 German troops were dealt with and many thousands non-Germans and Russians repatriated.

APPENDIX 5

FUTURE OF S.A.S. TROOPS

To:
Lt-Col W. Stirling
Lt-Col D. Stirling, DSO
Lt-Col R. B. Mayne, DSO
Lt-Col B. M. F. Franks, DSO, MC
Lt-Col I. G. Collins
Lt-Col E. C. Baring
Lt-Col The Earl Jellicoe
Lt-Col D. Sutherland
Lt-Col D. Lloyd Owen, MC
Major J. Verney, MC
Major R. Farran, DSO, MC

The Director of Tactical Investigation, Maj-Gen ROWELL, has been ordered by the Chief of Imperial General Staff, that his directorate should investigate all the operations of the Special Air Service with a view to giving recommendations for the future of S.A.S. in the next war and its composition in the peace-time army. The actual terms of reference were:

An investigation of S.A.S. technique, tactics and organisation without prejudice to a later examination of all organisations of a similar nature which were formed and operated in various theatres of this last war.

Brigadier Churchill is Deputy Director of Tactical Investigation and lives at Flat 110, 4 Whitehall Court, London, SW1 (Whitehall 9400 Ext 1632), just behind the War Office. The Officer immediately concerned is Lt-Col C. A. Wigham. Lt-Col Wigham has in his possession all the reports on S.A.S.

operations in W. EUROPE. The reports on S.A.S. operations in ITALY and in the MEDITERRANEAN Theatre are also being obtained and forwarded. I have given Lt-Col Wigham your names so that he may either have a talk with you to obtain your views and to find out about incidents which are not clear in the reports, or to ask you to write your views to him.

We all have the future of the S.A.S. at heart, not merely because we wish to see its particular survival as a unit, but because we have believed in the principles of its method of operations. Many of the above-named officers have had command of forces which have had a similar role to that of the S.A.S., as well as being in the S.A.S. at one time.

The object of this investigation is to decide whether the principles of operating in the S.A.S. manner are correct. If they are correct, what types of units should undertake operations of this nature, and how best to train and maintain such units in peace, ready for war. I will not start now by writing about the principles of S.A.S., which have been an intrinsic part of your life for the past few years, but I will mention what I think are some of the most important points which needed bringing out. The best way to do this is to consider the usual criticisms of the S.A.S. type of force.

1. 'The Private Army'

From what I have seen in different parts of the world, forces of this nature tend to be so-called 'Private Armies' because there have been no normal formations in existence to fulfill this function – a role which has been found by all commanders to be a most vital adjunct to their plans. It has only been due to the drive and initiative of certain individuals backed up by senior commanders that these forces have been formed and have carried out their role.

2. 'The taking up of Commanders' valuable time'

This has often been necessary because it has very often only been the Comds of armies who have realised the importance of operations of this nature, and to what an extent they can help their plans. The difficulty has been that more junior staff officers have not understood the object or principles of such forces. They have either given us every help as they have thought us something wonderful, or they have thought we were 'a bloody nuisance'. I feel that the best way to overcome this is, that once the principle of the importance of Special Raiding Forces operating behind the vital points of the enemy's lines is agreed to it should become an integral part of the training of the army at the Staff College, military colleges, and during manoeuvres, etc. Students should be asked not only what orders or directives or requests they have to give to the artillery, engineers, air, etc. but also what directives they would give to their raiding forces. There should be a recognised staff officer on the staffs of senior formations whose job it is to deal with these forces, i.e. the equivalent of a C.R.E. or C.R.A. This should also be included in the text books F S R, etc.

3. *'These forces, like airborne forces, are only required when we pass to the offensive, which - judging by all previous wars - is when the regular army has been nearly wiped out in rearguard actions whilst the citizen army forms, i.e. about 3 years after the beginning of the war'*
The answer here, I feel, is that it is just when we are weak everywhere that forces of this nature are the most useful, and can play a most vital part in keeping the enemy all over the world occupied. Also there is little difference between the roles of S. A. S. and 'Auxiliary Forces' who duck when the enemy's offensive rolls over them and then operate against the enemy's L of C from previously constructed bases. An S. A. S. formation, by its organisation and training, is ideally suited to operate in this defensive role.

4. *'Overlapping with S.O.E. and other clandestine organisations'*
My experience is that S.O.E. and S.A.S. are complementary to each other. S.A.S. cannot successfully operate without good intelligence, guides, etc. S.O.E. can only do a certain amount before requiring, when their operations became overt, highly trained, armed bodies in uniform to operate and set an example to the local resistance. S.O.E. are the 'white hunters' and produce the ground organisation on which S.A.S. operates. All senior officers of S.O.E. with whom I have discussed this point agree to this principle.

5. *'S.A.S. is not adaptable to all countries'*
This has already been proved wrong. S.A.S. is probably more adaptable to changes of theatres than any regular formation. Also, as I have said in 4 above, S.A.S. work on the ground organisation of S.O.E. It is for S.O.E. to be a world-wide organisation with an organisation in every likely country. Then when necessary, S.A.S. can operate on this organisation using their guides and intelligence, knowledge, etc.

6. *'Volunteer units skim the regular units of their best officers and men'*
Volunteer units such as S.A.S. attract officers and men who have initiative, resourcefulness, independence of spirit, and confidence in themselves. In a regular unit there are far less opportunities of making use of these assets and, in fact, in many formations they are a liability, as this individualistic attitude upsets the smooth working of a team. This is especially true in European warfare where the individual must subordinate his natural initiative so that he fits into a part of the machine. Volunteer units such as the Commandos and Chindits (only a small proportion of the Chindits were volunteers

although the spirit was there) have shown the rest of the army how to fight at a time when it was in low morale due to constant defeat. A few 'gladiators' raises the standard of all. Analogies are racing (car, aeroplane, horse, etc), and Test teams.

7. *'Expense per man is greater than any other formation and is not worthwhile'*
Men in units of this nature probably fight 3 or 4 times more often than regular units. They are always eager for a fight and therefore usually get it. If expense per man days *actually in contact with the enemy* was taken into account, there would be no doubt which was the more expensive type of formation. I have found, as you will have done, the 'old familiar faces' on every front where we have seen trouble. I consider the expense is definitely worth it without even taking into account the extra results. One S.A.S. raid in North Africa destroyed more aeroplanes in one day than the balloon barrage did during 6 years of war.

8. *'Any normal battalion could do the same job'*
My experience shows that they definitely cannot. In NORWAY in 1940, a platoon of marines under a Sgt ran away when left on its own, although they had orders to stay, when a few German lorries appeared. Mainly owing to the bad leadership of this parade ground Sgt, they were all jittery and useless because they were 'out of touch'. A force consisting of two Gurkha Coys and a few British troops of which I was one was left behind in 1942 in Burma to attack the enemy in the rear if they appeared. The Commander, a good Gurkha officer with a good record, when confronted with a perfect opportunity (Japs landing in boats onto a wide sandy beach completely unaware of our presence), avoided action in order to get back to his Brigade because he was 'out of touch', and could not receive orders. By avoiding action, the unit went into a waterless area and more perished this way and later by drowning than if he had attacked.

My experience with regular battalions under my command in Burma was that there were only 3 or 4 officers in any battalion who could be relied on to take positive action if they were on their own, and had no detailed orders. This 'I'll 'ave to ask me Dad' attitude of the British Army is its worse feature in my opinion. I found the RAF and Dominion officers far better in this respect. I have not had experience with the cavalry. They should also be better. Perhaps cavalry could take on the S.A.S. role successfully? I admit that with training both in Burma and North Africa there were definite improvements amongst the infantry, but in my opinion, no normal battalion I have seen could carry out an S.A.S. role without 80% reorganisation. I have written frankly and have laid myself open to obvious criticism, but I consider this such a vital point I do not mind how strongly I express myself. I have repeated this for 5 years and I have nowhere seen anything to change my views, least of all in Europe.

I have mentioned some points above. You may not agree with my ideas but I write them down as these criticisms are the most normal ones I know. Other points on which the D. T. I. wants to obtain information are:-

1. *Obtaining of recruits.* Has anybody got the original brochure setting out the terms and standards required?
2. *Obtaining of stores and equipment.* Here again, I imagine S.O.E. has been the main source of special stores. My own HQ is producing a paper on this when in England.
3. *Signal communication.* This is of course one of the most important parts of such an organisation and it has, as in other formations, limited the scope of our operations.
4. *Foreign recruits and attached civilians.*
5. *Liaison with R A F. and Navy.*
6. *Command.* How is an organisation of this sort best commanded and under whom should they be?
7. Suggestions re survival in peacetime including auxiliary formation, command, technical development, etc.

You may expect a communication from Lt-Col Wigham. Please give your views quite candidly. They certainly need not agree with those I have written down. I am sending Lt-Col Wigham a copy of this letter so that it may give you something to refer to if necessary. I hope, from the army point of view, and for all that you have worked for and believed in during the last few years, that you will do everything you can to help Lt-Col Wigham to obtain all the information that he requires. We can no longer say that people do not understand if we do not take this chance to get our views put before an impartial tribunal whose task it is to review them in the light of general policy, and then make recommendations to the C. I. G. S. Send along any reports or documents you have got. Lt-Col Wigham is thirsting for information.

Sloe House,
Halstead, Essex.
12 Oct 45.
JMC/LGM.

J. M. CALVERT
Brigadier,
Commander,
S. A. S. Troops

APPENDIX 6

COLONEL WOODHOUSE'S LETTER, 9 DECEMBER, 1981

The Secretary,
S.A.S. Regimental Association.   9th December 1981

Dear Sir,

In view of the extreme pro and anti views on the Malayan Scouts S.A.S. ... I feel obliged to express an opinion. My qualification is that I was the only officer to serve from the formation of the Malayan Scouts in 1950, who also served on subsequent tours until December, 1964.

The first Squadron to form, and there was only one in 1950, contained many good soldiers. Three of the first four troop Commanders in my opinion would have done well in that capacity at any time subsequently when I was serving. There was also a minority of all ranks who were unsuitable. It is true that operational standards in the early years were poor compared to those gradually attained over the next decade. This is neither surprising, nor should the junior officers and soldiers be blamed. Apart from the not entirely relevant experience of veterans of the Burma war we had no skilled instructors and very largely taught ourselves ...

Before excessive criticism is made of the CO, Mike Calvert and other senior officers, it should be remembered that the situation in Malaya was bad and getting worse. Calvert was under pressure to get results and get them quickly. The training of A Squadron was not extensive; subsequent squadrons almost literally were trained on operations. I commanded in quick succession all three British squadrons and was never in my life faced with so hard, even impossible, a task.

The Rhodesian Squadron in 1951 had a three weeks' training exercise before operations, advised by me and one NCO, with perhaps nine months' jungle experience between us. A case of the blind leading the blind! This Squadron with a high percentage of potentially outstanding S.A.S. soldiers never realised its full potential in Malaya because it was never properly trained. The same mistake was not made with the New Zealand S.A.S. Squadron when it joined us in 1955.

Perhaps the strongest and most justified criticism of the Malayan Scouts was poor discipline, in and out of the jungle ... Numerous widely publicised, sensational and mainly true stories circulated for years and very nearly led to the disbandment of the unit. Calvert's comparison was that a building site can be a rough and mucky place until construction is finished. But if Calvert must accept much of the blame, he deserves credit too for his far-sighted perception of the broad strategy and tactics of counter-insurgency, which I learned mainly from him, with subsequent additions from the splendid Z Reserve of the wartime S.A.S. whom I met at Otley in Yorkshire in 1952 for two weeks T.A. camp. It was their example which inspired me to spend as much as possible of the rest of my military career in the service of the S.A.S. ...

yours truly
J.M. Woodhouse

APPENDIX 7

BRIEF HISTORY OF DEVELOPMENT IN S.A.S. CAPABILITY FOR PARACHUTE OPERATIONS IN THE JUNGLE

The Malayan Scouts were formed in 1950 and were used for deep jungle penetration. They were joined in 1951 by a squadron of S.A.S. which was parachute-trained. In September, 1951, efforts were made to start a parachute training school in Singapore and in January, 1952, the Far East Parachute School was formed at Changi.

The first parachute operation was carried out by B squadron in January, 1952, on to a padi field DZ. By a dropping error all but a few men landed in the jungle with only a few casualties. From this experience it was realized that it was possible to jump into trees without alarming casualties and experimental descents were made, first into rubber trees, and then in May, 1952, into primary jungle.

In these early days soldiers jumping into deep jungle carried 100 feet of rope knotted every eighteen inches; when caught up in the trees they had to climb down this thin rope hand over hand, but this was found to be very fatiguing. As a result, a crude form of lowering device was evolved based on a mountaineer's abseiling gear. Although this was better than climbing down a rope, many snags were encountered. In January, 1953, B Squadron carried out an operation (EAGLE) into primary jungle with an abseiling device with a 240-feet lowering line made of 1¾-inch webbing with a 1000 lb breaking strain. This lowering gear was used on three further operations, but in operation SWORD in January, 1954, three fatal casualties occurred through snags in this equipment. Further development was carried out and six months later a much improved system was used on operation TERMITE when 177 troops of three squadrons were dropped into the Perak jungle with only four minor casualties, despite inaccurate drops.

This equipment was evolved for use in primary jungle only and it was not possible to land into bamboo, rocky ground, newly felled ladangs and bomb blasted areas. The jumper crashes through the top jungle canopy and hopes that his chute will be caught so that he will then hang below the canopy from where he can get out of his harness and abseil down to the ground.

Parachuting allows a commander to deploy troops into deep jungle where altitude, terrain or security do not allow the airlifting of troops into the area by helicopter. The helicopter of those days carried only a few men and at any altitude this could be reduced to one man only.

D Zs were marked accurately by Auster aircraft using smoke flares.

The speed which a troop or squadron takes to rally depends on the accuracy of the drop and the concentration of sticks on the ground. Five-six men was the usual number in each stick and thus each aircraft would make several runs over the D Z.

Troops rallied at R Vs, which had natural features, eg: stream junctions, ridges etc. Vocal signals were used and some represented birds not found in Malaya. The average time for a Squadron of 60 men to rally was about one hour.

Each party after dropping had its own parent Auster for communication by relay to HQ. The troops in the jungle call first for their fixed drop of radio sets and other equipment. Requests for evacuation of casualties by helicopter were also made through this Auster.

The advent of larger helicopters with improved performance coupled with a change of role for the S.A.S. in later years reduced the need for these parachute operations.

INDEX

Y048054